A Daughter of Isis

About the author

Nawal El Saadawi was born in a village outside Cairo, Egypt, in 1931. A trained medical doctor, she wrote landmark works on the oppression of Arab women including *Woman at Point Zero* (1973), *God Dies by the Nile* (1976) and *The Hidden Face of Eve* (1977). After being imprisoned by Anwar Sadat's government for criticising the regime, she founded the Arab Women's Solidarity Association in 1982, before being forced into exile in later life due to death threats by religious extremists. She returned to Egypt in 1996, running for president in 2005 until government persecution forced her to withdraw. Saadawi died in Egypt in 2021.

A Daughter of Isis

The Early Life of Nawal El Saadawi,
In Her Own Words

NAWAL EL SAADAWI

Translated by Sherif Hetata

BLOOMSBURY ACADEMIC
LONDON • NEW YORK • OXFORD • NEW DELHI • SYDNEY

BLOOMSBURY ACADEMIC
Bloomsbury Publishing Plc
50 Bedford Square, London, WC1B 3DP, UK
1385 Broadway, New York, NY 10018, USA
29 Earlsfort Terrace, Dublin 2, Ireland

BLOOMSBURY, BLOOMSBURY ACADEMIC and the Diana logo
are trademarks of Bloomsbury Publishing Plc

First published in Great Britain 1999 by Zed Books Ltd.

This edition published 2024 by Bloomsbury Academic

Cover design: Adriana Brioso
Cover image: © The Estate of Nawal El Saadawi
Author photo © Tom Pilston/Panos Pictures

A catalogue record for this book is available from the British Library.

Library of Congress Control Number: 2024931641

ISBN: PB: 978-0-7556-5156-6
         ePDF: 978-0-7556-5157-3
         eBook: 978-0-7556-5158-0

Typeset by RefineCatch Limited, Bungay, Suffolk
Printed and bound in Great Britain

To find out more about our authors and books visit www.bloomsbury.com
and sign up for our newsletters.

Contents

Foreword

This publication marks the fourth edition of *A Daughter of Isis* (first published in 1999). I intially met Nawal El Saadawi in Springfield, Missouri in 2007. Unaccompanied, at 75, she radiated a petite and elegant, but powerful aura. I was immediately reminded of her admission in the book that her mother believed that 'I could walk into danger with a brave heart' (2). She had been invited to give a series of lectures on creativity and dissidence at Missouri State University. During her stay, I requested an autograph for my copy of *A Daughter of Isis*. She wrote 'To Adele who made me feel at home in a homeless world, Nawal.' I was on guard to verify that Nawal, the actual person, was the likeness of the character in the autobiography. Was she the complicated activist her work paints her to be? Was she as fearless as the work portrays her?

Her autobiography begins with a preface that foregrounds the importance of naming for women. In 2007, Saadawi wrote an article supporting the position of naming children according to the maternal line that her daughter Mona Helmi advanced in an article. Traditionally in Egypt, a child receives a personal name and then the names of his/her father and grandfather. Because of her support for Helmi's article, in 2008, Saadawi was accused of apostasy, and her books were banned in Egypt. She and her husband Sherif Hetata fled Egypt after her name appeared on a death list in January 1993. She completed the autobiography while working as a lecturer at Duke.

In the preface, she immediately declares war on God and the patriarchy. She reasons early in her life that 'the illiterate God' was in league with her father. She was greatly influenced by her mother's perspectives and beliefs. Although not openly defiant, on many issues Nawal could count on her mother's support in thwarting patriarchal ideas and traditions. She later in the work admits that deep down inside her mother possessed 'the seeds of rebellion' (189). The other notable feature here is that she alternately demonizes her father's traditional practices and praises his forward thinking in such cases as educating his female children. She also expresses contrasting feelings for her mother. She explains, 'But my childhood was not always happy. There were things that made me suffer, caused me pain. At such moments I was filled with hatred against my mother' (9). Nawal would be the first to acknowledge the complicated nature of human beings. They are never all one thing. If one has the capacity to love deeply, one also has the capacity to hate deeply.

She goes on to advise the reader of her approach to the work. 'I cannot live the same moment twice, cannot transform past into present let alone express reality in words written on a piece of paper. Truth changes, is never the same, like the sea, like the movement of water, of air and soil . . . This is the difficulty whether in autobiography or in fiction, for it lies not in the limitations of language. Imagination, dreams, reality, memory are all imprisoned, surrounded by walls, slower than the changing truth' (6). That is the brilliance of Saadawi. In life, she freely married reality to fiction employing her imagination with great aplomb. Her works (fiction, nonfiction, speeches) indiscriminately draw on her imagination to affect meaning. Her activism and her works were two parts of a whole. She thought it inconceivable to limit oneself to the scientific realm alone. For a person to be whole, she believed that the two parts must be unified. She adds, 'The moments of my early childhood are alive, are always being renewed, are inseparable from my adult life. Past and present fuse' (6).

In effect, Saadawi is telling her reader that her autobiography is the sum of what she remembers, how she has changed, and the tools her imagination puts at her disposal. Another hallmark of the work is her studied ambivalence. Continuing the idea of duality, she acknowledges that there are always two sides to a coin and the people in her life. This is especially true of the people she adored like her mother, who could also inspire her hatred. I believe that it is this tension between the good and the ugly, the angelic and the demonic that informs much of Saadawi's writing. In her public appearances and essays, she also advanced this notion, often acting as the devil's advocate to free her audience of binary thinking.

Her play *Isis* enlarges on the theme of an illiterate God in league with the patriarchy. Isis, for Nawal, was the ultimate goddess. She references her many times in the autobiography. At the age of 11, Nawal was selected to play the goddess on stage. Isis was magical, a healer, and cunning all at once. She'd have to be to survive the male deities. Greed, discord, and control characterize the males in the play and the males in her autobiography.

Of her plays, H. Oby Okolocha pronounces they 'are, to say the least, bold, fearless, unconventional, much like the author. The issues she addresses are audacious and barge into areas where "angels fear to tread"' ('Religion, Capitalism, Politics' 64). Saadawi often said that if she does not tell the truth, she did not deserve to be a writer. When I questioned her about the veil and Middle Eastern women, she responded by asking me about Western women and their use of makeup, many of whom, she charged, would never leave the house before applying it thereby contributing to the billion-dollar cosmetic industry. Bold truth telling (laced with imagination) is the hallmark of this work. From the beginning and continuing to its conclusion, Saadawi invites the reader to interrogate the condition of all women in the world. Her autobiography is about her personal triumph and her journey to agency. Saadawi died on March 21, 2021 at the age of 89. She was, until the end, the complicated activist she paints in this work.

By Adele Newson-Horst

WORKS CITED

El Saadawi, Nawal. *A Daughter of Isis*.
Okolocha, H. Oby. 'Religion, Capitalism, and Politics: The Revolutionary Imagination in the Plays of Nawal El Saadawi'. *African Literature Today* 40. Ernest N. Emenyonu, editor.

The Gift

My First Words

It was my mother who taught me how to read and write. The first word I wrote was my name, Nawal. I loved the way it looked. It meant a 'gift'.

My name became a part of me. Then I learnt my mother's name, Zaynab. I wrote it down next to mine. Her name and mine became inseparable. I loved the way they looked, side by side, and what they meant. Every day she taught me to write new words.

I loved my mother more than my father. But he removed my mother's name from next to mine, and wrote down his instead. I kept asking myself why he had done that. When I asked him, he said, 'It is God's will.' That was the first time I heard the word God. I learnt he lived in the heavens. I could not love anyone who removed my mother's name from next to mine, who abolished her as though she did not exist.

In my mind God had become responsible for that and I felt it was unjust. But father said to me that God was just. I did not understand what that could mean so I wrote a letter to God asking him. It was the first letter I had written in my life and it began as follows: 'O God, if you are just, why do you treat my mother and my father differently?' I thought God had written the Qur'an since my father said it was God's book. But mother said to me that God did not read or write. After my mother told me that, I did not write to him again. Instead I wrote letters to my father for I now realized that between him and God there must be some relationship. However, each time I wrote a letter to him I burned it, and so none of my letters ever reached him.

In my memory, the distant childhood years, the 1940s, seem closer than the 1980s. Memory, like wine, grows mellow with time. The impurities settle into deep forgetfulness. Body becomes mind transparent, and I can see things to which I was blind.

As I write, moments of the past emerge into the light. Body memory becomes one with my spirit, with my blood. I discover the past, rediscover it again and again, try to catch hold of the moments, but they escape me like fish in a mercurial sea, enveloped in the darkness of night.

I cannot live the same moment twice, cannot transform past into present, let alone express reality in words written on a piece of paper. Truth changes, is never the same, like the sea, like the movement of water, of air, and soil. We do not swim in the same sea more than once, so how can I cast it in a mould of three letters on to a sheet of paper? This is the difficulty whether in autobiography or in fiction, for it lies not only in the limitations of language. Imagination, dreams, reality, memory are all imprisoned, surrounded by walls, slower than the changing truth.

The moments of my early childhood are alive, are always being renewed, are inseparable from my adult life. Past and present fuse. The smell of the air here and now is the smell of the air in my village nestling quietly into the embrace of the River Nile.

My relationship with my mother decided the course of my life. I used to think that my father's influence on it was greater than hers. I discovered while I was writing that this was not true. The spinal column that has held me up was built on what my mother said when I was young: 'Throw Nawal in the fire and she will come out unhurt.' After hearing that, I could walk into danger with a brave heart. Maybe that is why I was able to escape death more than once.

At the age of ten I could have been trapped in a marriage were it not for her. Sometimes she used to weaken under pressure, and then in addition to struggling against my father, my grandmother and all my aunts and uncles I had to struggle against her. There was hatred in their eyes when I stood up to them. All except mother. Her eyes would shine with pride and happiness as she watched me fight my battles against them. Now and then she would give me a quick sidelong glance to back me up, or whisper a word of encouragement in my ear.

If it were not for her I would never have continued my education and become a medical student. Father believed in the importance of education for girls as well as boys but sometimes under financial stress his resolve would weaken. He had to pay school or college expenses for six girls and three boys.

One day he said to my mother: 'Zaynab, the work you are doing at home has become too much for you. Why not take Nawal out of school so that she can give you a helping hand?' The answer came right back without a moment's hesitation: 'My daughter will never be made to stay at home. I don't need help', pronounced in a ringing voice which still echoes in my ears.

My mother spent her whole life caring for nine children and their father. Not one of her six daughters was deprived of an education, which went up to university level. She died a young woman at the age of forty-five, and spent two whole years in bed suffering terrible pain. But since the father alone gives his name to the children, bestows legitimacy and honour on them, her name was buried with her, is lost for ever. For in this class patriarchal world of ours a mother's name is of no consequence, a woman is without worth, on earth or in the heavens. In paradise

My mother in Giza, in the spring of 1956.
She died in 1958.

a man is promised seventy-two virgins for his sexual pleasure, but a woman is promised no-one except her husband, that is if he has the time for her, and is not too busy with the virgins who surround him.

My mother made my childhood very happy. I used to bury my face in her breast, smell the odour of her milk, of the hot soup she prepared on winter nights, of corn cake rising in the oven. Her voice in the stillness of the night was like the voice of God, and her laugh in the morning a ray of sunlight. It made me run towards her, lift my arms up in the air so that she would take me to her breast, and we could play or sing together: 'The sun has risen, a light more beautiful than any light. The shining sun.'

The smell of my mother's body is a part of me, of my body, of its spirit, of the hidden strength I carry within me. She is the voice that speaks to me if something's wrong, rescues me just in time, encourages me in moments of despair.

My father in Giza, January 1959, less than a month
before his sudden death.

But my childhood was not always happy. There were things
that made me suffer, caused me pain. At such moments I was
filled with hatred against my mother, wished that she would die,
against my father, and my grandfather and everyone else in the
family. Then something would come along and wipe it all away,
delete it from my memory, banish it from history. My mother
would be at her best, once more a shining star, the real mother
that I knew, her head held high, a woman full of pride, a goddess like Isis, a halo of light around her head, like a full moon,
a silvery crown that the ancient Egyptian goddess wore above
her brow. When I watched her move it taught me to be proud, to
dream of better things, of a place for myself in this vast world.

I did not know from where arose her strength, her pride. Did
it come from an unknown woman I had never seen, a grandmother, or a female antecedent of hers born many years ago, a
descendant of Isis or her mother Noot, goddess of the heavens

five thousand years ago? For was it not Noot who, speaking to her daughter, had said before she died 'I say to you, my daughter who will inherit the throne after I am no longer here, be a merciful and just ruler of your people rather than a goddess who depends for her authority on sacred power.'

My father was a just and kindly man, who never raised his voice to her. He worked all day, and when he came home gave her a helping hand, laid the table, made the salad, and washed the pots and pans. He sat up at night sometimes to darn his socks, told us that the prophet, peace be with him, repaired the leather sandals that he wore, and sewed his own clothes. He followed what the Prophet did if he believed he should, but the Prophet was not a model for him in everything. The Prophet had several wives, but my mother was my father's only wife and he would never have behaved towards her like Abraham, who gave away his wife as an offering to the pharaoh to escape his tyranny.

My father opposed the king and the coterie of men through whom he ruled. He stood up against the British occupation of Egypt and colonial rule. He was loyal to his country, faithful to the woman who shared his bed, and believed that a man could not betray his wife and at the same time remain loyal in his dealings with the outside world.

Four months after my mother died, his coffin travelled to the village and we watched it as it was lowered into the ground. Before he died I used to see him sitting silently on the verandah, a fleeting look of sadness in his eyes, before he smiled quickly at me. He loved my mother dearly, never raised his voice when speaking to her, except that day when I woke up to hear him shouting in angry tones at her. She was dressed as though ready to go out and I heard her say in a voice that shook with anger: 'I'm ready to go from house to house washing clothes, rather than live with a man who allows himself to shout at me.'

My mother was not a doctor, or a writer. She had no job, no income of her own, no place in which she could live apart from her husband's home, but she preferred to leave him rather than sacrifice her self-respect and pride.

Mother had a happy life in many ways. But she was not like the other women in her family. She regretted being just a house-wife. Ever since her early school-days she had dreamed of other things. Sometimes when we sat together and no-one else was around she used to whisper: 'I wanted to be a musician, and play music, or to finish my education and find a place where I could experiment and invent something useful. I dreamt of galloping on a horse to the horizon, of riding in an aeroplane to see the world, but your grandfather Shoukry took me out of school and married me off to your father.'

My father's dreams were different. He wanted to liberate his country from colonial rule, free himself from the bondage of his government job, become a poet, or a writer. He died without achieving any of these, without writing anything, lived a life of semi-exile in faraway corners of the country with nothing to keep him going except his love for his family and an inner pride, the feeling that he had never given up, had always struggled for what he believed was right.

Did I inherit the dreams I heard them talk about, sometimes with enthusiasm to others in a tone of wistful sadness? I was proud of them despite the dreariness and pain that marked much of their life. I was proud of my country despite the almost constant alienation I felt towards the society in which I lived. I dreamt of another world on earth and in the heavens. It was as though I had come into the world from an unknown planet, could not believe that the earth and the heavens were two separate things, would not believe in a country which robbed me of my pride and freedom, in a husband who did not treat me as an equal, in a God who made me only half a human being.

I was proud of my dark skin. It was a beautiful brown, the colour of silt brought down to my land by the waters of the Nile. I never hid it under make-up or powder, or pastes of any kind, did not believe in a femininity born with slave society and handed down to us with class and patriarchy.

My mother rebelled against many things but still she held on to certain traits of femininity which I did not share with her. Moments before she died, she stretched out her hand to a little flask of *kohl*, pulled out the rod and drew a line of black around her eyes, painted her lips with a baton of rouge, sprayed perfume around her neck and behind her ears, and combed her hair. She wanted to meet God fully made up, completely feminine, as though she was going to meet the only man she would ever meet again, like a nun who has been locked up in a monastery for years and dreams of meeting Jesus Christ, for she had been brought up in a school supervised by nuns and had mixed with them for years.

When she died, I saw her eyes open wide full of a sudden childish surprise, as though she were discovering the truth for the first time, realizing for the first time all that had happened to her in her life just a moment before she closed her eyes, never to open them again and look out at me with that shine. Her lips parted for a moment perhaps to express what she had now found out, but death was quicker, snatched her away before she could say anything.

In our life there is always a missing link, something which can be completed only by death. Perhaps not even death can do anything about it, and the circle of our life is never completed, remains open, continues as two parallel lines which never meet even at the horizon. This world of infinity, this infinite world, does it have an end and, if so, when and how?

I learnt my first lessons in philosophy, my first lessons in religion and politics, from my grandmother. She had not read the book of God, had not been to school, but I heard her say to the village headman as she waved her big rough hand in front of his face: 'We are not slaves and Allah is justice. People have come to know that through reason.' My father used to repeat what my grandmother said, but he used different words. 'Allah

My uncle Sheikh Muhammad, my father's half-brother,
attending the wedding of my sister Hayam in 1963. My
daughter Mona, then seven years old, is to the right.

is our conscience which tells us we have done something wrong
when we do not stand up for justice. God's voice comes to us from
our depths and not from the pulpit of the mosque.'

Were it not for my grandmother, my father could have become
like his half-brother. He had the same father but a different
mother, and taught religious jurisprudence in Al-Azhar.* I
called him Ammi Al-Sheikh Muhammad (my uncle Al-Sheikh
Muhammad). He always addressed me using the slang word *bit*
(short for *bint*). It means 'You, girl', and expresses contempt.
He did not believe in girls going to the university, in their
mixing with boys and men. He grew a long thick beard around
his face which made me wonder what relation there could be
between the strength of men's faith in God and the thickness
of the beard on their faces. He used to slip the prayer beads
through his fingers with a slow movement as he muttered the
ninety-nine names of Allah. He believed that God permitted
men to punish their wives by staying away from the marital
bed, or scolding and beating them at will. He had a wife in the

---

* Based in Cairo, this is the most important religious university in the Muslim
world.

village who baked buttered pastry loaves for him, and a wife in the city who cooked him meals made of lambs' feet or stuffed tripe. He did not darn his socks like the prophet did, but he followed the prophet's ways in other things, like marrying several wives and punishing them if they did not please him. He did not care whether his country was free, or under foreign rule, never opposed the government or the king, gave a sermon every Friday morning in the mosque, at the end of which he prayed that Allah protect King Farouk, whom he described as the pride of all our countrymen.

The Forgotten Things in Life

Memory is never complete. There are always parts of it that time has amputated. Writing is a way of retrieving them, of bringing the missing parts back to it, of making it more holistic.

My memory started to awaken, after the deaths of my mother and my father. I was twenty-eight when one day I suddenly remembered the earlier years of childhood. Now they no longer seemed so distant. I could not describe what I felt in simple language so I wrote a poem in which reality was a dream, disappeared when it emerged under the light, was like an elusive flash, here one moment gone the next. Reality is something which changes all the time, something I cannot pin down or express in words on paper. When I try to draw it, it takes on the form of a collection of dots which become more dense at the centre. I say to myself maybe this is the truth, and maybe it is not, so I try to draw it, as I would like it to be, not how it really is.

What makes writing a source of wonder and beauty is its complexity which is simplicity itself, is the frenzied movement of the earth yet which remains so still that we do not feel it moving under us.

In my secret diary I noted down a poem which I wrote in my early youth:

> My memory has remained a blank page
> Since childhood
> A mountain hidden under water
> With a single eye which stares at me
> The eye of God or Satan
> For they are one
> And I fear both of them.

The most difficult thing to write about is what people call sex. It is hidden behind a cloud of smoke, behind an inability to break the code hidden in the subconscious depths, in that obscure grey matter we call the brain. When I deal with sex I lose my mastery over language. This is the case especially with Arabic. Arabic is the language of the holy Qur'an and cannot be used easily to talk about what is considered sacrilegious. In English I can write down the word penis as simple as that, but in Arabic it is called the masculine rod, which sounds obscene. It is even worse when I write about the female sexual organs, especially in the colloquial slang used by the street urchins.

In my early youth writing, rather than reveal the things that people do not speak about, concealed them, served as an additional mask with which to hide the private shameful parts. Everything in a woman's life was seen as shameful, even her face. She often hid it behind a piece of material, or the edge of her shawl, or behind the shutters of her window. Literary criticism in our country is under the control of a small group of men and a few women who think and write like them, who say there is no such thing as an issue related to women's rights. For them the only important issues are related to the nation or to people in general, irrespective of sex. They call this humanizing the issues. They conceal the gender oppression of women behind brave words about human rights or the human being, distinguish between the liberation of our country and the liberation of women who are half of society, apply the norms and values created by the class patriarchal system and their signifiers in both spoken and written language.

At the age of thirty I was incapable of writing about many painful and sensitive issues in my life. It needed another thirty years before I developed enough courage to get rid of the fear and the feelings of shame rooted in myself. There had to be thousands of miles between me and my homeland, I had to be cut off completely from the past, the present and the future, all of which had weighed heavily on me, to feel that I no longer had pressing needs, and could do without almost anything, that the limitations, the bonds that held me down like invisible chains had fallen away, and left my fingers free to move my pen in any direction, before my memory could start to recall. Step by step, what had been enveloped for so long in dark cloud started to reappear.

At the age of five I had my first experience of sexual pleasure. The experience, deeply marked by guilt and fear, was lost in the deep tunnels of my memory. Sometimes the remembrance came back to me while I slept, in the form of a dream, or a nightmare, of a strange creature pursuing me, a body that could be that of a human being, yet was not, had not the eyes of an angel, but the horns of a devil, an old man who resembled my grandfather, the gardener who lived in a hut at the back of the house, a youth like the son of our neighbour, a student in the boy's school, my elder brother, or the youngest of my uncles.

The dream was real and ever changing, like reality, and this childhood experience comes back to me when I look into my computer, see the moving dots inside an atom densely packed together at the centre. I say to myself maybe the electron is here and maybe not, and then reality seems to me like imagination, for it is never still.

I do not know why I forgot. I used to hear people around me say, you are a grown-up girl. Ever since I was five years old they would say I was grown up, and so it seemed to me that I should be held responsible for everything that happened to me whether in real life or in my dreams. Was I not the daughter of Eve, responsible for what I had done, for sin?

When I was six, the *daya* (midwife) came along holding a razor in her hands, pulled out my clitoris from between my thighs, and cut it off. She said it was the will of God and she had done his will. It was as though there was some relation between this and what had happened to me in that other experience, but I did not know what it could be. Perhaps the devil had whispered to me in the night, had been sent by God, like the angel who visited the Virgin Mary before she gave birth to Jesus Christ. In those early years I felt I was like her, pure and chaste, thought my belly could never swell with child unless it was the promised Messiah or Jesus Christ. Later, when the innocent days of childhood were over, I forgot about the Virgin Mary and all that.

Thirty-five years later I remembered how the *daya* had come along and circumcised me. I was in a place called Kanya Kumari at the Virgins' Rock, the southermost tip of India, where the Indian Ocean and the sea of Arabia meet, at a spot seven thousand miles from where I was born.

That day it all came back. I picked up a pen and wrote one page about my circumcision, then tore it up. The pieces of paper flew up into the wind, then dropped to the surface of the ocean, floating up and down until they were out of sight.

I have not written yet about the sexual experience I had at the age of five. Maybe I shall write about it soon, moved by the earth as it goes round and round, by the waters and the winds when they reveal a new layer of the iceberg hidden in the depths of the ocean.

Writing My Life

On 8 January 1993 I said farewell to our small flat in Giza. I had lived in it for thirty-three years but now we were ready to leave. Sherif was strapping the bags in the hall. Since the day we had married more than thirty years ago the government authorities had not given us a day's respite. Every time we started something, a magazine, an association, a cultural society, a publishing project, after five or six years and sometimes before,

Nawal and her husband Sherif Hetata, 1989.

they would close it down. They destroyed everything we built, snuffed out every candle we lit. Now I was on a fundamentalist death list, guarded by the very police who had hunted us down throughout the years, caught in a cross-fire not knowing from where the bullet could come.

I moved through the flat taking a last look, as though bidding each room goodbye. My daughter, Mona, stood in the hall waiting. She took me in her arms: 'Peace be with you wherever you go, mother', she said. 'Phone me as soon as you arrive.' My son, Atef, stood beside her, embraced me in turn. 'Take care, mother', he said, 'take care of yourself.' Then they embraced Sherif, their smiles concealing the tears in their eyes.

Sherif carried the bags out of the door, moving in that steady, quiet way of his which reminded me of my father, of the day when, seven years old, I watched him as he strapped the bags, and carried them out of the house, ready for our journey. The government was sending him away from Alexandria into semi-exile because he had participated in a demonstration against the British and the king.

My daughter Mona Helmy, creative writer and poet, in 1988

Sherif and I walked out of the building carrying our bags. In the plane Sherif put his arm around me, held me close to him and said: 'Nawal, we are going on a wonderful journey. It is going to be a new experience and another exciting stage in our life.' We embraced, suspended between the earth and the sky as the huge Boeing aircraft headed north, piercing its way through the clouds.

Little did I know that now over sixty years old, and here in North Carolina, I would write the story of my life.

I

Allah and McDonald's

Since January 1993, I have been in this small house overlooking Duke Forest with its dense masses of tall cedars,
pines and oak trees: an inundation of green. The sight is not a
familiar one to me. The word 'forest' is strange to the ears of a
woman who has spent her life in Egypt: the valley of the Nile, the
tranquil river, its waters slipping by, never overflowing, never
flooding, the ribbon of green fields winding through the yellow
sands, shrinking as the desert and concrete walls close in on it
from every side.

In front of my home in Giza, there was a tree (Giza is as-
sociated in the minds of tourists and Egyptologists alike with
pictures of the Pyramids, the Sphinx, the tombs of the pharaohs
like Tutankhamon, and with the camels and donkeys that the
tourists ride guided by the mischievous local children, whose
faces are scorched by the sun, their heels cracked and black as
they walk along under the admiring gaze of the tourists, who
want to see so-called differences of race and culture). I used to
open my window and look out at this solitary tree. My eyes are
drawn to green, my lungs breath it in. Green is converted in my
lungs to oxygen.

I spent my childhood and my youth in the countryside, in the heart of the Delta, moving between my village Kafr Tahla in Al-Kalyoubeya province and the town of Menouf in Al-Menoufeya province. My eyes became used to seeing fields of crops, and orchards. My chest seemed to expand, to open up in order to embrace the green expanses reaching out before my eyes.

One day during the year 1977, I opened my window. The lonely orphan tree was no longer there. A bulldozer had come along and uprooted it. Two concrete walls started to rise until they blocked out the sunlight from my window. Over one wall rose the tall minaret of a new mosque bathed in the white of neon lights. Over the other hung a billboard for McDonald's surrounded by revolving neon lights. On the ground floor appeared other circling lights for something new called Disco Club.

I started to keep my glass windows and wooden shutters closed day and night, but the din of noise and the pulsing lights kept going through my body, mingled with the smell of hamburger, the thump of disco beats and the cries of 'Allah is most great... Come to prayers.'

During the painful sleepless nights, I wondered whether there was some pact between Allah and McDonald's to chase away the sleep heavy on my lids, or drive me out from where I lived.

Duke Forest is a flood of vivid green trees. My eyes seek their colour like dry soil seeks water. The sun comes through my window as I sit writing. Two years have gone by in this remote place almost ten thousand miles from Egypt, where Duke Forest is part of the university in this small village-like town called Durham in North Carolina, on the east coast of the Atlantic Ocean.

I raise my head bent over the paper, put down my pen for a moment. Why am I writing this autobiography? Is it a longing for my past life? Is my life over, or is there something of it left? Are words the last resort when one wants to hold on to what has passed by in life before it is gone forever? To fix images in one's memory before they vanish and can no longer be replaced? To struggle against death, to exist now, or even forever?

When I was a child, when I was still young the word eternity held for me a magic, like that of the gods. Now its spell has gone. The very word makes me impatient. Things that never end are only boring, and were it not for death, life would be an impossible burden.

Am I trying to discover what is buried deep down inside me, to reveal what is hidden through fear of God, the father, the husband, the teacher, the male or female friend or colleague, through fear of the nation to which we belong, or those we love?

It is normal when we show anger and rebel against those whom we hate, but when our anger and rebellion are directed against those whom we love, what will the words be like when we express them in writing?

When I was a child, the word God for me meant justice or freedom or love. How did it become a sword over my head, or a veil over my mind and face? I sang songs to my nation, to my country in my childhood and my youth. How has my country become a prison, or a policeman wearing a fez, a skull cap, a turban or a hat, speaking English, or classical or colloquial Arabic, or a dialect from the Gulf states as he pursues me day and night?

With other girls I sang of love. On moonlit nights, we would sing of love all night. How did the word love become the four blackened walls of a kitchen in a falling house called the matrimonial home? And medicine too, and science or art or literature, words I dreamt about like a small bird dreams of flying, how have these words become chains that drag me to the ground or under its surface?

From the day I was born until the age of sixty I lived in Egypt. When I try to recollect what happened when I was born, all I know is that I was born a female. I heard people say God creates the male and the female, that long before I was born female infants were buried alive. Then a verse descended in the

Nawal El Saadawi, aged two months, in Egypt 1931.

Qur'an from above, which said: 'And if the infant girl who has been buried alive is asked for what sin was she killed...' I could have been one of those infants who were buried alive had I been born at that time. This is what I heard people say to me when I was four years old.

But I was born in better times. Nothing happened to a female when she was born. Life just came to a standstill. People were simply sad, and sorrow is easier to bear than infanticide. The sorrow might conceal a latent desire to bury the female infant, but it remained sorrow, just a darkness of the face, masking what is repressed beneath.

During the first days of her life the female infant does not see this sadness. Her eyes which open for the first time on this world are too young, too innocent, unable to see the hidden.

I was one of those female infants. Like them I did not take in the scene with my own eyes. The original images were not registered in my memory. I have tried to retrieve them in my imagination through the words I seem to have heard from my grandmother, and with which I have painted a description of those sad moments when I emerged from my mother's womb.

2

The Cry in the Night

With the first light of dawn creeping through the night of that month of October, before the sun came up over the piece of land demarcated by a speck on the map almost invisible to the eye on the curving line, fine as a hair, known as the Nile, which pushes its way through desert sand, from south to north, and with the last stroke of four dropping like a dying gasp from the ancient clock on the wall, rose a cry, coming from the four-poster brass bed pushed up in a corner of the innermost room in the house, the cry of a woman in labour which went through the night just once. Then there was a long heavy silence, as though both the woman and the child had died.

In the hall, the throng of people gathered outside held their breath. First, the family of Shoukry Bey, noble descendants of a lineage going back to the great Tala'at Pacha of Istanbul. Then the family of Al-Saadawi, from Kafr Tahla, with their dark, dusty faces, and the bare skin of their cracked heels looking out from under the hem of their long garments. The smell of mud and sweat in the threadbare *gallabeyas*, the long robes worn by peasants, mingled with the sweet scent of French perfumes in the flowing silk dresses and the smell of whiskey and dark tobacco rising from the foreign cut suits made of English wool.

My peasant grandmother Sittil Hajja, my father's mother,
in 1947 in the village of Kafr Talha.

All sound stopped in the narrow hall, even the sound of
breathing, or the early whiffs of the creeping dawn, reluctant
to advance, unable to go back, even the exhausted ticks of the
old rusty clock handed down from the era of the Khedive Ismail.
The sun too refused to come out, as though held back in the
entrails of the earth.

Perhaps such a moment seems unreal, but that is what happened as told to me by my grandmother Al-Hajja* Mabrouka, the
mother of my father, whom we addressed as Sittil Hajja.

Her breathing also stopped, held back in her throat closed
tight after the first and only scream died out. She looked into the
room through the door, left slightly ajar, and suddenly glimpsed
the small round head showing through the slit, wedged up between the thighs, refusing to come out. An obstinate head, hard
as stone, dark as night, round as the earth, resting motionless in
the wide open vaginal slit, stretched to its limits, to a complete
circle like the setting sun, as red as clotting blood.

But after that one and only shriek rising from the innermost
depths of the mother lying on the bed, the dark obstinate head

---

* A term of respect for older people, although strictly applying only to those who
have made the pilgrimage to Mecca.

thrust out slowly, gently, then stopped again, held back at the neck, undecided whether to continue on its way out, or go back. But the muscles of the vagina contracted tightly round the neck, threatening to throttle out its life. There was no way for this being to save itself except to go out into the world as quickly as it could.

And so it did, curled around itself like a ball, like a porcupine, its arms and legs wound around its body. Two broad, horny palms caught the rounded head in their grasp, long sinewy fingers pushed the straining thighs apart. As quick as lightning, and as hard as rusty nails, the hands of these *dayas* had been trained to do so ever since the Turkish occupation.

The two small thighs of the newly born baby were held tightly closed, one against the other, with a force which seemed almost superhuman. It was as though between them lay something which had to be hidden, something which was a source of shame. But the steely fingers of the *daya* pushed one thigh away from the other as if they were the legs of a chicken, eager to reveal whatever good or evil lay hidden between them, to be the first one who would let out a screaming 'Yoo-yoo' if her eyes fell on a penis ('May the name of the Prophet protect and guard it'), if she glimpsed the sacred organ bestowed by Allah on males alone, or to be the first to lower her head, show a solemn face, and become as silent as the dead if all she could find was a cleft – that unhappy vaginal opening accursed in this world since sinful Eve.

No yoo-yoo of joy shrilled out from the mouth of 'Um' Mahmoud' the *daya*, no eyelid was lifted by the mother to glimpse the thing born of her that night. I happened to be that thing which the *daya* turned over between her hands sucking at her lips with a sound of deep regret before she let it drop to drown in the basin full of water.

No one from the family of Shoukry Bey or the Al-Saadawi kin stretched out a hand to save me. They probably all disappeared

---

* Mother.

into thin air, leaving me to the hands of Um Mahmoud, that *daya* trained over centuries of time to deal with such catastrophes. She had feelers that detected the unspeakable things lurking in the eyes. The newborn female child would live or not, for all depended on God's will, and she was on good terms with God, and knew his will. Did He not visit her when she slept, just as He had visited the Prophet and the Holy Saints? Did He not reveal to her what was hidden to others so that she was able to tell the sex of any infant, as it lay inside the womb? Did not God guide her hand as it felt its way up, to pull out the child, so that at times the cord would twist around the little neck and throttle out its life, or it would bleed and bleed until no drop of blood remained and the little female body let out its final breath. Did not, did not, did not... So many things could happen, and all were willed by God. No one could challenge Allah's will, except the wicked Satan.

My mother did not open her eyes. She left me to kick inside the basin. I do not know how I foiled death during the first moments of my life. Maybe a Satanic will took hold of me. At the time I did not know who Satan was. At the age of five I was told his name was Eblis, that he was the only one who had possessed the strength to disobey Allah's commands, and wave the banner of rebellion in his face.

Maybe my mother opened half an eye (after the *daya* left). The moment she saw my brown complexion with a tint of indigo in its depths like those of the peasants in the Al-Saadawi family, she closed her lids as though forever, pressed her lips tightly together until the blood in them turned blue. Silence reigned, a silence heavier than the earth itself. It crept out of the small house, to the whole village huddled beneath the banks of the Nile, then on to the capital city Al-Kahira (Cairo, the triumphant) the oppressor of its people since way back in time, since the age of slavery, the oppressed by the guns and bayonets of many invaders until the 1882 British occupation. The giant city that lay below the Mokattam Hills, the pyramids, the tomb

My mother's father, Shoukry Bey, before his death in 1945.

of the pharaoh, the outstretched feet of the giant Sphinx, the greatest of all gods in stone.

The mother of the newborn child shut her eyes and curled up around herself like an embryo, pressing the soft flesh of her white thighs over the open bleeding cleft. Her arms did not stretch out to enfold me, to hold me to her breast. She left me to shiver by her side wrapped in an old rag so tight around my belly and chest that I almost suffocated, and went into a kind of daze, a feverish state where the pain and bleeding took her back to her wedding night. She advanced to the beat of drums, at a slow, heavy pace, her feet stumbling over the high tapering heels of her shoes, catching into the tail of the long wedding gown with its cascades of folds and frills. The drum beat into her ears like hammer blows. Her thighs trembled as she pressed them tightly over the cleft between them, shorn of its pubic hair, of pride and self-respect. She was fifteen. Her father had chased her out of school with a stick. Her bridegroom was sixteen years older than she was. All she had seen of him was his back, as she peered through the slats of the window shutters. Her face under the white coating of powder was as white as chalk, and under the electric light it took on a shifting sickly, yellow hue. Her high cheekbones were painted bright red like the sugar dolls of the Moulid.* Her honey-coloured eyes shone with a childish gleam and the pupils turned round and round like mice in a trap searching for a way out. Her name was printed on the invitation card in black ink:

Miss Zeinab Hanem† Shoukry, the dutiful daughter of
the most Honourable Mahmoud Bey Shoukry,
Director General of Military Conscription
to be married to Al-Sayed Effendi Al-Saadawi,
the teacher in the Ministry of Education.
The wedding ceremony will be on the evening of
25 March 1929, in the residence of
Shoukry Bey, Villa No. 6, Zeitoun Street,
Zeitoun Hamlet, Suburb of Cairo.

Her memory stopped all of a sudden with her feet, as she came to a halt on the threshold of the bedroom. She could see the yellow brass bed with its four posts and a tall, broad-shouldered man standing upright like one of the posts. She had never seen his face before. From behind the shutters she could glimpse only the back of his thick neck, its hair shaven with a razor blade, his head surrounded by a turban like that of the Fikki‡ reciting verses from the Qur'an in the cemetery for the souls of the dead in exchange for a few dry cakes.

After a moment, she would be lying on the bed in this man's arms, her eyes closed, being impregnated with her first child, without taking off her clothes or opening her eyes, so that she could give birth to that child nine months later, followed by another impregnation before she had time to wean the first,

---

* The anniversary of the Prophet Muhammad's birth is celebrated by all sorts of festivities, including sweets made in the form of sugar dolls.

† A term of respect used by the Turks for the women of high-class families.

‡ A man of religion hired to recite verses of the Qur'an for the dead, or recently deceased.

again in the dark of the night without taking off her clothes, or pressing on the switch to see the face of the man who climbed over her. So year after year, in the dark of the night, my mother became pregnant ten times, gave birth to nine children, and induced an abortion with the tenth before she had reached the age of thirty, without ever having known that thing which is described as sexual pleasure. Then she died, a young woman, holding my hand in her hand, her childish honey-coloured eyes looking at me with astonishment, discovering that, for the first time in her life, she was holding my hand, that her five fingers were folded around it in the same way as my small fingers had clutched her hand when I lay beside her on the bed, the night I was born.

In the mirror I can see my face, long and pallid like my mother's face when she lay dying. She was still in her youth but I am now over sixty-two. Thirty years have passed since my mother died, and yet it is as though she died yesterday. My tears are falling slowly. I let them fall. I used to hold them back. I was afraid that my mother, or my father, or someone else, would see me crying.

I move the pen in my fingers over the sheet of paper. The veins in my hand are swollen, like they were in my grandmother's hand. Sixty-two years of my life have passed without my knowing. Parts of my life have fallen into oblivion. I try to bring them back, to haul them out of the clutches of the past. Those moments that try to escape, to disappear from my memory, or to hide from people's eyes, moments of pain and despair, of weakness and decay, when I forgot the day, and the hour and the place where I would be, when I forgot my name and the names of my mother and father, and the village where I was born, moments of anger that took hold of me, so that I wanted to kill, moments when I would walk the streets not knowing where I was going, glimpse my face in the mirror, or the glass window of a shop, as I came to a sudden stop, struck with bewilderment at what seemed another woman's face, dark, and pallid, and sad, looking out into the world from brooding eyes, as black and as dark as the night.

I would close my eyes trying to escape from my face, trying to bring back my mother's face when she laughed. I do not remember how old I was when I first heard her laugh. She had a very special laugh that belonged only to her, and resembled no other laugh in the world. It rang out in the house, swept through the walls into the street, into open space filling the whole universe. I could hear it as I walked along by my father's side. Its ring in my ears was wonderful, like the ring of sweet, limpid water in a vessel of pure silver or crystal. I used to hear it before I entered our house. My hand would slip out of my father's long fingers and I would run up to her. She would sweep me up in her arms, hold me to her breast, feed me. Her smell has never left my nostrils. It is as though it were the smell of my body. It belongs with the smell of fresh milk and hot bread and of steam rising from soup in the cold of winter.

She lay sick in bed for two years, in the yellow brass bed with the four posts. The same bed in which she lay on her wedding night, and in which she gave birth to nine children: three boys and six girls. The first child was one year older than me, and they called him the eldest brother. I was the second, the eldest daughter who carried her mother in her arms when she lay on her deathbed, held her up to her breast and fed her. None of the males ever carried her in his arms, or held her close to his chest.

I glimpse myself in the mirror, and wonder at how the years have fled by so that here I am feeding my mother instead of her feeding me. In the mirror I see the spoon in my hand come close to her mouth. Her head lies on my chest just as my head used to lie on hers while I whispered my dreams to her, and now she is whispering her dreams to me. Her voice is halting, her breathing weak, her words disjointed, cut short, incomplete. I strain my ears, fuse all my senses into the one single sense of hearing. I pray that time, that the hands of my watch, go slower, let her say what she has to say. I bring my ears to her lips, try to wring words out of silence, to help her find them just as she used to help me find them and speak. She opens her mouth, tries to pronounce them but they escape her, just as time escaped her, just as everything else escaped her and turned to nothing.

In the mirror, I can see my face and the pen in my hand as it moves over the sheet of paper. The time is ten o'clock. The place is Durham, a small city in the state of North Carolina near the southeast coast of America. More than ten thousand miles lie between it and the village where I was born. More than sixty-two years separate me from the moment when my head thrust out from the vaginal opening of my mother into the world, and more than thirty years have gone by since my mother passed away from this world. It is as though she died yesterday, as though I am still sitting on the edge of the yellow brass bed. I still feel the spoon in my hand, the touch of her head is still on my chest as I feed her, and the smell of her milk as she suckles me from her breasts is still in my nose, like the smell of my own body. My face has grown longer, my complexion darker and more sallow, the shine in my black eyes is no longer the same. Deep inside me lie moments born of nothing. I brush away the phantom of death with a movement of my hand, as though brushing a fly away from my desk, and glimpse a white envelope with my name on it, Doctor El Saadawi, Visiting Professor at Duke University. The word Duke echoes strangely in my ears, but even stranger is the echo of the name El Saadawi. 'Who is Al-Saadawi?' I asked Sittil Hajja, 'who is he?' She said he was a man of unknown origin. He had been carried down from Abyssinia by the waters of the Nile, in a canoe made of straw or bulrushes, like our prophet Moses, abandoned as a child by his mother, to be carried away to an unknown fate by the waters of the Nile.

I was six years old when I used to sit next to Sittil Hajja on the threshhold of our home in Kafr Tahla. In front of her she would have laid out the straw mat on which she spread the grains of wheat and rice, as I watched her picking out the tiny stones, and bits of chaff with her strong rough fingers. Every time a peasant man or woman passed in front of her, I would hear them greet her: 'Health and strength to you, O mother of Al-Sayed Effendi.'*

She would stretch out her long sinewy neck, its muscles standing out from years of carrying sacks and big earthenware jars or other weights. I could see the proud movement of her head when they pronounced the word effendi, hear her answer with a double greeting: 'I wish you twice as much strength and health, my sister.'

Then she would go back to picking out the stones and bits of chaff with her sunbaked fingers, to the story of Al-Saadawi, my father's great-grandfather and his antecedents who had lived in Abyssinia and of whom the only one ever to be mentioned was his mother, Habasheya.†

I listened to these stories, my mouth wide open, my mind floating with the small canoe, made of straw or bulrushes, as it rode over the waters of the River Nile, my grandmother's voice coming to me from a magic world:

His mother was called Habasheya, and he had no father, just like our Prophet Moses, and Jesus, God's peace be with them. He would talk about his mother as though she was, God bless her, our Mother Mary. He said she belonged to a noble family in Abyssinia, and owned more land and slaves than the Queen of Sheba owned in her day. Everyone in the village believed him, except my mother, God rest her soul. She used to say, if his mother was an Abyssinian of noble ancestry, why did God not mention her in the Qur'an the way he mentioned our Holy Mother Mary. And if she owned land and slaves like the queen of Sheba, why did the Qur'an omit to talk of her. Habasheya was certainly no more than a slave, or one of the Sultan's concubines. She hated Al-Saadawi like poison, said he was a devil, son of a devil. In the night his eyes gave out sparks of fire, and in the summer he disappeared as though swallowed up by the earth. Then in winter, he would come back, lie on top of the mud oven for warmth and call out to one of his women. He married,

---

* At that time, a term of respect for people who had risen from being peasants by means of education.
† 'The Abyssinian woman.'

and divorced and married again at will, and no-one knew how
many women he had. He would enter the house and leave it with
his underpants slung over his shoulder since he had no time either
to take them off or to put them on. The only verses of the Qur'an
which he knew were 'Marry as many women as seems good to you.
Your women are as land to be plowed by you, so plow them when
you wish', and 'Abandon their bedding and chastise them.'*

He had a son who was his living image with the same ugly
frowning face. He named him Habash after his mother Habasheya.
He married him to one of the women in the village. She died
after bearing two sons to him. I was still a child, my breasts had
not grown, and my period had not come when suddenly they
took hold of me and, hop, married me off to Habash. There I was
screaming at the top of my voice, 'Mother, where are you?' but
that unnameable woman, Um Mahmoud, that brazen daughter of
a whore, together with four other women, took hold of me, tied me
up as though she were trussing a chicken, covered my head with
a shawl and pulled my thighs wide apart so that she could tear off
my surface† below. I recited the Fatiha [the opening verse of the
Qur'an], for my soul, whispered 'There is no God except Allah
and Mohammed is His Prophet'. I looked death in the eyes as Um
Mahmoud tore off my surface, her finger going through it like a
nail cutting into my flesh with a burning pain, drums beating into
my ears like hammer blows. I said to myself, finished, everything
is over for you, Mabrouka, your soul has left your body, and this is
your deathbed, not your wedding bed. Verily it is true, for Allah is
my witness, the wedding bed is a deathbed in this village of ours,
believe me, O daughter of my son.

She would stop short, burst into sudden laughter, a strange
jerky, gasping, muffled laughter almost like sobbing, which
shook her long wasted body, then pull at the edge of her black
shawl, hide her nose and mouth with it, trying to suppress the
laughter until her voice choked and the tears welled from her
eyes as she dried them quickly on the edge of her shawl.

---

* Meaning, punish your women by not sleeping with them and by beating them.
† In colloqual Arabic pronounced *wesh*, which means face or hymen.

3

God Above,
Husband Below

When I was a child I did not know whether my grandmother was laughing or crying. She was probably laughing, for after she had wiped the tears away her eyes shone with a sudden light, and she would begin to laugh again, almost choking as she held the black shawl over her nose and her mouth and muttered 'Allah, let it lead to something good',* only to resume her laughing until the tears welled up in her eyes once more.

So I learnt from her that Al-Saadawi was the name of my great-grandfather who came from Abyssinia and that Habash was the name of my grandfather whose son Al-Sayed became my father. In the official register, the names of those three men were inscribed with my name so that it became Nawal Al-Sayed Habash El-Saadawi. Somehow the name Habash disappeared on my birth certificate and my identity card and I completely forgot that it had even been a part of it, only to reappear in the files of the Ministry of Interior and of the prison authorities. I discovered this in 1981, when I had already reached my fifties. In

---

* Accustomed to tragedy in their lives, village people are afraid to laugh, as though God may punish them for laughing, as though they have no right to laugh, so that when they do, they pray God that it might bring something good and not evil to them.

Nawal in prison

that year I became number 1,536 on a list of people arrested by
President Sadat. The authorities put me in the Women's Prison
located near Al-Kanatir Al-Khaireya, about ten miles north of
Cairo, near a barrage on the Nile. The officer in charge asked
me my full name. I did not mention Habash. He pulled out an
ancient register, flipped through the heavy yellowing pages
and extracted the name Habash, followed by Al-Saadawi, a man
whom I had never known, as though he were digging out two
bodies one after the other from their graves. Ever since I was
born the name of that unknown Al-Saadawi has been carried by
my body, inscribed on my school-books, my school certificates,
my certificates of merit, printed on my articles in newspapers
and magazines, on the covers of my novels and books written
with my ink, my sweat, my tears, my blood in the stifling heat
of summer days and the freezing winter nights, day after day,
night after night, for more than flfty years.

On my desk lies a white envelope with my name written on it:
'Dr El-Saadawi, Visiting Professor, Duke University'. The name
'Duke' rings strange in my ears like that of Al-Saadawi. Who was

'Duke'? A millionaire from North Carolina. Just before dying, he suddenly discovered he could not take his money with him to the grave, so he thought why not leave his name on a wall, or at the bottom of a statue? Why not pay whatever sum of money was required to ensure that his name would not be buried forever with him?

But my mother's name was buried forever. She owned nothing, had no money. According to divine and to human law, her children, including me, were her husband's property. So, I never carried the name of my mother. Her name was buried with her body and disappeared from history.

Ever since I took hold of a pen in my fingers, I have fought against history, struggled against the falsifications in official registers. I wish I could efface my grandfather Al-Saadawi from my name and replace it with my mother's name, Zaynab. It was she who taught me the letters of the alphabet: *alif, beh, teh, geem, dal*, all the way to *heh, wow, lamalif, yeh*. She used to press her hand on mine and make me write the four Arabic letters of my name. I could hear her voice like the song of birds, sing out Nawal, Nawal.

I hear her voice call out to me. I slip my hand out of my father's fingers, and run towards her. She carries me up in her arms, and holds me to her breast. The smell of her body is in my nose as though it were the smell of my own body. The sun is shining in the sky over Durham. It is a blue, blue sky. They call it Carolina blue. It is like the blue of the sky in my village, Kafr Talha, in the Delta of the Nile. The air in Durham in this month of October smells like the autumn air in Cairo. The past is one with the present, fuses into one long moment, which started the day when I was born a child crawling, then walking on the earth. My body remembers the smell of dust, the touch of the earth under my feet, the glare of the sun hurting my eyes. The plane has carried me thousands of miles across the Atlantic Ocean to the small city of Durham, and the years, more than half a century of years, have flown by. Yet the same smell is in my nose, and the same glare makes me close my eyes, and my mother's voice calling out to me, 'Nawal, Nawal', invades me with the rays of the sun through every pore. I surrender to this invasion by her voice, by her smell, by the dazzling light. I let them carry me back, once more a child darting like a butterfly through the open spaces of green under the blue sky. The sun drops gently down to the horizon, the sky throbs with red and orange colours, changing from moment to moment, the red and orange colours give way to a grey line of clouds, and the air on my bare arms and legs becomes colder and colder. But the earth still carries on it the imprint of my feet. I shiver with cold as the night envelopes me. My body feels tired, but I can still feel the warmth of the earth under my feet, so I close my eyes, lie down to rest on it, sink into a deep sleep, wake up, see the stars shining in the sky above me, hear the voice of Sittil Hajja still telling me the story of her wedding night, the 'night of entering the bride', how the blood gushed out between her thighs after the *daya* pushed her long sharp finger through her virginity, how the she-ass carried her from her father's home to her husband's house. All the way the blood kept flowing down from her over the saddle, the drums beating behind her as she went along. In the bridegroom's house she lay on a mat, shrinking into the new *gallabeya* embroidered with coloured threads and spots of blood. The bridegroom called out to her in a loud, rough voice: 'Get up girl and prepare supper.' She was slow in getting up, so the blows of his long thin cane rained down on her, the same cane with which he used to guide his donkey, and he shouted at her, 'Get up, girl, may your day of reckoning rise on you at once.'

This was the custom in the village. Every husband had to beat his bride on the wedding night before he did anything else. She had to try the taste of his stick before she could sample the taste of his food so that she would know that Allah was above, and her husband below, and she should be ready for a beating if she did not do as she was told.

On the night of her wedding Sittil Hajja was only ten years old. She had not yet had her period. Habash bore down on her as she stuffed her *tarha** into her mouth to stifle the screams. A bride should not scream or else she would be stung by a cane, or by the neighbour's tongues, and neither she nor her father would be able to face the village.

After several years, three or four, according to Sittil Hajja, her belly rose up in a first pregnancy and my father was born. She took care to make sure that the male organ was there between his thighs before letting out a resounding 'yoo-yoo'. She fought against the fever that seized hold of her and overcame it, thanks to her great joy at having given birth to a male child. After the blood ceased to flow, she performed her ablutions, then knelt in prayer to Allah for not having let her down by giving her a girl.

Sittil Hajja lived with Habash for eighteen long years before he died. She did not have a brass bed with posts, only a mat laid over the dusty ground. She gave birth to fifteen children on this mat: four boys and eleven girls. Three of the boys died, leaving only my father. Six of the girls died, leaving my five aunts Fatma, Baheya, Roukaya, Zaynab, and the youngest Nefissa who was still suckling at her mother's breast when her father Habash died at the age of thirty-eight. He died of bilharziasis, bleeding in his urine, like his father, like the peasants in the village had always done, throughout the ages, since the times of the pharaohs and the slaves of Egypt. The disease was a calamity sent by God as Sittil Hajja said, but biggest of all calamities were the eleven girls born to her, of whom to her misfortune only six had died, leaving five to live on. She would clench her five fingers into a fist, as though waving it in the face of an enemy, or of Satan and say, five girls. A catastrophe of girls!

When the eleventh girl was born it had been too much for Habash. He died of grief, so they carried him away to the cemetery in a wooden box called a *taboot*, like a coffin. Sittil Hajja

---

* Shawl, usually black in colour.

did not shed a tear for him. She waited until his body was buried under the earth, rose to her feet, heated a big tin full of water, performed her ablutions and knelt in thanks to Allah for ridding her of her husband. She had become a widow at the age of twenty-eight. She tied a black kerchief around her head, and swore that until the day she died she would let no man come near her again. Since her wedding night, she had hated all men, or since even before that, four years prior to her wedding night, when she was still a child only six years old and the *daya* Um Mahmoud came to their home.

The image of Sittil Hajja fades from my mind but her voice continues to reach my ears, as though rising from the depth of the earth:

I had just started to walk, go to the fields, and play with the children when that unnameable woman Um Mahmoud, that *daya*, that brazen daughter of a whore, came to the house, got hold of me and tied me up like a chicken with the help of four other women. She said: 'Now listen to me you girl, Mabrouka, I am going to cut off your *zambour*,* so that you will be pure and clean on your wedding night, and your husband won't run away from you in disgust, and you won't run after men.' Then she got hold of a razor, whetted it so sharp on a stone that it cut through me like a flame. I said to myself, it's all over with you Mabrouka, this is the end. I lay on the mat, the blood gushing out of me like from a tap. My mother recited the Fatiha three times for my soul as though I would die any minute. But after a few days God gave me a helping hand and I got up as full of life as the devil. You see, daughter of my son, girls have seven lives, like cats. But boys are not like girls. They have airy souls that fly away easily, and people give them the evil eye, and hang a charm around their necks. So every night I burned incense around him and recited incantations and the verse of Yaseen.† Poor thing, this child, the apple of my eye was so skinny and ate so little, not like those greedy girls. I used to hide food for him in a hole inside the wall, bring him milk straight from the tit of the buffalo, and fill a plate with cream for him. At dawn, before the sun came out, I woke up the girls and we

---

* Arabic slang for clitoris.
† Aa verse of the Qur'an recited to keep evil spirits away.

went off to the fields with the animals, laboured there until sunset
and came back carrying sacks on our backs. On Saturdays, I rode
to the market carrying whatever I could sell, and I went on putting
one piastre on top of the other until by the end of the year I had
three pounds, each one big enough to knock the other down. I hid
them between my breasts and when my son Al-Sayed came home,
I said to him, son, pride of my womb, apple of my eye, here are
three whole pounds, go buy a train ticket from Benha* to Cairo,
pay the fees of the school and the cost of the books, and the rent of
a room in the Citadel† and, pride of my womb, buy yourself a pair
of new shoes instead of the old ragged pair you're wearing. Yes,
there could be nothing less for your father than for him to wear
a new pair of shoes, walk with his head high, and enter Al-Azhar
and Dar Al-Oloum.‡ No way but for him to go to the best school
in Misr§ and become the biggest head in the whole country. Yes,
there was no way but for him to get out of the muck, never to be a
peasant like his father, and die of bilharziasis,¶ to live, and learn
and become educated and become Sayed Effendi, yes, no less
than Sayed Effendi, and even Sayed Bey like Shoukry Bey. Why
not? Was the belly that gave birth to Shoukry Bey any different
from your woman's belly, Mabrouka? I swore an oath, I swore by
Allah and the Prophet Muhammad, by Sayedna Al-Hussein and by
El-Imam Al-Shafei and Sittina Zaynab and Sittina Mariam.** I said
your son, Mabrouka, daughter of the woman from Gaza that you
are, your son is destined to marry one of the daughters of Shoukry
Bey, and you're not going to die, yes you will not die before you
dance at your son's wedding on the night when he will enter into
one of the daughters of those beys or pashas†† of Egypt. Why not?
The bellies that gave birth to the beys and the pashas are not
different from your belly, Mabrouka.

---

* Provincial capital about forty miles north of Cairo.

† District of Cairo near the religious institution of Al-Azhar. The Citadel itself
is a fortress palace built on a hill by Salah Al-Dine Al-Ayoubi.

‡ The higher institute for study of the Arabic language from which graduated
the teachers greatly esteemed when the national movement for independence was
growing.

§ Misr: Egypt, but here it meant Cairo.

¶ A worm which lives in the intestinal or urinary tract vessels and causes
bleeding, among other symptoms. Very common in Egypt at that time, especially
among the rural population.

** Bey: a title given by the king to notables. Mabrouka: Sittil Hajja's first name.
Al-Hussein and Al-Shafei: holy men (saints). Zaynab: wife of the Prophet Muhammad.
Mariam: the Virgin Mary.

†† A higher title given to members of the upper ruling class by the king.

The voice of Sittil Hajja echoes in my ears despite the passing of the years. I see her tall figure, her head upright as she walks through the village, treading firmly on the ground with her feet clad in *balghas*,* watch her knock with the flat of her sunburnt hand on the door of the Omda's† house and shout, 'Come out, Omda, and speak to me. I am Mabrouka, the daughter of the woman from Gaza and my head can reach as high as the head of any man in this village.'

---

* Pointed leather slippers open at the back, which it was the custom for villagers, especially men, to wear at the time.
† The village headman was very powerful at one time.

4

Thank God for
Our Calamities

As much as I try I cannot remember the features of my grand-mother Amna. All I can remember are her eyes. The whites of her eyes were coloured grey. The blacks of her eyes did not exist. I used to ask my mother where they had gone. Were they hidden under her lids or had they dissolved into the whites? I used to think she was blind, but she would follow everything from where she sat on the couch in the big hall. She wore a white silken *tarha* around her head. Between her hands rolled the yellow prayer beads, and her lips muttered verses from the Qur'an. She never spoke to anyone, nor did anyone speak to her, except when the servant came to tell her that the food was ready, or when her daughter (Oustaza* Fahima Shoukry) came back from her work at noon and sat down next to her for a few moments. Then a short exchange took place between them, more like silence than anything else:

'How are you today, Nena?'†
'I thank Him, my daughter.'
'Yes, Nena, we must thank Him,

---

* Term of respect for teachers, professional people, etc.
† Mother.

Thank Him for all things, Nena.
He is the only one who may be thanked
for the harm that may be befall us.*
Yes, Nena, He alone may be thanked for any harm.'

I often used to hear the phrase 'He alone may be thanked for any harm' being repeated by my grandmother Amna and my aunt Fahima, whom we called Tante (Aunt) Fahima, and who taught girls at the Teachers' Institute, so I asked Aunt Fahima who it was that alone could be thanked for the harm that befalls us. She emitted a long sigh, her bulging eyes grew even bigger behind the glass of her spectacles and she said angrily, 'Who else can it be but God?', stood up suddenly as though stung by a scorpion, and muttered, 'I beg of Thee Almighty God to forgive me for all Almighty sins',† then walked away, her iron heels striking heavily on the floor, as though she wanted them to go through it. When she summoned the male servant or the maid, it was always in a sharp, loud voice: 'Bring me a glass of water, boy.' 'Bring me my slippers, girl.' She never stopped giving orders to the servants, her voice echoing throughout the house. She imitated her father, Shoukry Bey, but as soon as he appeared at the outer door her voice dropped to a whisper, and her body quickly shrank into her room disappearing behind the closed door.

The house of my maternal grandfather, Shoukry Bey, was a villa composed of two floors in the Cairo suburb of Al-Zeitoun. It was surrounded by a big garden with a high fence. The lower half of the fence was made of stone and the upper half of iron railings, their ends rising like sharp, pointed knives. Bright red and dark purple bougainvillea and jasmine, with its small white flowers and delicate perfume, climbed over it. All through the garden lay beds of roses, red, yellow and white, and purple velvety pansies. At the edges grew tall sunflowers which opened

---

* Meaning that, since all things come from God, we should thank Him even for any harm that may befall us, and not rebel against Him.
† Meaning that the question itself bordered on a great sin since the answer should have been obvious.

their petals to the touch of the morning sun, and followed it in the same way as the earth circled round the sun.

A bell hung over the gate of the garden. It rang loudly every time the door was opened or closed. Each time it rang the wolf-dog rushed to the door barking fiercely, and eyes inside the house looked out to see who had come in or who had gone out. When my grandfather went out, my grandmother Amna sighed with relief. Her feet clad in black *pantoufles** shuffled from the bedroom to the hall. Her head was covered in a white *tarha* and her face was white with not a single drop of blood in it. Her eyes were grey and lustreless. No ray of light seemed to move in them. They were like the eyes of a corpse. There she sat in her usual place on the couch, rolling the yellow prayer beads in her hands, and muttering verses of the Qur'an.

My aunt Ni'mat would also open her door and come out, her face pale as a ghost risen from a cave, her eyelids swollen as if she had been crying all night. She stared at me from a distance with resentful, bilious eyes that saw in me the cause of all her sorrows. I was six years old. I had not known the meaning of real sadness. Over my skin passed a shiver of cold, as icy as the feel of the bare walls, as the dull colour of my grandmother Amna's eyes and the dead silence filling up the big house. Nothing broke this silence. Only the lash of sharp orders landing on the servants' heads, or the sound of the wind beating on the wooden shutters, or the dog barking whenever the bell rang out above the garden door.

When my aunt Fahima came back from her school, some movement stirred inside the house. Her heels tapped sharply on the floor. Her voice rose in the air as she quarreled with Ni'mat, her sister. They were sisters born of the same mother and the same father, yet they were different from each other in every way, had nothing in common except a mutual hatred. They shunned one another for days during which they exchanged not a single word. When they spoke it was to quarrel for the

---

* French for slippers. Usually closed and made of leather or wool.

smallest reason, or for no reason at all. It was enough for one
of them to raise a whiff of air as she passed by close to the
other for a quarrel to erupt. Sometimes it was just one of those
distant bilious looks which Ni'mat sent across the distance to
her sister Fahima.

Tante Ni'mat was in the habit of drinking a small pot of bitter
black coffee first thing in the morning, then she would tie her
head in a black kerchief, take her place on the couch, opposite
her mother, and throw bilious looks around through her red-
dened, swollen eyelids. At that precise moment, it might happen
that her sister Fahima would walk past on her way to the inner
hall. One of Ni'mat's bilious looks would fall by accident on some
part of her body. That was enough. She would come to an abrupt
stop, hitting the ground with both heels like a soldier saluting,
and pull her short, thin body up to its fullest height. Her eyes
would bulge out more than usual from behind the glass of her
spectacles, her hand would rise to her waist and suddenly her
sharp voice would shoot out as loud as it could:

'Why are you looking at me like that Ni'mat? Aren't I good
enough for you?'

'Yes, that's exactly it Fahima.'

'Why, my sister? I'm certainly better than you'll ever be.'

'In what way are you better? You're nothing but a grousy
whiskered spinster.'

'A spinster is better than the divorced woman you are my
dear Ni'mat.'

'Fiddlesticks. At least I found someone to marry me, but you
haven't found anyone to do even that.'

My Aunt Ni'mat would then stick out her long tongue taunt-
ingly, give her another of those sharp, bilious glares and repeat,
spinster, spinster. Aunt Fahima would tap on the floor again
with her iron-shod heels, stretch her arm out with clenched fist,
her index finger pointing out like an arrow which could fly out
at any moment into Aunt Ni'mat's eye, and repeat in her thin,
sharp voice, 'You're nothing but a brazen divorcee with no-one

to hold you back.' Aunt Ni'mat would retort, 'Spinster, who can't find anyone to marry her.'

I did not know the meaning of the word divorcee, nor did I know what to be a spinster meant. When I asked my mother, she pouted her lips and said, 'They're as bad as each other.' My mother was twenty-four, surrounded by five children with a sixth growing in her belly. She kept counting the days that were left for us to go home. Like me she hated this house and everyone in it, even her mother, that ever silent woman living in another world of muttering and prayers, and praises to God that went on and on like the prayer beads slipping through her fingers. Nothing brought this woman back to the world in which we lived except the sudden ringing of the bell above the garden door, a special ring unlike all the other rings that rose from it. Her ears recognized it even if her mind was wandering elsewhere, in that distant world of hers. They would twitch in a movement of sudden attention like those of a cat. She knew it was Shoukry Bey, her husband, who had opened the garden door. She could hear his footsteps over the path paved with stone leading from the outer stairs. His step was slow, his foot trod with its full weight on the stone. His body was short and thin inside the dark woollen suit. The collar of his shirt was starched white, surrounded by a shining silken necktie. His head was big for his body, topped by a red fez tilted slightly towards his right ear which protruded large below his white hair. But his nose was the most prominent feature on his face. It was a big nose, curved slightly, like a beak. Under his nose were a pair of thick, long-haired whiskers, as white as his hair. reaching across his cheekbones almost as far as the tip of his ears.

I stood in the main hall watching my grandfather as he climbed the wide marble steps. He would put his foot up on the step, hold his head high tilted slightly backwards on his neck, like a turkey cock, his fez as red as the cock's comb. I could hear him clearing his throat with a loud noise to announce his arrival. His black ebony stick tapped the stone floor of the verandah before he walked into the main hall, repeating, 'Allah, you are my power and my glory.'

Fahima and Ni'mat disappeared quickly into their rooms followed by the envious looks of my grandmother. She did not have a room of her own in which she could lock herself up. There was nothing she could do but get up from her couch and move towards this stranger who had slept in the same bed with her for more than thirty-five years.

My grandmother Amna was forty-four, but she looked seventy, with her shrunken body, her wrinkled complexion drained of all its blood, her swollen legs thrust into thick woollen stockings, her drooping features, her lids swollen over grey lustreless eyes like a surface of frozen water, under which had disappeared the irises and pupils.

I asked my mother what had happened to my grandmother to make her lose the black of her eyes. My mother clapped her hand over my mouth to smother my question and whispered to me to be quiet. My grandfather was in the house, and when my grandfather was in the house everyone had to be quiet.

But although my mother said nothing, I understood everything. It went through my body with a shiver. It was my grandfather and my grandfather was the husband of my grandmother Amna. He married her and she bore his six children, Ni'mat, Fahima, Zaynab, Hanem, Yehia and Zakareya, four girls and two boys. She was fourteen when he married her and he was eighteen years older. They had nothing in common except the written paper which said they were married.

'Marriage' was a mysterious word surrounded by secrets. Whenever it rang out in the air, my aunt Ni'mat's face went pale, and the lips of Aunt Fahima curled in scorn. Over my mother's face floated a misty sadness. Grandmother Amna would cease her muttering, the prayer beads circling between her fingers would come to a sudden stop, and her eyes became fixed, their colour changing to that of muddy stagnant water. They went so dark that not a gleam of light looked out of them. I could hear her whisper, 'Praise be to Him for He alone is to be praised for any harm which might befall us.' From the couch opposite her where my aunt Fahima sat would come the reply, 'Yes, Nena, we thank and praise Him for all things.' In the room across the hall I could hear my aunt Ni'mat sigh, 'What is apportioned to us, written on our foreheads, ordained, comes from Him, and for all that we praise and thank Him.'

I began to realize that the third person referred to by 'Him' meant God, and that all the calamities which had befallen this house had come from God. I was still a child and did not realize what the word God meant, but it became linked in my mind to the word calamity, which in turn had something to do with what they called marriage.

When I was six years old, I learnt these three words by heart and they were like one sentence: 'God, calamity, marriage.'

5

Flying with
the Butterflies

Nine months after her wedding night my mother gave birth to
her first child, a male, complete with all the organs needed to be
fully male. I had not yet come into the world, but I later heard
my grandmother say that the doors of Heaven were open to her
that day when she lifted her hands up beseeching God to bestow
a male child on her son, Sayed Effendi, a son who would lift the
head of his father high in this world and the next, and who would
be given the name of the Prophet Muhammad, Allah's prayers
and peace be with him.

Thus it was that Allah responded to Sittil Hajja's prayers,
and that my elder brother was born endowed with a skin as
white as milk like my mother and her relatives from Shoukry
Bey's family, all of whom had the fair skin of the Turks, honey-
coloured eyes and straight noses fitting well with the features
of their oval faces. He had only one fault, a fault inherited from
the ancestors of Shoukry Bey – the big protruding front teeth
which my paternal aunt, Rokaya, called a snout. I remember her
describing my mother in a whisper as the 'one with a snout' when
she was angry with her. My mother, of course, never heard her
say this, for Sittil Hajja quickly silenced her: 'Shame on you girl
… she's the wife of your brother, Al-Sayed Effendi.'

My elder brother became the darling of both my father's and my mother's family. Everyone described him as a lovely child. They said he had inherited the features of his maternal uncles, but my grandmother, Hajja Mabrouka, was not so happy with his features. She wanted her first grandson to inherit the features of his father, Al-Sayed Effendi, to take after his father, the man, and not his mother, the woman, to inherit his complexion burnt dark by the sun, a sign of manliness, and the large black eyes shining like pieces of the black precious stone in the Holy Sanctuary of Mecca. She wanted to name him Muhammad like the Prophet, but Shoukry Bey decided that his name should be Tala'at like his great-grandfather, Tala'at Pasha, who was buried in Istanbul.

'What have we to do with that foreigner from Turkey? We must give him the same name as our Prophet, may the Prophet bestow his blessings on him', my grandmother whispered into her son's ears. My father did not want to anger his mother, nor did he want to disappoint his father-in-law, Shoukry Bey, so he put both names on the birth certificate and named him Muhammad Tala'at, thus bestowing upon him one of those hybrid names so common in Egypt despite the fall of the Turkish Empire. At that time, feudal bourgeois families in Egypt still had grandiose dreams which drew them towards the glorious past of the Turkish rulers in Constantinople. The family of Shoukry Bey, even though bankrupt as a result of the world economic crisis and the collapse of the cotton market which left them almost penniless, still held on to glories that belonged to the past, and to the remnants of a feudal status now sinking to that of the middle class.

On the other hand, the family of Al-Saadawi were poor peasants who looked up to becoming civil servants in the government. My father was the first village man to have graduated from Dar Al-Oloum and the first to discard the *giba*˙ and *kaftan* for a suit, a tie and a fez. And the inhabitants of his village, Kafr Tahla, began to address his mother as Sittil Hajja, the mother of

---

˙ The long flowing inner and outer robe worn by religious dignitaries and sometimes rich villagers.

Al-Sayed Effendi.* When my father reached the post of Inspector in the Ministry of Education in the province of Al-Menoufeya, his mother bestowed upon him the title Al-Sayed Bey and the people in her village began to address her as 'the mother of the Bey'. She would sit on the threshold of her house, dressed in a black silk *gallabeya*, lifting her head with pride, her hair covered by a fine *tarha* made of black chiffon. Her legs were stretched out in front of her, her feet protruding from beneath the *gallabeya* to make sure that the passers-by would get a glimpse of the leather slippers she was wearing. They were made of real leather and her son, Al-Sayed Bey, had bought them for her together with the silk *gallabeya* and the chiffon *tarha*. They would greet her, saying: 'Health and strength to you Um Al-Sayed Bey.'

I would squat next to her on the threshold of the house, but my aunt Fatima would bring a cane chair from the visitors' room for me to sit on saying that 'the daughter of Al-Sayed Bey' could never be allowed to sit on the floor like a peasant.

My mother gave birth to me one year after my brother's birth. Sittil Hajja said that I burst out of my mother's belly like a shooting star. My aunt Ni'mat told me that I was born like devils were, standing on my feet. When I asked my mother, she told me it had been easy, without pain, but the birth of my elder brother had been difficult. He did not want to leave her womb quickly, enjoyed the comfort and the warmth of his mother's belly. When my aunt Rokaya became angry with him she addressed him as 'mother's boy'. When Aunt Ni'mat was not pleased with me she said I was the daughter of peasants. She called me the 'Slave Warwar' after one of her great-grandfather's slaves in Istanbul.

Sittil Hajja would stare at me silently. My skin was reddish brown as though it had been burnt by the sun reaching inside my mother's womb. My eyes were black, like two pieces of precious stone from the Holy sanctuary of Mecca. Sittil Hajja would hide her mouth behind her *tarha* and whisper into the ear of her

* A title of respect given to more educated people who usually became government officials.

daughter Rokaya, 'She's exactly like her father', then make a sucking noise with her lips to express regret before she added, 'if only she had been born a boy!' Aunt Rokaya would lift up her hands to the heavens and pray Allah to turn me into a boy. I could hear her say, 'God is great, and He can do anything', to which my grandmother would respond in a low voice, 'May the words go out of your mouth straight through the doors of Heaven, my daughter Rokaya.'

I would look up at the heavens fearful that the doors of Heaven would be open and that Sittil Hajja's prayers would go straight to the ears of Allah so that I would wake up from my sleep in the morning to find the cleft between my legs closed up and replaced with a male organ like the one my brother had. In the morning as soon as I woke up I slipped into the bathroom to steal a glance at my body. I did not dare look between my legs for I was afraid to part them more than was safe to get a glimpse of that forbidden area surrounded with shame and doubt, and fear of God. I was afraid that He might have really been able to transform me from a female into a male.

I was a child of six and had no way of finding out what was the power of God. My eyes would steal glances at the spot where I thought His power might manifest itself. But I was never able to see anything except a small dark area hidden deep up between my thighs, concealed behind dark clouds of fear and shame. It seemed so far away from me that I could not see it with my eyes, let alone touch it with my hands to find out what it was that God could have done with it.

Deep inside my heart I hoped that God did not have the power to change me into a male like my brother. I did not love my brother. I loved myself more than him. He seemed so big, used to beat me, pull the doll with which I played away from me, tear off her fine silken dress, her petticoat and her small knickers edged with lace, pull out her arms and legs and head, tear off all her clothes and leave her naked, open her legs as though he was looking for something, but there was nothing there. When the tears started out of my eyes, he laughed and made fun of me saying, 'Stupid, she's only a doll, not a human being.'

When we celebrated the Eid* my father bought me dolls. He bought my brother an airplane that could be wound up to fly away, or a boat with a sail, or a pistol which let out sparks. I hated dumb, lifeless dolls that could not move from their place like an airplane or a boat, or let out sparks like a pistol. If I held the pistol in my hand, my aunt Ni'mat would tear it out of my grasp, pout her lips and say, 'Nice girls play with dolls. Pistols are for boys.'

Aunt Ni'mat was short and fat, her breasts were fleshy and big, and her fat white legs showed bare under a short dress reaching down to her knees. She had a round face with a white complexion, from which rose the smell of powder and perfume and red lipstick. She was always chewing a piece of gum, pushing it out of her mouth on the tip of her tongue, or blowing it between her lips into a balloon before she sucked it back with a snap and started to chew again as she sat on a high chair, her legs stretched out, her feet dipping in a basin of warm water. Her toes were soft and smooth and swollen with flesh, and her toenails were painted red. My aunt Rokaya sat at her feet on the ground and with her long chapped fingers, burnt by the sun to the colour of the earth, she would carefully rub the pudgy soft toes of Aunt Ni'mat, and say, 'Your toes, Ni'mat Hanem, are so soft and round. May Allah smite that donkey of a man Muhammad Al-Shami, son of that mad woman Nabaweya, to the ground.'

Aunt Ni'mat would suck her lips regretfully and say, 'Our eyes cannot but see what is ordained, what is written on our foreheads.† Ever since I was born God seems to have fated me to suffer. My luck is as dark as soot, may God help me. He chose Muhammad Effendi Al-Shami for me, but the man didn't even enter into me. We just signed the marriage contract and the

---

* Religious festival after the fasting month of Ramadan, also known as the festival of the Sacrifice.
† Fate.

night we were to consummate our marriage, I received a summons to divorce by post.'

The fingers of my aunt Rokaya would come to a stop. She would lift her tired eyes to Aunt Ni'mat's face and exclaim with a gasp, 'That's terrible, Ni'mat Hanem. You mean to say you're still a virgin. May God smite him low wherever he may be. But never mind. Everything can be made up for, and everything is sent by Allah. Maybe God will send you a man worth much more than the likes of Muhammad Al-Shami, and his whole family too', at which Aunt Ni'mat would pull out a white silk handkerchief and wipe her tears, hiding her face behind the handkerchief so I would not see her cry. Aunt Rokaya would then lift the hem of her black *tarha* and dab her eyes, her mouth concealed behind it as she mumbled, 'I spent fourteen years of my life with that useless man, Muhammadein. Year after year he gave me hell, beat me every night before he swallowed his supper. Day after day I went from Sheikh to Sheikh hoping to bear a child. But what can one do, Ni'mat Hanem, if all is ordained, and written on the forehead? Everything comes from God, we praise and thank ye, God, for the sweet and for the bitter. All comes from ye, O God, and were it not for the fear of Hell, maybe a woman like me would have lost her faith a long time ago, or maybe from the very day she was born on this earth.'

I could see Aunt Ni'mat peering at me with red-rimmed bilious eyes from behind her white handkerchief, hear her say, 'Little girls should not be sitting with older people.'

I never felt I was a little girl. From the age of six I felt grown up. I often heard Sittil Hajja say that I was big, that my body was overflowing and that it would not be long before a bridegroom would come along. I was growing taller than my elder brother, and I ran faster than him when we played with our neighbours' children. At school, I did better than he did. He did not like school, and in the morning when my mother helped him put on his uniform, he kicked and cried. My father would walk up to him and say, 'Shame on you, a boy crying like a girl.' Then he would glance quickly at me where I stood upright in my uniform, my school-bag in my hand, eager to shoot out of the house with not a trace of a tear in my eyes. I could glimpse something looking out from under his thick eyebrows, something in his big pupils, something unsaid lurking inside, which said that I should have been the one to cry rather than my brother. My eyes would stare into his eyes for an instant, a fleeting moment in which it would seem to me that I read hatred, that he hated my body standing upright in its uniform, hated the eager gleam in my eyes, the desire, the impatience to be away and out of the house on my way to school.

Ever since childhood I wanted to rush out as quickly as possible from the house. I loved school despite the cane stick with which Ismail Effendi beat me over the tips of my fingers, but what I loved most was to run out into the streets or the fields, to play, to race as fast as the wind like a bird.

Ever since childhood, I have had one dream. To fly on two wings, escape from the house into the wide open spaces of the universe. But to escape where? When I was six years old I did not know. A heavy feeling like a burden, heavier than my body, seemed to pull me back to earth, pull me away from the green spaces, the sunshine, from flying with the butterflies, back to the stone house, to my room and its four walls, to the kitchen.

I hated the kitchen. In the kitchen my mother used to make me stand in front of the stove. There she would teach me how to cook, how to cut onions into rings with a sharp knife. The strong smell of onions burnt in my nose and brought tears to my eyes. Neither my brother nor my father entered the kitchen, or peeled onions or washed plates. The kitchen was the place where I knew the humiliation of being female.

School was the only place that saved me from closed walls and kitchen chores. No matter how hard the cane landed on my outstretched fingers, still in the early morning, I would put on my uniform, and shoot out of the house like a prisoner released from jail.

In the courtyard of the school, I played with the girls. The yellow sand, heated by the bright sun, felt warm under our feet. We sat on the wooden benches, or hid under them as we played hide and seek. We ran and jumped and raced one another, played 'The fox has passed by, its tail knotted seven times' or 'Camel driver, camel driver, where have your camels gone?' or 'A pinch of salt from the woman next door'. What I enjoyed most was skipping with a rope. I never stopped until the hunger pangs gnawed into my stomach. Then I would open my little basket and the delicious smell of bread and cheese and homemade pickles would fly straight up into my nose, as though my mother was hovering nearby.

6

Killing the Bridegroom

The more the years go by the greater my yearning for my mother becomes. I am over sixty and yet I often see her in my dreams. Sometimes I can feel her holding on to my hand, her lips parted, trying to let out words, but she dies, and the words remain unsaid. At other times, I glimpse her standing dressed in her silk dress with thin shoulder straps, laughing as only she could laugh while we sing together, 'De te tessa – de te tessa.'

I do not know what these letters or words meant, but my mother said that I used to sing them to myself before I learned to talk. My head would nod up and down when my mother sat me on the couch, perhaps because my head was heavier than my body. She surrounded me with cushions on every side. I was a quiet child, and would sit like that for hours without crying or screaming, not at all like my brother. All I did was nod my head up and down and sing or gurgle: 'De te tessa – de te tessa.'

I caught myself nodding my head and repeating the same refrain as I sat in Perkins library, my fingers moving over the keys of the computer as though it were a piano. Here I can close my eyes and dream up any book. I used to go round from library to library looking for books which I never found. But now they were at the tips of my fingers. I just had to touch the keys and out they would come on to the screen under some title or other. The world of computers was now part reality and part dream. I had learned the secret of the keys. I pressed down on the letters of my surname El Saadawi and in a moment there were the titles of my books, all of them, in English and in Arabic, shining on the screen in front of me. Under my ribs I could feel my heart flutter like that of a child. Happiness flowed through me as my fingers sought for the keys again and I repeated the same refrain under my breath: 'De te tessa – de te tessa.'

But it seems that my voice was loud enough to be heard. Eyes turned towards me, as I sat in the reading room. Next to me was an American professor, his beard long, the colour of ripe corn, his head bald, burnt red by the sun. I caught him staring at me, his eyes bulging behind thick glass spectacles like the eyes of Tante Fahima with a silent look of disapproval which chased away all joy, stripped me of my childhood, brought back the wrinkles of old age. Once again I remembered that I was more than sixty years old. I shrank back into my clothes the way I used to shrink into my tattered uniform in primary school. As a child I was ashamed of being poor, ashamed of my peasant aunt, tried to hide her away from the curious eyes of my schoolmates, like a stigma.

Now I am ashamed of my old age. I try to hide the veins that stand out under the skin of my hands. When someone asks me how old I am, I am silent for a moment, then in a small voice say 'sixty'. The word sixty stops in my throat. Its letters seem to curl up and get stuck, like a sob held back. I almost choke. Then I lift my head up, tense the muscles of my body, straighten my back, defy the age which I have reached, the years and the passage of time, put on my jogging shoes, and rush off to the country trail winding through the forest of Duke. I no longer run like I used to. Now it's something between a quick walk and a run. But I can still feel my muscles contracting, feel the firm tread of my feet on the ground. My feet are big like those of Sittil Hajja, and my steps are steady. They hit the ground exactly like hers did. I tense the muscles of my back, brace my shoulders, keep my body straight the way she did. To this day, I do not know where she drew her pride from, why her back was always straight, and her head high. Hers was a real pride, coming from her body, born with it, something in the blood, from her mother, or her grandmother, that woman from Gaza. I did not know who that Gaza woman was, or what she was like. All I can remember was that Sittil Hajja would stretch up her long neck and say, 'I am Mabrouka, the daughter of the Gaza woman', and immediately her mother and her grandmother would be conjured up before my eyes, looking just like the goddess Nefertiti or Queen Hatchipsut.

I loved Sittil Hajja much more than my grandmother Amna or any of the other women in my mother's or my father's families. But I used to hate her when she said: 'A boy is worth fifteen girls at least.' I would burst out in anger: 'No! Sittil Hajja, one boy is not worth fifteen girls at least!', and stamp my foot on the ground with rage. She would stretch out the long dark fingers of her hand in the air and add: 'Girls are a blight. A boy, the Prophet bless him, lifts his father's head up in the world, and in the next, carries his father's name, and hands it down. With a boy, the family household is kept running, but girls get married and go off, leaving the father's house, and their children carry the names of the men they marry.'

I stamped on the ground with my foot again and screamed out, 'I will never marry!' My grandmother would be seized with a fit of laughter until the tears ran down from her eyes, and then say, 'God has sent you a wonderful bridegroom, a man straight from Heaven and soon we will be celebrating your marriage and your wedding night.' I would stamp on the ground several times and shriek, 'I will never marry! Never, never, never, never!' My grandmother would start laughing again until the tears flowed from her eyes, and she almost choked, 'Marriage is your destiny like all girls. It is God's will, O daughter of my son.'

Her voice kept echoing in my ears as I slept. In my dreams I used to ask myself, 'What is the relation between God, marriage, and a husband?' God appeared in them dressed like a bridegroom. To me, a bridegroom was like one of the dolls which my mother made out of the remains of cloth, and stuffed with cotton or old rags, dressed in a dark jacket similar to the jackets worn by my father and my grandfather, and in long dark trousers tied around the waist with a ribbon of black taffeta, with a red fez made out of woollen material on its head. After she had finished with all that she inserted two black beads into the head for eyes.

In my dreams, God often appeared to me in the form of one of these dolls, dressed in a dark suit, with the red fez on his head and the two black beady eyes shining wickedly in the night. He used to hide in the shadow of the clothes-stand, then move out slowly from behind it. Sometimes he would appear with the upper half of his body only, and the red fez on his head, and shake his fist or his finger at me, his eyes all the while letting out little sparks. I would hide my head under the bed covers, until I could hardly breathe, then poke it out and peep quickly in the direction of the clothes-stand, but meanwhile he would have emerged with his whole body and I could see him creeping towards me. I opened my mouth to scream but no sound emerged, and at that very moment my eyes would open wide in terror, and I awoke.

My dreams often changed. Sometimes I would see him standing behind the window or the door. His long arm shot out to catch hold of me as I ran and ran. Sometimes I ran so far that I found the sea in front of me, plunged into it and swam like a fish. Then he would follow me into the sea, but not knowing how to swim, he drowned, and his whole body sank, only his red fez or the black ribbon of taffeta with which his trousers were tied around his waist remained floating on the surface of the water.

My younger sister Leila and I often played with the dolls together. She would throw the bride or the bridegroom out of the window into the street, and my mother would make us other dolls. I sat on the carpet with the dolls around me and told my sister stories about them. I do not remember the stories I told her, but when the bridegroom beat the bride to death, she wept bitterly. Then we covered the dead body of the bride with a white sheet, and caught hold of the bridegroom to punish him.

Punishment meant taking off his red fez, his jacket and his long black trousers. Taking off his trousers was not as easy as the rest, so we used a pair of scissors to cut through them from the waist down to his feet. I expected to see a piece of flesh dangling between his legs, like the piece of flesh my brother had, and which my aunt Ni'mat called the bird. But we found nothing. With the point of the scissors we delved further down for that piece of flesh which made the yoo-yoos shrill out of the throats of the women in the family, but still to no avail. There was no piece of flesh, neither was there that cleft which lay hidden high up between the thighs of girls. My sister Leila would say, 'He must be hiding his bird in his belly.'

So I would grasp the scissors and cut into the belly of the bridegroom only to find it stuffed with pieces of cotton, rags and straw. My sister would start to cry again because the bridegroom was now dead, pull the sheets off the head of the bride, and whisper into her ears to tell her that the bridegroom was now dead and done with, that he had gone to God in Heaven, so she should wake up because God would be sending her another husband much better than the first.

My mother used to get angry with us when she saw how we had split open the bellies of the dolls. She would hide the scissors from us, and we would look everywhere for them without success. But in the kitchen drawer we found a small sharp knife which my mother used to cut cheese. It had a shining edge like a razor blade, which cut into the bellies of the dolls just as well.

The young girls of Shoukry Bey's household never cut open the bellies of their dolls. A girl there would carry her doll in her arms close to her breast, rock her to sleep like a mother, put her to bed and cover her, then sit by her side and sing to her until she slept. When the doll woke up she would suckle it at her breast which had not yet budded out.

I did not like to play with the children of my mother's family. I much preferred the company of the children in my father's family. We rode donkeys and went to the fields together, ran through the green expanses chasing butterflies, took off our clothes and swam in the stream or in the Nile, kneaded water and earth into mud, and moulded it into houses or trees, or figures like human beings or animals or birds.

From the day I was born, the village remained closer to my heart than the city. The city was called Cairo, but people in my village called it Misr. My village was called Kafr Tahla but its inhabitants cut the name short and called it Al-Kafr. It was situated on a bank of the Nile but people called the River Nile 'Al-Bahr', which means the sea. The map showed that in fact it was only the Rasheed branch of the Nile. The Rasheed branch and the Damietta branch were the two tributaries of the River Nile. My village, Al-Kafr, was not on the map, but for me its existence was more real than that of Cairo.

I was still a small child when I first saw Cairo. I do not remember how old I was. It seemed a strange city to me, huge like some fantastic monster sprouting from the belly of the Nile. Everything in it seemed to be old, even ancient, as though it had already existed before the city was born, before the Sphinx or the Pyramid of Cheops. All the houses were made of stone, like the stones out of which the Pyramids had been built, big square stones one on top of the other. The walls around the houses were also made of stone. As a child I could not imagine how children could live like that behind walls of stone. In my imagination, I used to recall my village and make comparisons. The sky over the city was different from that which I looked up at in my village. The sun and the moon, too, were different. It seemed to me as though it was not the same sky, the same sun, or the same moon.

The strangest thing of all were the streets of this city. They were made of tarmac, were wide and ran up to the horizon piercing into the sky where God sat on his throne. At the time I thought that God sat on a throne like the king, on a big chair with a high back made of gold. To me it seemed impossible that the streets could reach as far as Allah, that the earth and sky could meet in that line visible to my eyes above the asphalt of the streets.

The house of my grandfather Shoukry Bey was a big house also made of stone, surrounded by a high stone and iron wall. It had a big garden with a dog that looked like a wolf. It was a savage dog that could bite me, not like the friendly dogs in the village. I used to hold on to the hand of my mother with all five fingers afraid lest her hand slip out of my hold. When I walked through the streets I kept looking around me as though I was walking through a city over which a spell had been cast. The end of each street ran into the beginning of another street and all of them looked the same, dividing the city into big regular sections. Each section was bigger than the parts out of which it was made, and all of them were built out of stone and cement and iron.

Was the Cairo which I saw in my childhood another Cairo, a different Cairo to the one I got to know later on? It looked unreal to me. People's faces were pale, almost white, as though made of chalk. The cheeks of the women were a bright red like the cheeks of dolls, and their lips too were painted red.

The village was much closer to me. Its little houses made of mud snuggled together. It was real mud, and I could hold it in my hand. The streets were narrow alleys, and I could see where they began and where they ended, and the dust which lay over them was real dust. The faces of people were real, their skin burnt brown by the sun. Their *gallabeyas* were made of cotton and smelt of the human body, of sweat and dust, of gooseberries, and maize, and pastry, and wheat. The waters of the Nile ran in the fields, irrigated the green plants. I ran through the fields with the other children. We plucked sweet figs, and Navel oranges, from the bushes and the trees, ate cucumbers, munched big green fava beans, filled the hollow of our hands with water from the river and drank. But the water in the city came out of a metal tap, had a metallic taste. Everything in the city, even the fruit and the vegetables, seemed artificial, manufactured, unreal.

At that time I was only a child. I knew nothing about the city or the village. I did not know that despite the differences between them, there was one thing which did not differ. It was a sameness which I could see looking out through the eyes around me, something I could not exactly define. I felt it in my body like a shiver of cold: I had been born a female in a world that wanted only males. This realization, this fact, ran through my body like a shiver of cold, a dark shiver, as murky as death.

Later I would pick up a pen, write down letters and words, leave them free to express themselves, so that there should be no difference between the letter of the words and the truth, but the words written down on sheets of paper were never the truth. The struggle between me and words was never-ending. Letters and words, instead of being a means of communication, put a distance between me and things as they were.

Sometimes I would snap the pen between my fingers, tear up the paper, and stop writing. But it was not long before I went back to writing, like a child to the breast of her mother. Writing to me was life, like the embrace of my mother, like love, and love, if real, happens without reason, but since then I have never stopped trying to discover the reason. Why do I write? Why have I spent my life writing short stories and novels? Maybe I wanted to do something, to draw a true image of myself and make the world see it, bring back the image which had been obscured by another image, make the silent child hidden in my depths speak up. I had not yet learned to speak, but my body was able to feel the shiver creep up, able to understand the silence in the eyes, to see the words staring out. I wanted to get hold of something sharp, like scissors, or a razor blade, or a pen, plunge it into those eyes, open them the way my sister and I split open the belly of the bridegroom doll when we played with it.

I used to take hold of the pen and press down with its pointed nib on the sheets of paper. I made my younger sister talk. I made my sisters speak up despite all the people around us who were forcing silence on their voices. I made the silent child within me express herself through the characters I put down in black ink on the sheets of paper.

I was a silent child. I looked around me with eyes full of wonder. What is it that dazzled my eyes since the day I was born? To me the world seemed a magic world. It was unreal. Behind the magic world hid a real one and I had to find it.

Perhaps the whole of my life has been this search for the real hidden behind what is false. When I was a child, I could not tell from where came deception, from where came the lies. Was it my eyes that could not see, or was it the people around me describing things in a way which was unreal, including that self which was me?

I would look in the mirror, try to see myself as I really was. When I was a child I could not tell who was lying to me, who was drawing an image of me which was not myself, not the original. Throughout the years of my life I wrote trying in vain to abolish the distance between the image and the original, for letters, words on paper are not the body, can never be the body with which I live.

7

Daughter of the Sea

Every day in the early morning I walk a distance of seven kilometres along the path winding through Duke Forest. I walk with a rapid stride just as I used to do around the Nile in Giza. Here I am alone in the dark shadows of the tall trees, the pines, the conifers, the elms. The air is still, the sky is grey. No rain, no rustle of leaves, no sounds, just the tread of my feet, dub, dub, dub, on the ground, a repeated sound which reminds me of the knocks on the door that night of June in the year 1992. It was after midnight, around two o'clock in the morning. I was asleep in my bed. One of those hot humid summer nights in Cairo. Not a breath of air, and those repeated knocks resounding in my ears like a dream, or a nightmare.

They stood outside the door, well-armed, polite. Eleven years had passed since September 1981 and they were back. Last time they had broken in with rifle butts. This time they rang the bell. I did not hear the ring, did not open the door, so they knocked. I can see their faces through the mist far away there, across the ocean, crossing time into nowhere, going beyond reason, for reason is a crime. Since I started writing I have understood my crime. My crime has been to think, to feel. But writing for me is like breathing in the air of life. I cannot stop.

Nawal, aged seven (*right*), with her brother Tala'at,
her younger sister Leila and the two younger brothers
in Alexandria in 1938.

I wrote to bring back my mother's face, to describe it as it
was. Sometimes her features were lost as though I never had a
mother, as though she never lived. At other times, I could see
her features stand out clearly. I had not learnt to speak. I cried
to make her take me out of bed and sit me up. Sitting on the
couch I could see her face more clearly. She put cushions all
around me to prevent my falling off. She held my head and put a
soft cushion behind it. Her hand was smooth over my cheek and
had that smell of mother which I knew so well. The smell was
hers, belonged to no-one else. It came to me in coloured rings.
The rings melted into one another, fused with smell and touch.
I touched the coloured rings with outstretched fingers, sniffed
them with my nose, tasted them with my tongue, sucked at them
with my lips around her breast, my eyes fastened to her face.

Her face had the roundness and the whiteness of her breast.
Her eyes were big and full of light. They were two circles of pure
white around two honey-coloured circles breathing warmth.
They were tender, touched my face like milk flowing from her

breast, which filled me up with sleep, so that my lids closed by themselves. I floated over expanses of white light. I swam in the sea, never reached the land, then woke up on my mother's breast reaching shore at last. It was the only shore I knew in this vast expanse. Beneath its smooth surface I could feel her heart. It beat with mine. She and I were one heart beating in the body which was us.

On the sea-shore she taught me how to walk. My eyes searched the ground as I felt my steps. My head, now lighter than my body, was held up. My eyes took in the sea, a broad expanse of blue floating in the sun. I filled my lungs with air, breathed in the odour of sun, of salt and seaweed and of mother's skin.

My mother's breast was smooth like sand on the sea-shore. Our breathing rose and fell in a movement that was one. The air went in and out between her chest and mine, carrying with it the smell, the tang of salt and fresh sea air. I lay on the shore wearing a swimsuit with shoulder straps. It was green, with blue and red and orange bands, but in the photograph the colours change to black and white.

The only remnant from this period is a photograph, taken by a chance photographer in a chance moment of my life. Fifty-eight years have gone by since then. The photograph has survived in an envelope in the bottom drawer of my desk. The small rectangle of paper has lost its shine. The words written on the back have faded, but the handwriting of my mother still stands out. Thirty-six years have passed since my mother died, but her letters are still there on the photograph: 'Chatby Beach, Alexandria, 18 June 1935.'

In the photograph I can see myself lying on the sand wearing the swimsuit with its bands of black and white. My mother is sitting next to me wearing a swimsuit also coloured black and white. It covers her belly and her chest, with shoulder straps on either side. My younger sister, Leila, is sitting between her legs and is wearing a swimsuit which is smaller, but is just like mine. My father is sitting a little distance away, his chest and belly are bare, his swimsuit has no shoulder straps, and next to him is my brother wearing a swimsuit which covers only a small part of his body below his navel and above his thighs.

My mother used to hold me up on the surface of the sea, teach me how to jump or float over the waves. I thrash the water with my arms and legs, and laugh. I drown under the waves with laughter. My mother pulls me out, laughing all the time. Our laughter rises in the air above the waves. The waves rise up, then break into white surf. The white of the surf melts into the blue of the sea, and the sea fuses with the sky, travels to where they meet far away at the horizon. My mother's arms carry me high up, and my head touches the heavens.

My mother used to swim alone like a wave in the sea. I imagined she was the daughter of the sea who, born of its waters, had given birth to me. She and I had emerged from its warm blue depths, on to the smooth white sands, under this pure blue sky, bathed in this golden sunlight. This was our air, our sun, our sea. This was our land, and it belonged to her and me. When we laughed our voices were carried by the air, transported through the waves from one wave to the other, from one country to another, on and on, endlessly.

Her arms embrace me, hold me high up over the waves, leave me free to swim alone, then encircle me again, so that her body becomes my body, before she lets me go once more, her body separate from mine. Over the waves and under them we continue this never-ending game of becoming one, fusing and separating from each other again.

In the photograph my father is sitting far away from me, and near him is my brother. My father always kept a distance, his distance separated between us in the photograph, on the seashore. Sometimes in my dreams, my arms would stretch out and embrace my father, but his arms never stretched out to me. He always maintained this distance between us. He occupied his own space away from me. His body was tall, his head far above, unreachable. He had a dark, square moustache over his upper lip. When he stood up on the sand, his body hid the sun and sea from me. He stood there, a tall giant who never came near, never bent down to kiss me on the cheek. Throughout his life, he never kissed me once. He stood tall, his big bones jutting out under the skin, brown as the colour of river silt. His muscles stood out under his skin, moved under the hair which covered his chest and thighs. When I knocked against him, I could feel them hard and cold under the drops of salty seawater.

Against the white sand, the contours of my father's body were well-defined, emphasizing its existence, an independent, solid existence in a world where everything was liquid, where the blue of the sea melted into the blue of the sky with nothing between. This independent existence was to become the outer world, the world of my father, of land, country, religion, language, moral codes. It was to become the world around me. A world made of male bodies in which my female body lived.

I lay on the sea-shore of the Mediterranean in my swimsuit. It was made of an elastic material which pressed tight on my chest and my belly and prevented the air and the sun from reaching them. My father stood with both his chest and his belly bare in the sun.

I used to pull down the straps from my shoulders, uncover my chest and my belly, but my aunt Ni'mat would raise her hand and slap me. Her sharp voice pierced my ear, 'Shame on you.' I would point to my brother and say, 'Why him?' and back would come the answer, 'He is a boy and you are a girl.'

This phrase bored repeatedly into my ears from the day I was born. My mouth swallowed it with the sea-water and I choked: 'He is a boy and you are a girl.' I could feel the bitter tang of salt burn my throat. It was a strange bitterness as though the blue of the sea had turned into crystals of pure salt, as though the sun was burning my skin. All the colours, the green, the red, the golden, turned grey or black.

Maybe it was the anger which had started to grow inside me like weeds grow in the sea. I could see the weeds, their dark shiny ribbons floating in the clear blue water. They sank to the bottom, floated up, were pushed out by the waves along the shore, then withered under the sun to become like dead snakes, or catfish.

My anger was still nascent, growing inside me like tender green shoots. Their tender green turned blue, and the blue turned black. The colours intermingled, fused into the black colour of anger, and of the other feelings growing out of it.

My brother bared his chest to the air and sun, but I had to cover mine, because my chest was a stigma, a shame, that had to be hidden from people's eyes. The word 'stigma' pierced my ear like a nail. It was an ugly word. My chest was as flat as that of my brother. I was a small child, younger than my brother. I had not yet learned to speak, to answer back to grown-up people like my father, yet I had become a part of the big world, a part of my father's world, and my place in it had already been fixed just because I was a girl.

My father would look up at the sky. At night he would sit on the balcony and look out over the city at the stars. My mother would be in the kitchen preparing the evening meal. My brother sat next to my father gazing at the stars with him. My father spoke to my brother but said nothing to me. He read out of the Qur'an to him, told him about God.

When I was a child, I thought that the God they talked about belonged to my father and my brother and that I had nothing to do with him. I also thought that the sky, with its stars belonged to them. My father would point with his finger to a trail of stars and say, 'That is the Milky Way', then to single stars and say 'That is the planet Mars, that is Venus, and that, over there, is Jupiter.' With his finger, he would name each star for my brother, just as God taught Adam the names of things. God did not tell us in His book that he taught Eve anything. God did not address women in His book.

My father often told us about Adam, how God elevated him above the angels and ordered Satan to kneel down and worship him, and how the sun and the moon and the stars and the heavens bent low before the Prophet Joseph. I used to listen to my father, my mouth open, my eyes staring wide at him. The world of the Qur'an was like the world of my father, the affair of men only. I dozed to the sound of my father's voice as he told us these stories, slipped into sleep, as though drowning in the sea, sunk deeper and deeper until I touched bottom and swallowed bitter salt water. My mother was now absent. Her arms were no longer there to pull me out. There was no-one to reach down and lift me out of the deep waters. I woke up in the morning with the bitter taste of salt in my mouth. Under my body the sheet was wet with salty water that smelt like urine. I would get out of bed, my body shrinking with shame. I wrapped my arms around my breasts to hide the stigma budding out. I pulled the heavy covers over the wet sheet so that nobody could see, but Aunt Ni'mat was there to pull them off, to run through the house shrieking my shame to the universe.

Gradually, my mother was withdrawing from my life. I no longer saw her except in the kitchen. I no longer heard her speak. Most of the time she sat listening to my father's stories as he moved from Allah and the Prophet Muhammad to the British and the king, then he would go on to the headmaster of the school in which he taught, for at that time we were in Alexandria and my father was a teacher in the Abbassieh secondary school for boys. The headmaster of the school was called Al-Nazir (superintendant or inspector).

The distance between my mother and me grew bigger and bigger, and the distance between my father and me smaller and smaller. My mother began to sit at the far end of the couch. Year after year the gap between us increased. My father stretched out his long legs and occupied the whole space. The space taken by my mother was shrinking all the time. She sat there, her body hiding in her clothes, her breasts hanging down as she suckled one child after the other. Her waist disappeared as her belly became swollen with child. Fat crept around her body, showing pale through her skin. She no longer belonged to the world which I shared with my father and my brother. Her world was another world which made me shiver every time I thought of it, the world of the kitchen, smelling of onions and garlic, filled with smoke or soot rising from a kerosene-burning stove.

The world of my father was the northern balcony, overlooking the flower nursery, open under the starry night, with Allah, and the Prophet Muhammad and the British and the king looking down on us. I used to hear the voice of my father echoing in the night as he said, 'Empty the ink pot over your report Oustaz' (headmaster).

The voice of my father vibrated through space as he sat on the balcony. It echoed in the house, in the whole universe, as though it was the voice of God. I would close my eyes as though avoiding light, despite the dark night all around. I was hiding something from my father, perhaps hiding my eyes, lest he look into them and see what was inside, glimpse the dark weeds floating deep at the bottom with their ink-coloured tendrils.

On the northern balcony of our home in Alexandria I sit listening to my father. Our flat is on the ground floor of a tall building. From the balcony, steps lead down into a small garden surrounded by a high wall. Beyond the wall I hear the rumble of a train as though it is arriving from another world, so powerful that the floor under my feet trembles, and the walls of our house shake violently, so that I feel they might collapse at any moment. But my father says that the building is big and solid and will never give way.

I used to believe everything my father said, learn his words by heart, listen to his stories as if they were the truth itself. I would gaze up at his huge body thinking that I was the daughter of this powerful man who was victorious in all his battles, and there were many of them: now with the owner of our building, or the headmaster of the school, before with the British, or the king, or the Germans, or other enemies unknown to me.

The first time I went to school was in Alexandria. I can remember only its name, the Muharram Bey School for Girls. The
street on which we lived was called Muharram Bey Street. It was
a long, frightening street which led to the other world where
all of us would go. I used to run from home to school, and from
school back home without stopping for a moment, fearing that
some thief might kidnap me. I had heard many stories about
thieves. In Alexandria the story of Raya and Sekina* was often to
be heard on people's lips. Both of these women had died before I
was born, but their story continued to go the rounds for over half
a century. Every time the police arrested a man or a woman who
stole small children, people remembered Raya and Sekina.

Before I left for school in the morning my mother would
remove my small golden earrings, saying that Raya and Sekina
used to steal children wearing such jewellery. Children were of
no importance to thieves if they did not wear golden earrings. At
night when I went to bed, I tugged at them, trying to pull them
off. Each earring was provided with a slender nail locked into
a clasp behind the lobe of my ear. It kept scraping against the
pillow when I moved my head, so I pulled at it. In the morning
my mother would notice the drops of blood on my pillow. The
lobes of my ears were often swollen and the small holes for the
two nails bled at their edges. I thought I was born with these
holes in my ears, that all girls were born with them so that the
earrings could go through. I would look at my brother's ear out
of the corner of my eyes. There was no hole in it, no nail passing
through to hurt him at night.

Later I found out who it was that had done this to me. It was
Um Muhammad who had almost drowned me in the basin of
water the day I was born. She had come back one week later,
holding a long sharp needle between her thick, coarse fingers

---

* Two women who lured children, especially girls, into their home, stole whatever jewellery they had on them, murdered them, cut them into pieces and then fed
the pieces into a mincing machine to hide all traces of their crime.

which she put in the fire until it turned red, then pushed it through the lobes of my ears.

Did she see in me an enemy? Was it some kind of feud between her and the female sex? Did she hate herself so much? There was a strange gleam in her eyes when she pierced the ears of a young girl, or cut into her clitoris, as though deep down she gloated over her victim, felt a mixture of joy and revenge at what she did. Her fat body sagged inside her black *gallabeya* reeking with the smell of dry blood, stale sweat, black and red henna, iodine, methylated spirits, alum, incense and raw gum. She dyed her hair with red henna, and plaited it with twisted strands of goat's hair or sheep's wool into two thin braids, wound a black kerchief around them, and pulled it as tight as she could to make a knot above her eyebrows.

In the village when the women gathered to mourn, or walked in a funeral procession, I used to see these black kerchiefs tied around their heads. On the second day of the Eid, in the early morning they would tie their heads with these black kerchiefs and go off to visit their dead in the cemetery. Over every brow protruded the knot, but the knot jutting out over the eyebrows of Um Muhammad was not the same as any other knot. It was pitch black, larger than any other knot, with four sharp serrated flaps sticking out. It moved with every movement of her head, crouched like a black scorpion in the middle of her forehead, staring at me through a single eye without lashes.

Before she came into the house through the outer door I could hear her call out in a loud voice, 'Folks whose house this is.' Sittil Hajja would sit up and exclaim abruptly: 'Uzrain [Israel, the angel of death] has come.' 'Who is Uzrain?' I asked. 'He is sent by God, descends from Heaven down to earth, and spirits people away before they realize what is happening to them', answered Sittil Hajja.

Whenever I heard her voice I disappeared. Ever since I was born I had seen her staring at me with that single eye, open wide, like a circle with a lid that never blinked. The eye narrowed as it dropped down below my belly, somewhere between my thighs, always probing for that piece of flesh called *al-zambour*, or in learned language known as *al-bazar*. She kept searching for it, as though eager to see it emerge from its depth, as though just one look from her eye at the place where it hid could draw it out. Then she would pick up the razor, hold it between her thick coarse fingers, sharpen it on a piece of stone, back and forth until it turned red like fire, pull at the *bazar* and cut it at its root with the blade, bury it in a hole, and cover the hole with dust, as she called on Allah three times to protect those present from the devil, after which, reciting the Fatiha three times, she washed the blood off her hands in a basin of water. Reciting the Qur'an over the bleeding wound had the same effect as iodine. It killed the germs, sterilized the wound and cleansed it of all sin. It was purification, a *tahara*,* and it was the *daya* who carried it out.

In 1937, at a time when I had just reached the age of six, all girls were circumcised before they started menstruating. Not a single girl, whether from the city or the village, from a rich or a poor family, escaped. Grandmother Amna, the wife of Shoukri Bey, and my mother Zaynab Hanem were both circumcised. My mother did not rescue me from this operation, nor did she rescue any of her other daughters, but I was able to protect my daughter, and many other girls, from undergoing it, when I started writing over forty years ago.

At the age of six I could not save myself from it. Four women, as hefty as Um Muhammad, cornered me, and pinned me down by the hands and feet, as though crucifying me like the Messiah by hammering nails through his hands, and feet. I had learnt from a Coptic† classmate in school that the Messiah had been crucified. 'Who was the Messiah?' I asked. My father explained to me that he was our Lord Jesus, and had not been crucified but,

---

* Circumcision among ordinary people is called *tahara*, which means cleansing, or purifying.

† Egyptian Christian. The majority of Christians in Egypt belong to the Egyptian Coptic Orthodox church (Copt from Egypt).

as the Qur'an said, people had been brought to believe that he had in fact been crucified, whereas this was not true. My aunt Ni'mat described my Coptic classmate as a Nousraneya,* a blue bone,† and said she would end in Hell.

My school friend was called Mariam and she was six years old. One day the *daya* pounced on her also and cut off the *bazar* from between her thighs. Girls who believed in the Messiah did not escape any more than did those who believed in Muhammad.

My paternal aunt, Rokaya, said that the Prophet had ordained that the *bazar* of girls be cut off. Yet I could not imagine that Prophet Muhammad, or Jesus, or any other prophet could ordain that such a thing be done. Could any prophet be like that? How could the prophets carry such a hatred for the *bazars* of young girls, and if they did, why was it so? The word 'why' stayed with me throughout my life. It led me to read what prophets and gods had written, starting with the God Amoun in ancient Egypt right down to our Lord Muhammad, the last of the prophets.

Since I was a child that deep wound left in my body has never healed. But the deeper wound has been the one left in my spirit, in my soul. I can not forget that day in the summer of 1937. Fifty-six years have gone by, but I still remember it, as though it were only yesterday. I lay in a pool of blood. After a few days the bleeding stopped, and the *daya* peered between my thighs and said, 'All is well. The wound has healed, thanks be to God.' But the pain was there, like an abscess deep in my flesh. I did not look at myself to find out where the pain was exactly. I could not bear to see my body naked in the mirror, the forbidden parts steeped in shame and guilt. I did not know what other parts in my body there were that might need to be cut off in the same way. So at night I lay in bed, my eyes wide open in the dark. I had no idea what fate had in store for me. Only Allah could see into the

* A non-Muslim, a foreigner or alien.
† Copts are secretively or sometimes insultingly called 'blue bones' by Muslims because of a bluish tint in their dark skin. Amongst friends the term may be used jokingly.

future, and the future was full of danger. Now my body, like all the bodies that moved around me, had turned against me, and might face me with terrifying things.

When I reached the age of nine I noticed blood coming out from between my thighs. In scholarly language it was called *maheed* or *heid* (flow), which means menstruation and is mentioned in the Qur'an. A verse says: 'And they ask you about menstruation. Say it is an offence, so keep away from menstruating women until they are cleansed.' The offence caught me by surprise that day. I opened my eyes in the morning to find my knickers soaked in blood. Had the *daya* sneaked up to me during the night and cut off something else from between my thighs? Or was it a jinni, or a devil that had slipped in under the bottom of my door and torn the membrane of chastity which God had created in the body of girls, so that people could tell who was a virgin and who was a married woman, and so that its presence could serve as a proof of good morals. When I talked it over with my school friend Mariam, she told me the story of our Lady the Virgin Mary, how God sent his representative (a spirit) to her, and how after that she gave birth to the Messiah, son of God.

I was only nine the day I saw blood in my knickers. I did not know that this was my first menstruation. I thought that maybe God, instead of sending someone to represent him, had come to me himself and torn the membrane of my chastity. When I saw him in my dreams he looked very angry. At that time my sister and I played with dolls, and when the Lord doll sank in the sea and drowned we were happy. Had God wanted to punish me? Had he afflicted me with bilharziasis so that I would go on bleeding until I had lost all my blood, and die? My great-grandfather Habash and his son Al-Sa'adawi had both died of bilharziasis.

I hid under the covers and prayed God to forgive me for my sins, then crept out of bed to the bathroom where I could wash away all traces of my guilt and shame and conceal them from everyone, even my mother. Would God answer my prayers before anyone in the house found out? God's forgiveness lasted half an hour, or an hour at most, but praise be to Him for small mercies. After that, my underwear was again soaked in that dark red colour. So I washed it all off again, did my ablutions, and prayed, burying my head in the wool of the prayer rug, fervently asking God Almighty to forgive me for my almighty sins, kneeling and prostrating myself again and again.

In the midst of one of my prostrations something gushed out from between my thighs onto the prayer rug leaving a big stain, yes on that sacred carpet brought back by Sittil Hajja from the Hejaz. It was a small grey carpet made of Persian wool, with the design of the sacred Kaba* worked on it. How could I have allowed the pollution of my blood to sully the sacred shrine? My humiliation was great. All the neighbours learned what had happened. Tongues wagged in my father's and mother's families, spread to the whole village, and throughout town.

But I kept asking myself: how could the blood of my body be polluted, be unclean? This was the first time I had heard the word polluted or unclean. Menses, people said, were unclean blood, and when a girl menstruated she was not allowed to touch anything sacred, such as the book of God, not permitted to pray or to fast or to read from the Qur'an. Her tongue became unclean, her hands too. If someone who had done his ablutions shook her hand, his ablutions and his prayers would no longer be acceptable to God.

I kept going to the bathroom. The red stain refused to go, and when it did it left a dark, or yellow patch behind it, something like a shadow. If the patch disappeared then there always remained an odour, a smell, like some evil spirit hovering around my body.

I was seized with something like an obsession, a kind of neurosis. I kept washing my hands with soap and water all day. It was a neurosis which affected many girls, whether Muslim, Coptic or Jewish. I had a Jewish classmate who, like me, never stopped washing her hands. For in the Torah God speaks of menstruation and calls it *Al-Tamth*, an unclean secretion. During the days of

---

* The holy black stone which pilgrims kiss when they go to Mecca.

Al-Tamth, a woman is unclean for seven days. She should not touch anything sacred, not come anywhere near it. If a woman becomes full with child, and bears a son, she is not purified of her blood until thirty-three days have passed. But if she gives birth to a female child, she remains unclean for sixty-six days. Once she is cleansed she must slaughter a lamb, and a female pigeon or a female dove, and offer them to her God, so that she be forgiven for her sins, and cleansed of her blood.

In the Qur'an, menstruation was described as no more than something which offended others. The word 'offended' seemed innocent to me in comparison with what was said about it in the Torah and the word *heid* seemed better to me than the word *tamth*, where the blood is twice as unclean if the child is a girl. Besides, how could the impure blood be cleansed by offering a roast chicken, or a roast lamb, to God? In the Qur'an, Allah did not request women to offer him a roast chicken or a roast lamb in order to be cleansed. I thanked Allah many times for having created me a Muslim and not a Jewish girl.

As far as I knew it was God who created fathers, and gave them their religion, and I thought that Muslims believed only in the Qur'an. But my father explained to me that the Torah and the Gospels, like the Qur'an, had been revealed by God as a guidance, and a light to lead people in their lives, and that Muslims had to believe in all three books. When I learnt that, it was as though my father had poured a pitcher of cold water over my head on a winter's night.

8

My Revolutionary Father

I believed everything my father said. We sat around him on the
north balcony of our house in Alexandria listening to what
he said. As he spoke to us he kept looking towards my brother
Tala'at as though he were addressing no-one but him. He never
turned to me unless he was thirsty, or felt his throat was dry:
'Get me a glass of water, Nawal', or when my mother rose to set
the table for supper, 'Get up and help your mother, Nawal.'

I did not get up. I wanted to listen to his stories, especially the
story of Saad Zaghloul,* and the revolution of 1919 in which my
father had participated. He was a young man of twenty at that
time, a student in Dar Al-Oloum,† in Cairo. He marched out into
the street with the other students, shouting out slogans against
the British and throwing stones and bricks at them. Bullets
started flying through the air and he was hit in the foot by a
fragment. His companion carried him to the first-aid station,
and he arrived in Kafr Tahla on a donkey cart drawn by a she-ass,
to be met by scores of women who advanced to meet him trilling

---

* Leader of the Wafdist Party and the Egyptian revolution of 1919 against British
occupation.
† The religious school attached to Al-Azhar University, from which teachers of
Arabic graduated.

their high-pitched chorus of 'yoo-yoos'. For the villagers he had become a hero, no less important than Saad Zaghloul.

Whenever he pronounced the word hero, his eyes sparkled. Since childhood he had never stopped dreaming of himself carrying a sword and smiting the enemy to liberate his country. He had heard his mother sing with the other women: 'Aziz, Aziz [Precious one, precious one] may a plague take Al-Ingliz [the British].' She was a child only two years old when the British occupied Egypt in 1882. And my father often told us about his grandmother, 'the woman from Gaza', who had died before he was born. He had heard her story from his mother and from other women in the village, how she was very tall and always walked with an upright body, how every day at the crack of the dawn she left her hut with a hoe on her shoulder and returned when the sun was setting, how she laboured all day on the parcel of land she had inherited from her mother. She worked for no-one, but no-one had ever seen her squatting or lying around in her house. She gave birth to her child, when the time came, in the field, put it in a basket and carried it home. When the British invaded Egypt the men and women in the village gathered around carrying their hoes with her standing in their midst, and all of them ready to fight the invader to the death, for was not their life no more than a living death?!

My father described to us what happened in Dinshwai,* told us about the revolution led by Orabi before the British occupation of Egypt, about the Khedive Ismail, King Fouad and the first Egyptian constitution established in 1923, followed by the first general election in 1924, after which Saad Zaghloul was appointed prime minister, how Nahas Pasha later took over from him after his death, to be replaced by Sidki Pasha in 1930. Under Sidki Pasha, peasants and workers suffered hunger, and demonstrations and strikes flared up all over the country, the

---

* A village in Sharkeya province where a hunting expedition of British officers clashed with the villagers. In trying to escape, one of the party died of sunstroke in the desert. An Egyptian court under British supervision condemned several of the villagers to death, and they were hanged after a few days.

most serious of which was the railway workers' strike, which continued for months. Sidki Pasha then declared martial law and ordered the troops to fire on the workers. Many were killed, but his government fell and the Wafdist Party returned to power, with Al-Nahas Pasha at its head. Negotiations started with the British, and the treaty of 1936 was signed with them, but the demonstrations and strikes went on.

When we were in Alexandria, peasants from the family of my father used to visit us. Some of them, through force of hunger, had migrated from the village to work in the textile mills of Mahalla,* or in the factories of Shoubra Al-Khaima,† and Cairo, or in the tramway company of Alexandria. As workers, they earned very low wages, three piastres‡ a day and so they started to join in the strikes, or in the demonstrations, side by side with the students protesting against British occupation.

In one of these demonstrations the students gathered in the big courtyard of Abbassieh Secondary School. The headmaster tried to stop them from demonstrating but they refused to obey, shouting, 'Down with the headmaster', upon which he retreated to his office and held an emergency meeting of teachers. During this meeting he said to my father:

'Sayed Effendi, you are liked by the students. They will listen to you and we'll be finished with this riot.'

'Headmaster, sir, this is not a riot. It's a patriotic demonstration.'

'Sayed Effendi, the students must go back to class.'

'Headmaster, sir, the whole country is out demonstrating, even peasants and workers. Why stop the students?'

'Sayed Effendi, students are expected to study and do nothing else. Politics are not their business.'

'Headmaster, sir, students are part of the nation.'

---

* One of the earliest industrial towns, specialized in spinning and weaving cotton and making textiles. Founded in the 1930s.
† A northern suburb of Cairo, also specializing in textiles.
‡ A piastre is one hundredth of an Egyptian pound.

'Sayed Effendi, this is hardly the time for a discussion. You must go down to the courtyard at once and make them go back to class.'

My father did as the headmaster told him and went down to the courtyard where the students had collected. They immediately thronged around him and started to shout 'Long live Al-Saadawi.' They lifted him up on their shoulders and carried him out into the street. He found himself repeating with them at the top of his voice: 'Down with the British. Down with the government. Long live free Egypt.'

'What did the headmaster do?', we children sitting around him asked in awe, our breathing fast, the heartbeats under our ribs now racing, now faltering.

At that moment my father would be on his feet explaining to us how the headmaster had written a report against him and tossed it down on his desk for him to read, upon which he picked it up and tossed it back to the headmaster's desk: 'You might as well empty the inkpot on your report, Mr Headmaster.'

There I would be sitting somewhere in the corner of the balcony gazing at my father's tall figure, at his eyes shining with pride. I was the daughter of this patriot, this courageous man who feared no-one, neither the headmaster, nor the king, nor the government, nor the English, nor the village headman back in Kafr Tahla. 'I fear no-one except Allah the Almighty, the exalted.' That is what he always said, adding: 'I fear neither headmasters nor government ministers.'

That was in 1938. I was seven years old, but my father's voice made its way deep into my memory and I never forgot his words. From then on as the years rolled by, I also learnt not to fear anyone except God within me, my conscience, my inner voice. If anyone wrote a report against me I would repeat in the same tone of voice: 'Empty an inkpot on your report.'

How many reports were written against me after I joined government service, there was no way of knowing. According to the law, such reports were supposed to remain a secret. They were written by higher officials against lower officials, or by mean people seeking to ingratiate themselves with the authorities, or because they hated me, or by spies. In every ministry there was a police unit, called the security office, that wrote reports and raised them with the Minister of the Interior or the office of the Head of State.

When I was a child, the village headman was for me like a head of state. Village people described him as the 'biggest head in the country'. He used to walk along the embankment of the Nile, surrounded by men. The walls of his house reached high above the elevated embankment of the river. It had three tall storeys built of red bricks and was called Al-Dawar. At the very top was a tower with small, circular windows which overlooked the minaret of the mosque with its small mud-brick balcony on which Sheikh Marzouk used to stand and call out to prayer.

Like the mosque, the houses of the village were built of mud bricks, made from clay mixed with straw. A small stable or pen for animals was part of every house. The dust floor was bare, covered only by a straw mat, and there was no furniture, only an earthenware jar filled with water from the river which villagers called 'the sea', a colourfully painted wooden chest usually pushed up against a wall in which were kept old and new *gallabeyas*, including the woman's wedding gown still stained with the blood of her bridal night.

No peasant's house had more than two storeys. It was called *Al-Dar*. A narrow stairway made of mud or wood joined the two storeys and continued up to the roof, on which were piled mounds of dry maize or cotton stalks, cakes of dung laid out to dry in the sun, earthenware jars of salted cheese harbouring small white maggots deep inside, and jars of various pickles.

The river embankment rose high, higher than the houses in the village, and extended from Kafr Tahla to another village, Tahla, about one kilometre away. The village houses were huddled together, supporting one another, a dark mud-coloured mass lying in the embrace of the embankment.

I often walked on the river bank with my cousin Zaynab, the daughter of my paternal aunt, Baheya. She was the same age as I was. She would stare at a house that stood much higher than that of the village headman and say: 'That's Olama Pasha's *dawar*. They are the richest family in Tahla. They own a thousand feddans* and fifty slaves. Your grandfather, Shoukry Bey, your mother's father, was the son of the eldest Sheikh Tahlawi, and had as much land and as many slaves as Olama Pasha, but he lost the land and the slaves and now his family own nothing in the Kafr except for the *dawar*.

The *dawar* of my grandfather Shoukry Bey still stood where it had always been. It was a huge house with two storeys built of red bricks, a big inner courtyard, balconies and finely decorated lattice windows made out of beechwood. The outer entrance was closed by a big double door which was never opened. No-one in my mother's family had ever visited the village except during the war, when people in the city migrated back to the village until the conflict was over.

When my maternal aunt, Hanem, married a trader from Al-Mouski,† she brought him to the village for a two-day visit. She wanted him to see this time-honoured relic of her distinguished family. There still remained four or five of these *dawars* owned by big landowners, together with the small *ezbas* (hamlets) in which their tenants lived. Their lands and fields stretched out parallel to the embankment as far as Tahla, or Al-Ramla or even Benha, the capital city of Al-Kalioubeya province. The headman, on the other hand, had authority but had no, or little, land. He obeyed the landlords, and his henchmen were supervised by the chief of the village guards who operated also as a night watchman.

Egypt was still living in a semi-feudal age. The big landowners possessed 98 per cent of the agricultural land area around the village. The remaining 2 per cent of the land was owned

---

* Acres. A lot of land in a country where there is perennial irrigation.

† A trading centre near Al-Azhar where are gathered many traditional crafts.

by 80 per cent of the peasants. The property of a poor peasant never exceeded three feddans. The remaining 18 per cent of the villagers owned nothing at all. They worked as day labourers on the land of others and many of them did seasonal work at certain periods of the year when their labour was needed (harvesting, rice growing, cotton picking, and so on).

Sittil Hajja belonged to the class of poor peasants. She owned a piece of land, three feddans she had inherited from her mother, the woman from Gaza. There were three million poor peasants like Sittil Hajja who owned or rented land. They were better off than the day labourers, and their children did not die of hunger. They died of diarrhoea, of respiratory or of gastro-intestinal infections. Their food was not dry bread, with no sops to dip it in. They could eat their bread with salted cheese or pickled cucumbers or small pickled green lemons.

The price of land continued to go up, but the income of the peasant continued to fall. Speculation on the cotton market benefited the big landowners and the British, while speculation in land raised rents so that the landowners profited all the time at the expense of the peasants who toiled to grow the crops.

Sittil Hajja laboured on her piece of land for twenty long years, but all she was able to put aside were the costs of my father's education. This money could perhaps have bought her another feddan. 'The land may increase or diminish by one feddan, daughter of my son', she would say to me, 'but the miserable life of a peasant does not change. Education is the sweetest of all things. It opens the door to a job in the government and helps a man to become full in his clothes.'*

Sittil Hajja was an illiterate woman. She could not read. Throughout her life she had not read a single book, had not read the Qur'an, but she would say to the village headman: 'I know God better than you, Omda. God is justice, and people have come to know that by using their reason.'

---

* A popular expression. A man full in his clothes is not miserable and shrinking but prosperous, respected and dignified, that is, a real man.

One day she took me to the Omda, the village headman. I was only seven at that time, but she had reached her fifties, and was very tall. Next to her stood the village headman, short and fat, his fleshy body sagging in his kaftan, his skin white, protected carefully from the sun. He held out his hand to me. It was small and smooth and flabby compared with my grandmother's big, rough-skinned hand. His fingers had never known the feel of a hoe. Between them he held a string of shining yellow prayer beads, and in his other hand he carried a Qur'an with letters written in gold.

He sat reclining in a high-backed armchair, enveloped in his black kaftan, its edges trimmed with golden thread, while Sittil Hajja stood in front of him clothed in a dusty *gallabeya*. Behind her thronged a small crowd of peasants, men and women, their faces thin and emaciated, drained of blood, their skin brown and cracked like fallow land that has not seen water for a long time. Sittil Hajja's face, however, was not thin or emaciated like the others, but her hands were like theirs, big and rough, with cracked skin. She lifted an arm high up in the air and waved her hand in front of the headman's face: 'To keep one's word is a matter of honour. What have you done with your promises?'

She was a peasant woman like the others but had a strength which seemed to be inborn. She owned land and worked for no-one, and after her husband died had become fully responsible for her family.

She was not the only widow in the village, there were many others, and yet she was much stronger than any of them. Why? 'Sittil Hajja inherited the strength of your great-grandmother, the woman from Gaza', people used to say to me.

After her husband died, Sittil Hajja worked the land alone, laboured with her hoe from the moment the sun rose to the moment it set. Her labour pains would come upon her as she stood in the field. Then she would squat on the ground, open her legs wide apart, to look at the head covered in dark hair wedged up between her thighs, take a long deep breath to fill her chest with air, let it out with all the force she could muster in her body, pressing down at the same time on her belly with the flat of her hand, and the child would shoot out sprawling on the ground. After that she would reach out with her long arm for the hoe, and with one blow sever the umbilical cord, followed by a second blow to cut the cord which attached her underpants around the waist, so that she could tie it around the navel of the child. Once over with that, she leant her arms on the ground, took in a deep breath to fill her chest once again with air before she breathed out slowly as she pressed on her belly with the flat of her large hand. This time it was the placenta that shot out, looking like a loaf of clotted blood. She buried it in the ground, wiped the blood off her thighs with dry maize husks, struggled back into her white calico underpants, tied them around her waist with the remains of the thin cord, lined one of her baskets with a nest of soft grass and lay her baby in it, covered him with green maize leaves, lifted the basket on to her head and walked home, with the buffalo following behind her.

One day her son Al-Sayed (my father) came home bleeding from his nose. He was only two years old but the chief of the village guards had given him a beating. She wiped away the blood with an old rag, pulled off her black shawl from where it lay covering the basket of bread, wound it around her head and rushed out of the house like an angry tigress. She found the chief of the village guards standing surrounded by his men. She lifted her big rough hand high up in the air, and shouted: 'The one who can beat my son has not yet been created', then brought it down on his face with all her force.

That night the story went round the village. Mabrouka, daughter of the woman from Gaza, had struck the chief of guards. The men and women spoke about her in whispers: 'A woman with guts born of a woman with guts. A woman worth twenty men. Never before in the village has a woman slapped the face of the chief of village guards.' She became a figure that inspired awe, and everyone sought her assistance.

But the mother of Sittil Hajja, described as the woman from Gaza, was famous for something else. She had humiliated the village headman as he stood in front of the entrance to his house surrounded by his men, and after that, one dark night he sent someone to her, a man who wore a big turban around his head, goatskin sandals on his feet, and who held a long yellow staff in his hand divided into sections by black bands.

In the morning they found the door of her hut open. In the entrance lay her dog, Marzouk, his head twisted on his neck to one side. She was lying on the dirt floor, her eyes wide open, staring at the heavens. They carried her away on their heads, a long procession of men and women, their bare feet soundless on the dirt road as they advanced line after line in their threadbare *gallabeyas*.

At the entrance to the village they dug a grave for her and lined it with the green husks of maize, and above it they built a monument of stone and cement.

9

The Lost Servant-Girl

Many were the stories that I heard about Sittil Hajja and her mother, the woman from Gaza. Women have an unwritten history told orally by one generation to the other. I used to sit next to Sittil Hajja and listen to her stories, hold onto the tail of her gallabeya when she went to the fields, and come back still holding on to her in the same way, follow her into what she called the store room, and which was filled with grain almost to the ceiling, listening all the time.

At that time she had stopped growing the corn herself, but she continued to spread it out on a straw mat, to pick out the small pebbles and straw, after which one of my aunts carried it to the mill where it would be changed into soft white flour. Then Sittil Hajja would knead it with water into dough in a large flat earthenware basin called a magoor, cut the dough into small round balls, and throw them into an oven heated by a live fire from which the balls would come out as large, flat loaves of bread.

I did not realize that Sittil Hajja was in fact a poor woman. She seemed to me very rich, for out of her oven came those countless loaves of bread, and when I bit into one of them it melted in

Nawal (*far right*) at school in Alexandria, aged seven.

my mouth almost at once. Never in my life have I eaten bread anything like hers. No other bread ever had the taste or the smell of her loaves. I could hear them crackling inside the oven before she pulled them out and let them drop, hot as fire, on the palms of her big hands.

And never in my life have I seen a palm as big as hers, bigger than that of the village headman, of the king, bigger than that of my father or our Lord Muhammad, or our Lord Abraham.

When I reached the age of seven my father taught me how to pray. I began to hear the stories of the prophets from him – our Lord Abraham, who seized hold of an axe and with it destroyed the stone idols of Quraish; our Lord Moses, whose wooden staff was transformed into a huge snake which swallowed up the serpents of the sorcerers in the court of the pharaohs; our Lord Joseph, whose brothers threw him into a deep well, and then returned to tell their father that a wolf had eaten him up; our Lady Mary the Virgin, who had through a spirit sent to her from

God given birth to our Lord Jesus, who, though still a new-born baby, had called upon her to shake the palm tree and eat of its succulent dates; our Lord Muhammad, to whom the Angel Gabriel had descended with the message: 'Recite in the name of the Lord who created. Who created man from a worm. Recite! Your Lord the most generous taught by the pen', upon which our Lord Muhammad returned to his wife shivering and said to her 'Wrap me in my clothes, wrap me.'

There I used to sit in the corner of the balcony, my imagination wandering with my fathers' stories, my eyes gazing at the sky. I could see Allah far up behind the clouds and near him our Lord Muhammad, and Moses, and Jesus and our Lady Mary.

From our north balcony I got a glimpse of the sea, and could sniff its smell with the early morning breeze. But during the summer days we went to the beach, and the sea became something I could touch, smell and really see.

To get there we rode in an open horse-drawn cab. My brother Tala'at and I tussled over who should climb up to the high seat near the driver, for there I could hold the horse's reins and see all the way down to the end of the long street called Kom el-Dekka. We passed in front of my brother's school, Kom el-Dekka School, and in front of the big terraced gardens rising up the hill. The horse panted as it climbed the slope, but its hooves rang merrily as we descended towards the sea-side Corniche. Like the horse, I breathed in deeply, inhaling the fresh sea air. The horizon opened up revealing a vast expanse of water, which stretched out as far as I could see to meet the sky.

Maybe in some previous life I had been a fish living in these waters. Then, they pulled me out of them, against my will, with a hook, for when I saw the sea for the first time, and every time I see it again in any part of the world, I am seized with this feeling of intense joy, with the desire to go back to the embrace of the blue water, to the embrace of my mother.

On the beach of Al-Shatby, we had a small wooden cabin in which we changed our clothes and put on bathing suits. But the servant-girl Sa'adeya did not take off her gallabeya. She sat on the sand under the umbrella, guarding the big bag bulging with the food packed inside it.

'Why doesn't Sa'adeya swim with us in the sea, mother?' I asked.

'Because she hasn't got a bathing suit, Nawal.'

My mother's answer seemed convincing. Sa'adeya could not swim in the sea without a bathing suit. It appeared to me that swimsuits could not be bought on the market. They were something granted by God to children who had mothers and fathers.

At night I slept in my bed under warm covers but Sa'adeya slept on the floor, on a mat or an old rug, and sometimes when I opened my eyes I would find her crying. She was a child, perhaps a few years older than me, but no-one saw her or treated her as a child. To me she did not seem like other children. She had neither a father nor a mother. One day she said to me:

'I want to see my mother, Miss Nawal.'

'Do you have a mother, Sa'adeya?'

'Yes, of course, Miss Nawal.'

'And where is she?'

'She's in our village.'

'Where is your village, Sa'adeya?'

'I don't know.'

'What is it called?'

'Kafr Al-Sheikh.'

I began to think of Sa'adeya. I doubted that she had a mother, for how could her mother leave her to live in the house of strangers? Sa'adeya stood at the sink to wash the dishes after we had eaten, and her fingers were red and swollen from soap and caustic soda. She sat in a corner of the kitchen eating from a plate on which there was nothing but leftovers. At the beach she sat clothed in her gallabeya of the village guards who operated also as a ni, guarding our food and dripping with sweat while we swam and rollicked in the blue sea.

One morning I sat beside her on the sand and we began to play together. Then we built a big sandcastle shaped like a pyramid. Each time the castle collapsed on itself, Sa'adeya laughed and her eyes gleamed with joy. But all of a sudden the gleam would disappear. She would stare down the beach with eyes as sad as those of my grandmother Amna then say: 'People tell me that if I walk along the shore and keep going straight I'll get to Kafr Al-Sheikh' by the end of the day.' 'You silly girl', I said, 'if you follow this shore it will take you not to Kafr Al-Sheikh but to Italy.'

I had heard my father and mother say that beyond the sea lay a country called Italy. Sa'adeya did not believe anything my father or my mother said, and continued to insist that her village was to be found down this shore, and could be reached after a day's walking.

We woke up one morning to find no Sa'adeya. My father went out to look for her. Before the day was over the coast-guards found her walking along the shore on the way to her village.

She came back to us her head lowered to the ground. When she stepped into the house she lifted her head, and our eyes met. For the first time in my life I understood the meaning of sorrow. There were no tears in her eyes. There was a complete dryness, a total despair.

Sometimes when I look into the mirror it is Sa'adeya's eyes that I see staring at me. They are my eyes in moments of sorrow, or despair, in moments of shame or remorse. A question keeps returning to my mind. Why did I not try to help Sa'adeya?

One morning we awoke to find her gone. Months passed without the police finding any trace of her. Had she lost her way somewhere along the endless coast? Been pounced on by the likes of Raya and Sekina? For from her ears hung two tiny earrings with a fine nail and clasp just like mine. Two tiny earrings made not of gold but of tin.

I was seven years old when I saw my first political demonstration. I was returning home from school alone. Suddenly Muharram Bey Street was flooded with a sea of bodies, with thousands of long legs enveloped in trousers. All of them were men, their voices resounding like thunder, their heels pounding on the tarmac road. I fled before them in panic, and fell under their legs. I do not know how I got to my feet, perhaps with the help of hands which were stretched out to pull me up. Meanwhile I had lost my school-bag, but I kept on running without looking behind me until I reached home.

My mother was waiting for me at the door. She held me tight in her arms. I was sobbing and kept saying: 'My bag has gone, mother.' 'What matters is that you're safe', she said, 'Never mind the bag.'

She stood there looking out at the street, her eyes restless as she searched among the faces in the crowd for my father. 'May our Lord God bring him safe', she kept repeating.

My father came home very late that day. I fell asleep before he arrived. I dreamt I saw him drowning in a sea of bodies, but the waves carried him high up to the sky. He was shouting 'Down with the government' when a bullet hit him in the chest. He went down under the waves and was trampled under the feet of the crowd. They carried his bleeding body to my mother and he died in her arms. She sobbed loudly for a long time, then dried her tears and quieted down. A moment later she took her suckling baby in her arms, lifted my sister up on one shoulder and my younger brother on the other, and stepped out into the street. My elder brother and I walked behind her clinging to the tail of her dress, wearing tattered clothes like beggars.

I woke up in a state of panic thinking that my father was dead, killed by the British or by the government, and that my mother had been sucked down into the sea of bodies carrying my brothers and sisters with her. Here I was all alone left to walk on an endless shore and be lost for ever like Sa'adeya.

10

The Village of
Forgotten Employees

During the year 1938 I woke up one morning to find my mother and father packing our bags. The government, wishing to punish my father, had transferred him to a place called Menouf. My father said a more appropriate name would be *manfa*, which means an exile. It was a village, or a small town, and was not to be found on the map although I searched for it several times.

We lived in this town for ten long years, from 1938 to 1948. During that whole period my father was not given a single salary increase and was deprived of all promotions. He had been put on the black list, included in a category known in the Ministry of Education as 'forgotten employees'.

Thus, from the city of Alexandria, from the bride of the sea as it was called, we moved to this silent gloomy town.

In compulsory primary education schools, poor children were recruited to learn by force of law. My father became the inspector for these schools within the province of Al-Menoufeya. When people saw him walking with his tall upright stature down the road, they would point him out and say: 'The Bey, the Inspector.'

In Alexandria no-one pointed him out. There he carried only the title of effendi. It was people in Menouf who bestowed upon him the title of bey. And I became the daughter of the 'Inspector Bey'. After Sittil Hajja visited us in Menouf she returned to Kafr Tahla carrying the title of Um Al-Bey.

After that my father was wont to repeat a verse of poetry which says: 'Better live as head in a village rather than as tail in the city.'

I asked my father who were the people we could describe as tails and he said, 'They are *al-nuzara* [headmasters] and *al-wuzara* [ministers], my daughter.'

Then I asked him, what does it mean to be a minister, so he answered me with a play of words, as he often did: '*Wuzara*', he said, 'comes from *wizr*, which means crime. But *zanb* also means a wrongdoing and *zanab* means a tail, so that to live as a tail is to live among the henchmen who are ordered to commit wrongdoings or crimes.' When he saw me all puzzled he burst out laughing and started explaining it to me all over again.

Menouf was not a village like Kafr Tahla, and did not have a village headman. It was the *mamour*, or senior officer in charge of the police, who was the most powerful person in the community. In the town there was a police station, a mosque, a church, a school, a court of law, a health bureau, a railway station, water tanks, a Jewish quarter, a goldsmith's shop, Yanni's pharmacy, Gramino's coffee shop, Zachari's grocery, Mikhali's store for spirits, a small shop which sold roasted peanuts and watermelon seeds, and a 'One Thousand and One Items' store.[*]

Our home was on the first floor of a small building, and looked out over open fields stretching as far as the cemetery. I could not see the cemetery from our balcony, called the verandah. It was hidden behind the maize fields, but when the peasants had harvested the crop, and cut down the maize stalks the rounded domes of the graves appeared, looking like white devils lurking under the clouds.

---

[*] Gramino's is probably Italian; the other three names are Greek.

The owner of the house was named Al-Hajj Mahmoud. He had not finished building the second floor but he lived in it, together with his second wife, Um Muhammad, and eleven children, five boys and six girls. They lay down to sleep in rooms without windows or doors. In winter they all piled into one room, lying on the dust floor after they had covered the door and the windows with old garments nailed into the walls.

Hajj Mahmoud was a travelling cloth merchant who went from one market to the other riding on an old she-ass. The ass's body was skinny and emaciated, her hair was falling out, and her bones jutted out beneath the skin marked with wounds which had not yet healed, and with the deep red stripes of heavy whip lashes. On her back she carried a huge pile of different cloths wound around long cylinders on top of which sat Hajj Mahmoud, dangling his legs on either side, boring into her flanks with his bony knees, or pulling at her neck with a rope, or lashing her back with a cane stick, all the while coughing and clearing his throat before he spat on the ground. 'Pull yourself together, Aziza.* Shee, shee.'†

Hajj Mahmoud was skinny like his she-ass and was also losing his hair, which had the same grey colour as his Aziza. His long loose *gallabeya* was made of gabardine, and he wore a skull cap which he had brought back with him from his pilgrimage to Al-Hegaz. It was embroidered in a style called the Prophet's Window because the stitching left many little holes in it.

Every morning I would hear his cough coming from beneath the railing of our verandah, and watch him as he emerged from the narrow path between the fence of our house and the adjacent fields. He and the she-ass looked like twins. Their breathing drew white circles in the early morning mist. The cold wind lashed at their noses with the same violence, and their coughs resounded in the same way. But the cough of the she-ass would rise gradually until it merged into a laboured bray. Then he

---

* The name he had given to his she-ass, which means 'precious one'.
† A sound meant to encourage the she-ass, to make her move more rapidly.

would hit her on the rump with the tip of his stick, so that she quickened her pace, panting and foaming with a whitish saliva resembling sea surf which exuded from her mouth, her nose and her ears. At that point she stumbled, and fell, dragging him to the ground with her. When he got to his feet he cursed her and her mother, called her 'daughter of a whore', upon which she left him and ran on ahead, while he followed behind, holding the hem of his *gallabeya* between his teeth so that he could catch up with her, cursing all the time, panting heavily. By that time, he would have caught up with her, and she started to bray again, but her bray seemed to choke in her throat, and she gasped heavily, white tears dropping from her eyes. He leant over her, patted her on the neck gently with his blue-veined hand, brought his mouth close to her big ear, now standing erect, and said in a wheedling voice 'Never mind, don't take it so much to heart. I'll make amends to you, Aziza. Never mind, never mind. Shee, shee, come on, shee, shee', making a clicking sound with his tongue. The she-ass would respond, shake her head once, or twice, then gasp out a choking sound which resembled his voice when he said 'Shee, shee never mind, never mind.'

Khadija was the daughter of Hajj Mahmoud. She went to primary school with me. We played *siga** together in front of the house, skipped with a rope and ran after butterflies in the fields. When I had chewing gum, or a stick of molasses candy which we called *caramella* (caramel), I always gave her a piece.

For the big Eid my parents used to give me one millime to buy what I wanted. I learnt at school that one pound was worth one hundred piastres and that one piastre was equal to ten millimes. I felt that one millime was a lot of money, and when I was given this 'great millime' I used to hold it tightly in my fist. It was a red copper disc and shone brightly in the sun. On it was engraved the picture of the king, and when I carried it with me I would keep looking around in fear of thieves. As soon as it was given

---

* A popular form of checkers played with pebbles which are moved between small pits dug in the ground.

to me, I ran off to the roasted peanuts shop, then to the store of 'The One Thousand and One Items'. I bought balloons, whistles, firecrackers and filled my pockets with white and dark melon seeds, shelled peanuts, chickpeas and carob.

At dawn on the first day of the Eid, the butcher arrived to slaughter the sacrificial lamb, and my father would tell me its story. How God wanted to test our Lord Abraham, and ordered him to sacrifice his son Lord Ismail. And how the father laid his knife over the neck of his son, ready to slay him, when at that very moment a lamb descended from the heavens.

In my sleep, I dreamt that God had decided to put my father to the test. But this time no lamb descended from the heavens, and I felt the knife cutting through my neck and woke up with a start in a state of terror. I rushed over to my mother and in a low whisper told her my dream. She reassured me, saying: 'That was a long time ago, Nawal. But now, praise be to God, He knows everything in people's hearts without needing to test them.'

However the word test continued to frighten me. I felt God would never stop making these tests, and did not believe everything my mother told me. I had never seen her read the Qur'an, and she did not know the stories that my father told us about the prophets. In addition she did not pray five times a day. All she did was to fast for the month of Ramadan.

The Eid Al-Sagheer (small feast) came after the month of Ramadan. I enjoyed the small feast much more than I did the big one. There was no slaughtering of lambs, no sacrifice, no Godly tests. Instead there were delicious *kahkes*, shortbread biscuits on which my mother made a design of birds spreading out their wings, and *ghurayeba*, a thick shortbread which melted in my mouth like sugar.

During the feast, our home would be crowded with relatives and visitors. Most prominent amongst them was Sittil Hajja, who sat cross-legged on the sofa in the parlour. The red millimes jingled in the lap of her loose flowing *gallabeya*, colliding with a musical ring. We children would gather around her, competing for the festival presents she distributed to us.

She began with the boys, with my three brothers. She gave two millimes to each of them. But to the girls she gave only one millime. Angry, I threw the millime back into her lap. 'God has told us that a girl is worth half a boy, light of your mother's eye', she would say to me.

My elder brother, Tala'at, would stare at me, a gleam of arrogant pride in his eyes. I did better than him at school, and the only thing that soothed his feelings of frustration was the verse from the Qur'an echoing in my father's voice which said: 'To the male a share equal to two females.'

I retreated to my room, lay on my bed, buried my face in the pillow and wept. Could God be unjust? My brother played all the year round, and kept failing in his examinations. I worked at school and at home and never had a holiday, and yet what was the result of all my efforts? I was given one millime and he was given two.

I stayed in my room where no-one could see me. In the parlour, they were laughing, enjoying themselves at the Eid, while I was here alone harbouring my sorrow and my anger. My room was small, next door to the kitchen. On the window were rusty iron bars, and when I looked through them I could see Hajj Mahmoud's she-ass in the stairwell. She stared at me with her sad, weeping eyes. On this day of festivity, in all the wide universe she was the only one to share my sadness.

I slipped out of my room to wash my face, glimpsed the servant girl kneeling on the tiled floor of the kitchen, scrubbing at it with a brush. She was about my age, and her name was Zaynab. My mother too was called Zaynab, and it was not considered proper that the servant-girl carry the same name as the lady of the house, so we had changed it to Sa'adeya, after the name of the previous servant-girl.

When I passed near her, Sa'adeya lifted her head and looked up from the tiled floor. Her eyes were like the eyes of Hajj

Mahmoud's she-ass, sad and full of tears. It seemed that on this day of festivity there were other creatures even more sad than I was: girl servants and she-asses.

But the question of God's justice continued to occupy my mind, and my thoughts about it made me feel guilty. On the one hand, God was justice, and people's reason had led them to this understanding. On the other hand, God seemed unjust. He favoured my brother, and was not fair. I questioned His justice: 'Is God just, mother?' 'Of course, Nawal.' My mother affirmed that God was just, and what she said relieved me. I did not want God to be unjust, to be like the village headman in Kafr Tahla.

II

God Hid behind the Coat-Stand

During the days of the festival I hid my tears from my mother. I could hear her laugh full of joy ringing out in the parlour, and see her honey-coloured eyes shining with happiness. But there was a moment when I saw tears in her eyes. I went through the open door into her room. She saw me in the mirror as I came in and quickly dabbed her eyes with a handkerchief.

'Are you crying, mother?' I asked her. 'No, of course not.' 'But why are your eyes red, then?' 'I was putting eye-drops in them.' There was no bottle of eye-drops in her hand. I felt she was hiding something from me, something that gave me the shivers. Could it be that she doubted God's justice, wondering why he always privileged males.

God hid in the dark behind the coat-stand, or the cupboard. Lying in bed I felt His presence, wondered whether I should hide my head under the covers or just keep still. Then I would hear His footsteps on the floor, jump out of bed in a fright, rush off to do my ablutions, and prostrate myself on the prayer carpet, repeating again and again. 'I ask Almighty God for His forgiveness for every almighty sin', until my throat went dry.

I became a model of good behaviour and piety amongst the girls of my father's and my mother's families. Everybody was happy with the grace which had descended on me from heaven. Happiest of all was Sittil Hajja. When she saw me kneeling on the prayer carpet, my face flat on the ground, she would say of me that I had now reached the age of reason, had come to know God, matured like a fig when it ripens and that God would send me a bridegroom from heaven to pluck me like a fruit from the tree before I fell to the ground and rotted.

My mother, however, was not thinking of a bridegroom for me. She was too occupied with other things, with her belly which once more had become swollen, so that once more the nurse came to our house, and I heard mother's shrieks resound. A child emerged from mother's belly, but I could not understand how in the first place it got in. If I asked a question, the eyes of people around me warned me off. The life of women remained for me a strange thing, surrounded in mystery, and when I saw bellies swell I was scared.

My father believed in education just like Sittil Hajja did. For him education was important for girls as well as boys, but for her it was only for boys. She educated her son, and the son of her husband from another woman. However, she did not educate a single one of her five daughters. They stayed with her in the village, lived a peasant's life, and married peasant men, except for the youngest, my aunt Nefissa, who did not go to school herself but sent her daughters as well as her sons to school.

In the town of Menouf there were elementary schools, a few governmental private schools, a middle school for trades and crafts, and a secondary school for boys. Apart from these, there was nothing else, but families who could afford the fees sent their children to private schools.

Sitting on the balcony facing the fields and surrounded by his children, our father told us of the new battles he was fighting. A struggle was going on over education between the political parties and within the government. There were members of parliament who were against compulsory education. One of them, a pasha named Badraoui Ashour, stood up during one of the parliamentary sessions and shouted at the top of his voice: 'Gentlemen, free education will transform the wearers of blue *gallabeyas* into people who wear ironed clothes. If the children of peasants are educated they will find it difficult to handle a hoe.' Another pasha, Waheeb Doss, said: 'Educating the children of the poor is socially very dangerous, and will lead to psychological rebellion. A third pasha, Tala'at Harb, declared: 'Education opens up the mind and will constitute a threat to the government of the country.'

My father stood on the balcony, as he had done before on the northern balcony of our house in Alexandria, and described the struggles in parliament between the Wafd Party* and the minority parties, between Al-Nahas Pasha and Ahmed Maher Pasha. Addressing his words to my brothers, to the boys in the family, I heard him exclaim: 'Can you imagine, this pasha of the Liberal Constitutional Party† wants people to starve to death and doesn't care even if they cannot get dry bread! He accuses Al-Nahas and the Wafdist government of showering benefits on peasants, workers, and government officials. Where are the benefits you're talking about, Pasha? Prices are increasing from day to day, but our salaries do not change, and even if they rise a few millimes, then we have only God to thank for His bounty.'

In the year 1940, the Wafdist government introduced a bill in parliament which put an end to the practice of sequestering the houses of peasants unable to pay their taxes. The feudal pashas, who constituted a big proportion of the deputies in parliament, shouted from their benches in a loud chorus: 'This is Bolshevism! This is Bolshevism!'

I asked my father what Bolshevism was and he answered that Bolshevism is communism. He said it meant that everything

---

* The nationalist majority party created in 1919 during the revolution against British occupation.

† A minority semi-feudal capitalist party allied to the king.

should be 'made common', but I was unable to understand what that was exactly. However, Sittil Hajja seemed to understand what it meant because she waved her big, rough hand and said: 'Those pashas are just like the headman of Kafr Tahla. They'll never be content until the peasants die of hunger, but God is on the side of the poor.'

'By Allah', said father, 'I'm wondering if the pashas won't say that God is a communist like Nahas Pasha!'

'It won't matter what they say, son. God will always side with the poor. He made the world "common", made it for all of us, didn't He?'

During the Eid, my mother's and my father's relatives gathered together and sat on the verandah. The Al-Sa'adawi family was headed by Sittil Hajja, or by my aunt Rokaya, who had a sharp tongue. The family of Shoukry Bey was headed by my aunt Hanem or Tante Fahima, or by my uncle Zakareya or Uncle Yehia. The verandah would be the scene of a struggle very much like the one which was going on in parliament. The peasants who constituted my father's family supported the Wafd and the government, whereas Shoukry Bey's family would take sides with the pashas such as Ahmed Maher and Al-Nokrashi, and with the minority parties.

My father was not a member of the Wafdist or of any other party. He maintained that all the parties were playing a game with the people, hiding behind the constitution, and what they called 'the democratic system.' At the same time, the religious sheikhs of Al-Azhar and the leaders of the Muslim Brotherhood were playing this game with the people in the name of Allah and religion. My father described Sheikh Al-Maraghi* as the 'sheikh with the beard': 'Can you imagine', he said, 'that that Sheikh with the beard is cooperating with the king and with the British in the name of Islam. He keeps saying: "Obey whoever is responsible for your affairs." When he addresses King Farouk he

---

* At that time he was the religious head of Al-Azhar, the university of Islamic theology.

says, "Allah is with you", and the king takes the cue from him and responds, "Yes, Allah is with us." This has nothing to do with faith or religion, Sheikh Al-Maraghi, this is just making fools of us.'

My aunt Hanem was enamoured of King Farouk and believed that Allah was on his side. On the other hand my aunt Rokaya thought that Allah was most certainly favourable to Nahas Pasha. The atmosphere between the two families would grow more and more tense. Aunt Hanem would let her eyes travel with scorn over Aunt Rokaya's worn *gallabeya*, and Uncle Zakareya would cross one leg over the other and speaking from the tip of his nose would say: 'Allah is on the side of the king. How can we possibly doubt that?'

At that point I would see Sittil Hajja wave her large blue-veined hand right in front of Uncle Zakareya's nose, and say: 'What does it matter? Allah can choose to be where He likes, Al-Nahas Pasha has all the people on his side.'

Everybody would burst out laughing, Sittil Hajja joining in the laughter until tears came to her eyes. She dried them on the edge of her black *tarha* and said in a whisper: 'I beg forgiveness of thee God Almighty. Make it that it bring good to us.'*

When the Second World War broke out, the British forced peasants to grow more wheat and grains in order to feed the allied armies. The production of cotton dropped quickly and speculation on the stock market increased to the benefit of the rich pashas and the British occupiers. The difficulties of the war interfered with the transportation of fertilizers and prices rose, but the British fixed an arbitrary price for cotton, lower than that of the international market, arguing that an increase in the price of cotton would be of benefit only to the pashas. The pashas in the Wafd and other parties were resentful of this measure and said that the British were sowing hatred between the classes, in Egypt, and encouraging communism and atheism.

---

* Popular superstition has it that laughter is a bad augury, stemming from the belief that sorrow is the lot of our people.

Taking advantage of this situation the king decided to deal a blow against the Wafd. He embarked on what, to all purposes, was a constitutional coup, and took over absolute power. He declared that no-one could sway him from this position because he believed that he was doing the right thing, working for the good of his people, fully confident in himself, fully reliant on his God who was the source of his inspiration and had been and would always remain on his side.

King Farouk was young, and was surrounded by pashas and religious sheikhs who were much older than him. They advised him to court the younger generation. At that time a young man, Ahmed Hussein, became leader of a new party called Young Egypt (Misr Al-Fatat). As *fatat* also meant girls, at the beginning I thought that members of this party were girls! Ahmed Hussein declared himself a supporter of the king and declared that the word of Allah was his banner. As a result a struggle broke out between Ahmed Hussein, as leader of Young Egypt, and Al-Nahas Pasha, the leader of the Wafd Party. Al-Nahas Pasha addressing Ahmed Hussein said, 'You are a conspirator, for to use the name of Allah as a slogan is deceitful, and to include Allah as a part of your political platform is nothing but sheer trickery!'

The British cooperated with the king and with the other parties against Al-Nahas. During the month of April 1940, Al-Nahas publicly accused the British of supporting the coup against the constitution, and demanded the evacuation of British troops as soon as the war was over.

12

The Ministry
of Nauseation

In 1940, I had reached the age of nine, and was in my second year of primary school. My father had avoided sending me to one of the government primary schools he was supposed to inspect, for in those schools the Ministry of Education crowded children into the classrooms like sardines in a tin, and many of the teachers were not only ignorant but also extremely harsh. They lacked the most elementary knowledge of the basic principles of education and often beat the children with big heavy sticks.

My father used to have meetings with these teachers on the verandah. He made efforts to instil in them the basic principles and methods of teaching, taught them grammar and syntax. Sometimes he threatened to deduct one or two days from their salary if they did not instruct their pupils properly.

I sat in a corner of the balcony listening carefully, taking in everything my father was explaining to them. If he asked a question I would put up my finger, and sometimes he would let me answer, for there were moments where one or more of them failed to answer his question. Then he would say with irritation, 'How is it that a girl in primary school knows more than you do?'

They sat on wicker chairs in a semicircle, wearing rumpled red fezzes on their heads, their eyes half-closed, their faces thin, their trousers baggy. The monthly salary paid to them was two to three pounds. These were the people whom the Ministry of Education described as the mentors of the rising generation who would build the glorious future of the nation.

My father always made fun of the Ministry of Education, punning on its name so that it became the Ministry of Nauseation. But the teachers were really the most nauseating thing about it. They were so dull and, to use a popular expression, could not distinguish between the first letter of the Arabic alphabet which resembles the letter *l* and a cob of maize. My father said sarcastically that they would most certainly go to Paradise for, God willing they would teach the rising generation how to make the future of the nation very gloomy.

During the days of the Eid, teachers were in the habit of making a round of visits to the headmasters and inspectors of the schools carrying gifts such as baskets of eggs, or oranges or figs, or slaughtered ducks, geese or chickens. It reminded one of the offerings which, according to the Torah, were made to the God Yahweh. The teachers felt that the spirits of the inspectors and supervisors would reach a new high when they inhaled the delicious aroma of roast meat, and out would come the secret reports with a rating of 'Excellent, deserves to be promoted.'

My father turned them out of the house, baskets, slaughtered offerings and all.

'But, Sayed Effendi', they protested, 'our Prophet himself accepted gifts.'

'Gifts are nothing but a form of bribery, gentlemen', he would say.

In Menouf, there was only one primary school for girls which was not run by the government administration. It was an English school, and combined more advanced instruction in English together with the governmental curriculum and programme.

Since the beginning of the British occupation of Egypt, English schools had spread throughout the country. Some of them were religious mission schools, and some were secular schools which followed the Egyptian educational system but were not subject to government inspection. The weekly holidays in these schools were Saturday and Sunday instead of Friday. They taught Islam and Arabic, as did the government schools, in addition to Christianity for Coptic children, and Judaism for Jewish children.

Menouf was what was called a *markaz*, a district town. It was not a village like Kafr Tahla, nor a city like Cairo or Alexandria. It was a small town and lay on the railway line to Shebin Al-Kom, but since it was small, express trains did not stop at the station. Most of the land in the town remained agricultural, and peasants continued to cultivate it. There were some small factories, mainly for tobacco and cigarettes, owned by the Al-Difrawi family. A few people who originated in Menouf had become prominent figures in politics and in the political parties. These included Sabri Abou Alam, who rose to a leading position in the Wafdist Party at the time of Al-Nahas Pasha, and Labib Shoukeir, who became president of the People's Assembly under Abdel Nasser.

One of the major streets in the town was called Al-Kenissa (Church) Street and was inhabited by a number of Coptic families. At the end of the street was a huge church, with bells that rang on Sundays, or whenever a member of one of these families died. A narrow street called the Lane of the Jews ran parallel to Al-Kenissa Street, and was lined on either side with small shops, many of them selling jewellery, and all packed close to one another. At the end of this lane stood the local tavern.

The biggest street was Al-Seka Hadeed (Railway) Street, on which the railway station was located. It extended from the station and the main market as far as a small square in which were to be found the post office and the water tanks supplying the town, then continued over the bridge to become Al-Kanal

(Canal) Street, which was always crowded with lots of people, for here were shops of every kind: tobacco and cigarette shops, candy doll shops for the Prophet's birthday, *konafa** shops which made the fine shredded dough, roasted-seed shops and shops that sold school notebooks and penny whistles for festival time. Street vendors called out their wares seated on donkey backs or on donkey carts, traders in cotton or clover plied their wares, festival and holiday musicians played their instruments or beat on their drums and tambourines, street performers swallowed fire or danced their monkeys round and round, town criers called out in praise of the Lord Prophet, professional women mourners wept and shrieked, professional women entertainers and dancers swayed in front of the taverns and bordellos, while policemen, beggars, the infirm and deformed sat or stood or moved around all mixing freely in the crowd.

Every day I walked along the main street to go to school, immersing myself in this sea of people, their faces seeming to float on the surface of the deep surging waters like seaweed thrown up by the waves.

The sun shone strongly all the year round. There was no thunder or lightening, no cloud or rain, except for a few days in winter. Rain was like a rare fruit. When it came I lifted my face up to it, absorbed it, like I absorbed the green of the fields. The peasants would lift up their eyes to the heavens and thank God for His blessings; if everything went dry, if there was no rain, they crowded into the mosque and, led by the Imam, they prayed, lifting their hands up to the heavens, asking God that the clouds gather, that the sky burst into thunder, flash with lightening, and pour with rain. And if the waters of the Nile sank low, they knelt to God, asked for His mercy, prayed that He unleash the flood of the Nile.

---

* An oriental sweet in the shape of a round flat cake made of fine shreds of dough with an internal layer of cream, or raisins and nuts. There is a range of variations of this classic form.

I would walk along the street, my school-bag tight under my arm. The main street ended in a big square on which were to be found Yanni's Pharmacy, Gramino's coffee shop, and a tiny store owned by a man called Shoukeir, who stood behind the wooden counter selling notebooks, pencils, pens and bottles of ink.

His son, Labib Shoukeir, sometimes replaced him behind the counter. One day when I went into the shop he said to me, 'You know, I am your brother Tala'at's classmate', but I did not answer and left without saying a word to him. My mother had told me never to speak to boys I did not know.

The father Shoukeir became one of the richest traders in Menouf. He kept adding one millime to the other until he accumulated millions, or so my father said. The people of Menouf and of Al-Menoufeya province in general were known for their thriftiness, and the common saying was 'The Menoufi (he who comes from the province of Menoufeya) is never friendly, even if you feast him on a lamb.'

Labib Shoukeir was a diligent student and did better at school than the sons of educated parents or government officials. When my brother failed in his exams, my father said to him, 'So the son of the inspector of education has failed, while the son of the man who sells nibs and paper passes his exams with distinction.'

After the days when I used to go to the Shoukeir bookshop in Menouf, I never met with Labib Shoukeir again until 1980, at an international conference in Beirut. He invited me to have lunch with him in a restaurant overlooking the sea and the rocks of Raouché. We reminisced about many things, and he said to me: 'Do you remember the days in Menouf? You used to ride a bicycle along Al-Kanal Street and the boys would run behind you shouting, "Look, look, a girl riding a bicycle!" We, the boys of Menouf, used to gather near the bridge so we could watch the daughter of the Inspector Bey riding a bicycle. Every single one of us had dreams about her and said to himself, "I must succeed in my exams and graduate as quickly as possible, so that I can ask for her hand."'

That was the last time I ever saw Dr Labib Shoukeir. I did not know him well and later I heard that he had died. On 15 May 1971, when Sadat struck out at Nasser's men in what he called the 'Corrective Revolution aimed at liquidating the centres of despotic power', Labib Shoukeir was the president of the People's Assembly, and one of Nasser's men. He was relieved from all his functions and exiled from public life, but he was not put in jail like Sha'rawi Gom'aa, Minister of the Interior, and other ministers belonging to the previous regime. Before becoming a cabinet minister he had been a professor of law, but he had succumbed to the glitter of politics and power.

The headmistress of the English language school which I attended was called Miss Hamer. She used to walk up and down the rows of girls standing in the morning assembly, and hit those she wanted to punish on the tips of their fingers with a ruler. Her victims were the girls who had not trimmed their fingernails. From behind the glass of her spectacles her eyes peered out, searching between our fingers and under our nails. She would part the hair of girls with the ruler, looking through narrowed eyes for lice small as a pin's head or for nits that were even smaller; she would thrust her long, curved nose with its red tip under the edge of a girl's uniform, using her ruler to lift it up and reveal a petticoat or the knickers which she wore, then smell her underwear.

With us in class was a girl called Fatima. She was the daughter of the *mamour*, chief of the police station. Her place in the morning assembly was always at the top of the line, and Miss Hamer used to look at her and say 'Good morning' then pass on without submitting her to the slightest scrutiny. She did the same thing with another girl, Isis, who was the daughter of the Health Inspector, and with Sarah, whose father, a man named Cohen, owned the jewellery shops in town. But Khadija, the daughter of Hajj Mahmoud, was always submitted to a very careful scrutiny. She never bypassed the girls who, like Khadija, came from poor families. She always stung them on their fingertips with the ruler, or made them step out of the line.

Her blue eyes swept over my face in a look of cold silence. She never smiled at me or wished me a good morning. But she also never searched my hair for lice or examined my clothes, for I was the inspector's daughter. True, my father was not supposed to inspect her school, but sometimes he would walk into her office with complaints he had received from the girls' parents alleging that the school was neglecting to teach Arabic or Islam in a proper way, or expressing fear over their Muslim daughters because they were made to recite from the gospels during the morning assembly.

Each day, before the assembly broke up, Miss Hamer climbed up on the platform holding an English-language bible in her hands and read a verse which the teachers and school-girls repeated after her: 'Our Father, which art in Heaven, hallowed be Thy name. Thy Kingdom come, thy will be done on earth as it is in heaven. Forgive us our sins as we forgive those who sin against us, and lead us not into temptation, but deliver us from evil, for thine is the Kingdom, the power and the glory, for ever and ever. Amen.' Then she would come down from the platform, one of the teachers would climb up in her place, read the passage from the Gospels in Arabic, and the school-girls would repeat it after her.

Unlike other parents in Menouf, my father found nothing wrong with reading from the Gospels. In fact he considered this a religious obligation. The Gospels were, for him, one of God's three books, and together with the Torah gave guidance to people, and lighted their path. That was what Allah had said in the Qur'an. In addition, he encouraged us to learn the English language, and said that we should learn the language of the enemy in order to be able to defeat him.

I loved the English language but my greater love was Arabic. My father made us familiar with Arabic literature at home, and often read poetry written by Aboul Alla' Al-Ma'ari and other poets as we sat around him listening. He had a big library in the parlour which contained old and more modern Arabic literature. In it were to be found *Al-Mu'allaqat, Lisan Al-Arab*; works by Al-Ja-hiz, Seebaweih, Al-Razi, Al-Asfahani, Kitab-Al-Aghani; poetry by Aboul Alla' Al-Ma'ari, Abou Nawas, Gareer, Al-Farazdaq; works written by 'Ibn Al-Muqaffa', collections of the poetry of Al-Khansa, Dananeer, Um Ja'afar Al-Hashimeya; books about Khadija and Aisha and biographies about other women in the Prophet's household; works by modern authors like Al-Mazni, Al-Manfaluti, Taha Hussayn, and Abbas Mahmoud Al-Akad; collections of modern poets like Hafiz, Shawki, and Al-Barudi; as well as many other books.

My father was a great admirer of Aboul Alla' Al-Ma'ari. When-ever he criticized Sheikh Al-Maraghi or other religious sheikhs in Al-Azhar he repeated Al-Ma'ari's famous saying: 'The inhabit-ants of the earth are divided into two categories. The first have brains and no faith; the second have faith and no brains.'

He encouraged me to think and to read. He made me love literature when I was still a child. I did not learn much from school. The teacher who taught us Arabic and literature resem-bled those who taught in elementary schools. He wore a rumpled fez and a suit which was all wrinkled, scratched at his head, and between the legs, and stung us with his cane stick on our but-tocks. We called him Mr Bogeyman. He looked as though made to frighten, with one eye smaller than the other, its black pupil disappearing under the upper lid, and a bushy black mustache speckled with white snivel from his nose which he wiped off with a large handkerchief patterned in blue squares. In class he sat cross-legged on his chair, and read to us from the Qur'an in a loud voice. When he read white spittle collected at the corners of his mouth, and drops of it flew out around him in the air.

Miss Hamer often went on inspection rounds to see what the teachers were doing. She walked on thick rubber- or crêpe-soled shoes, and made no sound as she moved or opened the door. Suddenly we would find her in the classroom. Ismail Effendi would jump to his feet, his hand would rise to his forehead, his thumb hitting his brow in a military salute introduced by the

Turkish occupation, before he wiped his mouth with the large handkerchief, and said: 'Good morgin, Miss Hamer.'

'Good morning, Mister Ismail.'

Miss Hamer did not speak Arabic, nor could she pronounce the letter *ayn*, transforming it into an *a* or a *y*. Ismail Effendi in turn changed 'morning' into 'morgin'. We made great efforts to prevent ourselves from bursting out in laughter.

Ismail Effendi then returned to his seat and to his readings from the Qur'an while she stood at the back of the class. He wetted his finger with the tip of his tongue and flipped through the pages hastily until he fell on the appropriate verse: 'So the angels said Mary, God sends you the glad tidings of a word from him whose name is the Messiah, Jesus, son of Mary. And we sent him the Gospels to be guidance, and light, and confirmation of what came before him in the Torah, to be guidance and admonition for the God-fearing. And Jesus, son of Mary, said "O Lord God send down from the heavens a table for us." And God said to me, "I am sending it down to you. Thus whoever of you does not believe will be punished more severely than anyone from all the peoples."'

Miss Hamer could not understand a single word of all this or maybe she did grasp the general meaning. But no-one could tell. I believed that she knew no Arabic so how could she understand what God was saying in the Qur'an. Besides, it seemed to me that God Himself spoke no other language than Arabic.

In my dreams I sometimes wondered whether Miss Hamer would go to Heaven or to Hell. Perhaps she might slip into Heaven in the same way as she used to slip into our classroom. I could not see her going to Hell since Satan spoke only Arabic, so that there was no way that Miss Hamer could understand him if he whispered evil temptations in her ears.

I also thought that, unlike Egyptian women, Miss Hamer did not menstruate, and did not urinate either. She always wore clean, well-ironed, silky clothes with a starched collar. Her corn-coloured hair was packed in a tight roll, and not even in the wind was a single strand blown out of place, her face was rosy red like the faces of all those who were from England.

To me, Miss Hamer was certainly richer than the chief of police, or even the king. Ismail Effendi had told us that it was God who made some people rich and others poor, and so it appeared to me that God must love Miss Hamer and the English people much more than he did Sittil Hajja and all the Muslims, since the English were rich and the Muslims were poor.

13

Dreaming of Pianos

Amongst my classmates was a girl who came from a family named Shakankiri. During the festival of the Eid she climbed onto a donkey cart and when the children started to sing she joined in. A few moments later the cart went over a railway crossing and was hit by a train. Hamida fell on the railway line and the wheels cut off both her legs. From then on she had to use wooden crutches and so while we did our physical culture, she sat on a wooden bench and watched us as we ran around the school-yard. Every now and then she would close her eyes and reach out with her hands for her legs, as though they were still there in flesh and blood.

I used to glimpse her crutches leaning against the wall when she put them aside and took a rest. A shiver would run down my body when I saw them or when I looked at her trunk on the bench. I could not bear the sight of her deformed body. Only bodies that were whole, brimming with health and vitality, attracted me.

The only classes I liked in school were those devoted to music and sports. Miss Yvonne held these classes in the open air, in the big courtyard, under the sunshine. There we played basketball, volleyball and ping-pong. Miss Yvonne was a young Egyptian woman from Upper Egypt, with a dark complexion like mine. She was the same height as I was, and she wore short dresses which reached above her knees and a broad leather belt around her slender waist. Her shoes were flat, made always of a soft leather, and her footsteps were light and quick as though her feet barely touched the ground. When her lips opened in a smile they revealed large shining white teeth which reminded me of my mother.

The music room was located at the back of the courtyard. Enthroned in the middle stood the huge piano looming black in the shadows with the white flash of its keys. Miss Yvonne took her place on the stool in front of the score and I sat beside her, singing out the notes and learning how to play 'do re mi fa sol la ti do'.

The music seemed to flow through my body in waves like warm blood, mounted to my head and dropped down to my heart beating behind my ribs with a new thrill. Was this love and if it was, was it my love for music or for Miss Yvonne? I often listened to music and songs on the radio. All the songs were about love, about love of a man for a woman, or the love of a woman for a man. Yet there was not a single man amongst those I saw around me who made my heart beat.

Walking down any street was enough to make me hate all males, all boys and all men. They never stopped gazing at me, with a stare that was like an arrow going through my chest. I hid my small breasts behind my school-bag, and ran to school, or back home, as fast as I could. Their eyes followed my everywhere, hunted me down from the doorways of the coffee houses, from the shops, from the corners of the streets and alleys.

Sometimes on my way home, father would catch sight of me walking quickly by, as he sat sipping coffee, or playing backgammon with the men in Gramino's coffee house, and call out to me to come and greet his friends. 'Nawal, Nawal, come say how d'you do to the medical inspector. This is my eldest daughter, a very clever girl. She's in Miss Hamer's school and wants to become a doctor', he would say proudly.

The word doctor had a magical ring in my ears. It seemed to rescue me from the stares of the men, carry me up to the heavens, where I soared like a winged bird. Yet I hated doctors, especially the medical inspector. He had clumsy fingers with which he used to grab my arm, before plunging his needle into my flesh. His breath smelt of methylated spirits, and his teeth were stained yellow with tobacco. If he examined my chest with the stethoscope, his finger was always tightly pressed against my breast, although I did not really have a breast at that time, just a small bud with a pointed tip so tender that it hurt me at the slightest touch, so what then if a finger like his was pressed hard against it?

I never saw myself as a doctor holding a syringe and plunging the needle into people's arms. In my dreams I saw myself seated at a piano playing music, or singing, or dancing, my feet beating on the ground, my head crowned with the disc of the sun, lifting it up like the goddess Isis.

At the end of the year the school organized a big celebration. Miss Yvonne singled me out from all the girls to play the role of Isis on the stage. I went over my part a hundred times until I knew every intonation, every word, every pause, by heart. She sat at the piano, hidden behind a curtain, while I stood on the stage dressed in a flowing white silk dress, an angelic, almost divine light dropping its rays on me. On my head I wore a crown shaped like the disc of the sun, with millions of stars radiating around it. I sang and sobbed over the death of my beloved Osiris, and the audience sitting in the courtyard started to sob with me. My father, my mother, my sisters, my brothers and all the girls of the school, everyone was sobbing. Then the miracle happens, the goddess Isis touches the dead body and suddenly it throbs into life. The beat of my feet on the stage floor is like a deep pulse, and my head is held high as I dance the dance of victory to the rhythm of the piano striking out its ringing music.

Nawal, aged eleven, on stage as the goddess Isis,
Menouf 1942.

At the end the audience crowded in the courtyard stamped
on the ground, called out in one voice, 'Bravo Isis! Bravo!', and
threw roses, Arab jasmine and carnations at me. After that,
whenever people saw me walking on the street they pointed me
out and said, 'There is Isis.'

'Nawal is gifted. She can become a great artist, Zaynab
Hanem', Miss Yvonne kept repeating to my mother whenever
she paid us a visit. Each time I heard her pronounce my name,
Nawal, my heart beat. My name was now no ordinary name. It
was as though I was hearing it for the first time, and the word
gifted coupled with it carried me above the clouds.

Sometimes Miss Hamer, accompanied by Miss Yvonne, paid
us a visit, or Miss Yvonne came alone. On such occasions my
mother opened the drawing-room. In our house it was treated as
a sacred room, remaining closed all the year round, the windows
and doors tightly shut, and never opened except to receive guests
who were not members of the family. Its armchairs were made of

beechwood, covered in red silk which felt like velvet. The wood was painted gold and so it was called *al-takm al-modhab* (the gilded suite). The armchairs were titled *fauteuils* by my mother, and were shrouded in white cloth covers to protect them from dust and light. On the floor was a brightly coloured Persian carpet which mother had brought home on her wedding night as part of the bride's trappings.

We children were not allowed to meet guests who were not part of the family. When Miss Yvonne arrived, she would ask: 'Where is Nawal?' and mother would call out to me, 'Nawal, come greet Miss Yvonne.' At that moment I was usually standing behind the door, straining my ears to hear what was going on, waiting for an excuse to go in through the door like a rocket.

In the drawing-room mother was a different woman to the one I used to see in the kitchen. With her silk dress, she put on another face, wore another body. Her long golden hair cascaded down over her shoulders. Her neck seemed to grow longer and finer, its flesh glowing like sculpted marble. Around it hung a diamond necklace, its stones flashing under the electric light. Her diamond earrings shimmered like stars with every move-ment of her head. She wore a yellow silk dress with thin shoulder straps which revealed the upper part of her bust down to the cleavage between her breasts. A brooch attached to her bodice nestled over her left breast like a small sun. On her left wrist she wore a tiny bracelet watch decorated with fine diamonds. Its figures were so minute that they could hardly be seen. Around her finger was a golden wedding ring with the name of her husband, Al-Sayed Al-Sa'adawi, engraved on it. On her right arm she wore several bracelets with stones that glittered brightly. They were her engagement present, offered by my father to his future father-in-law on the day they were betrothed.

In the drawing-room my mother could have been taken for the queen of Egypt, or a princess from the royal family. Her voice sounded radiant and pure like fresh water in a stream. Her laughter had a ring of silver, and when she laughed she threw back her head of long hair and flashed her white teeth. Her hand moved gracefully through the air as she spoke, or lay quietly in her lap when she was silent, its fingers clasping her other hand so that they looked like twin doves nestling against each other.

Sitting by her side Miss Yvonne looked even darker and thinner than she usually did. Her lips seemed pale compared to the full red lips of my mother. Her voice sounded more subdued to my ear than that of my mother. 'Nawal is gifted, Zaynab Hanem. I wish you could buy her a piano so that she can practise at home.' 'If God is willing, Miss Yvonne.' My mother said 'God willing' in a voice that made me realize that God will never be willing, and that no piano would ever enter our house during my lifetime.

My father often came into the drawing room to greet Miss Yvonne, and each time she asked him about the piano. On one occasion my father said to her abruptly 'What piano, Miss Yvonne? Things are getting more expensive every day but the salaries of the government officials do not change.' I shrank into myself with shame. Suddenly my father looked poverty-stricken in his long house shirt, or in his pyjamas made of cheap striped cotton. The heels of his big brown feet jutted out from the pair of old backless slippers he was wearing. I bent my face to the ground, hid my worn shoes under the chair. The Persian carpet seemed threadbare, its colours dreary. I hid the small hole which had bored its way through it with my foot.

At that time I was nine years old. Every night I had some dream or other about a piano. Very often it was the same dream, that of a piano dropping from the sky, and coming into my room through the window.

For twenty-six years I dreamt of this piano until the day when my daughter Mona reached the age of ten. That day I bought her a piano from an auction sale in Cairo. It cost me sixty-five pounds saved from my salary after I graduated from medical school. Sixty-five pounds accumulated over a period of eleven years in a tin money box.

Mona was living with me in my flat on the fifth floor of a building in Giza. I opened my eyes in the morning to see the piano coming in through the window hanging on a rope. The moment seemed imaginary, unreal. I had seen it night after night for twenty-six years, seen it for so long in my dreams that now the fact, the reality, seemed nothing but a dream.

14

To the Circus

Our house in Menouf had a spacious underground room known as a *badron* (cellar) where my mother used to store old things. My brother Tala'at kept his homing pigeons, as well as a huge dog named Fatty, in it. The dog looked very much like a wolf, and the girls who gathered around the pump to fill their jars with water screamed in panic when it emerged. My brother would smile with satisfaction, stretch his neck up like a turkey cock and pat his dog on the head as though he had chased away a tiger, basking in the sidelong glances full of admiration which the girls threw at him out of the corner of their eyes, as they loitered around, filling their jars, exchanging laughs and winks or trying to make jokes and clever remarks.

From the window above, Um Muhammad glared down on them, and then silence would reign, and they would quickly disappear one after the other.

'These girls of our latest times! They have no shame.' Every day, Um Muhammad made the same remark. Having no shame meant that the girls were not timid, or shy, that at the time when Um Muhammad herself was still a girl they had what was described as shame, meaning that they walked with their heads bent to the ground, never looked a man in the eyes, that their voices were never heard, that their laughter was never loud, not like the impudent hussies gathered around the water pump.

'In our days girls were well-behaved', confirmed my mother.

'Yes, mistress Zaynab Hanem, that's a fact. A girl was like a blind kitten, but in these troubled times of ours, a girl has no shame. Her eyes are so wide open, their look so brazen that a bullet could go through one of them without her batting a lid.'

Thus ran the conversation between my mother and Um Muhammad whenever she came to visit us. Tante Ni'mat or Sittil Hajja, or whoever of my maternal or paternal aunts happened to be there, would join in with her bit. They chatted, in no hurry to leave, sitting on the high-backed sofas sipping coffee or *mughat.** Um Muhammad read their fortunes from the coffee grounds left in their cups, or they played card games like *basra*, in which the jack or seven of diamonds takes all, and *cancan* (rummy). When they had finished playing, Tante Fahima took over, reading their fortunes from the cards while they chewed and snapped 'male' and 'female' chewing gum[†] between their teeth. Tante Ni'mat's hoarse laugh could be heard as she exclaimed: 'I love the male much more than I do the female', followed by soft prolonged feminine laughter left to continue unrestrained, or quickly suppressed to become something like a series of lascivious gasps. I could see my aunt Rokaya cover half her face behind a fold of her black *tarha* as she said 'May your mouth ever remain unhurt, Ni'mat Hanem'[‡] but Tante Fahima would pout her lips in disgust and reply: 'The female tastes better if it is young and fresh.' Sittil Hajja went on laughing until tears came to her eyes and voiced the opinion that there was nothing to match what was fresh and young.

---

* A hot drink made out of crushed fenugreek seeds to which is added ghee and sesame seeds.

† 'Male' chewing gum (*liban dahar*) is raw gum without sweetener, flavour or coating. The women are joking over the word *dahar*, which means 'male' in Arabic.

‡ Meaning that no harm should come to a mouth that speaks such words of wisdom.

At that stage Um Muhammad got up to get the bathroom ready and prepare the incense and the *halawa*, which was made by mixing sugar with fresh lemon and heating the mixture until it formed a sticky, elastic paste, while my mother started to hum one of Sayed Darwish's songs, 'Let's play cards on the balcony', followed by

> Perplexed, lost, flirting around O husband of many wives
> The white one says to the dark one
> 'I have no slave as dear to me as you.'
> The dark one says to the white one
> 'My walls are covered in whitewash and white turnips are
>   so cheap.'
> My husband loves only me.
> On your nights he stays away from you.

My mother's voice reached me in my small room as she sang in the parlour, and through the bathroom door penetrated the shrieks of Aunt Ni'mat, or Aunt Hanem, or Tante Fahima. They told me that Um Muhammad was removing the hair from their body with *halawa*. With this paste, women removed the hair from their bodies, from their arms and their legs, from their armpits and lower belly, and from around the cleft between their thighs.

They emerged from the bathroom, one by one, looking like skinned rabbits, their arms and legs and eyes all red, their eyebrows plucked and their eyelids swollen. One by one they sent angry looks in my direction as though I had unveiled something shameful, unmasked what should have remained concealed, revealed what humiliated them, dragged them down, made them kneel. In turn, each one of these women reached out with her hand to jab me with a finger-nail pointed and sharp like a needle, or to give me a cruel pinch in the lobe of my ear, or the flesh of my breast, a pinch which stung like the bite of a scorpion. I did not understand why they did that, whether they were trying to tease me, or to inflict a punishment on me. Their fingers were hard, strong pointed fingers that seemed to suffer from some deprivation or other and sought to compensate for it by digging themselves into the flesh of a child.

The ones who showed the greatest ire against me were Tante Ni'mat and my paternal aunt Rokaya. The two women belonged to different classes, were about the same age, and both divorced. At a distance they looked alike, but when they came closer one could see the contradiction between them. In one of the two, a pair of white hands which had stayed soft and smooth through lack of anything to do; in the other, a pair of large rough hands, the skin thickened and calloused from their grasp on the hoe. Both of them, however, believed in Allah and His Prophet. Both were in great fear of going to hell-fire, and both were submissive to the laws of marriage and divorce, read their futures in their emptied coffee cups, or according to the side on which a sea shell fell when dropped from the soothsayer's hand on to sand. Both attended *zars* (exorcism sessions) and gatherings where the spirits of the dead were summoned to appear, hung amulets around their necks to protect them from the evil eye, or from those who were able to cast spells on others. Both died surrounded by silence, without a sound, without anyone hearing of their death, abandoned by everyone, without children or even a home.

From this spot where I am now in Durham, thousands of miles from where we then lived, and after long, long years have passed, I can see them as they pass through a gap in the clouds on their very long journey to somewhere, two women who died many years ago, each of them still carrying her cross on her back, plodding on and on until it is time for them to throw themselves into hell-fire, submitting to God's will so that they can expiate for the everlasting sin of women that began with their foremother, Eve.

Nothing in the life of these women ever attracted me. I did not see myself becoming one of them, opening the cards to read my future, or pulling off the hair of my body and shrieking with pain. The life of women appeared to me to be full of pain. Around

it floated the odour of onions and garlic, of alum or incense, of
perfume mingled with sweat, of laziness and apathy.

I did not see myself in Tante Ni'mat or my mother. I felt I
resembled my father, I had inherited his dreams and to this day
I hear his voice calling out to me: 'Nawal do you want to go to
the circus?' 'Yes, yes father!'

My father belonged to the generation of the 1919 revolution.
He had received an education, and a higher degree. By dint of
his own efforts he had even picked up a few words of French,
including, of course, the phrase, *Je t'aime*, which he used to
write on a slip of paper and give to my mother after they got engaged. He described himself as being a modern *dara'mi*, meaning a modern graduate of Dar Al-Oloum. He was always fighting
battles against corruption in the government administration.
If he had befriended Sabry Abou Alam (a leading minister in
Wafdist governments), or Ahmed Maher or Al-Nokrashi (both
prime ministers of Egypt in the immediate postwar period), he
might have become Minister of Education. They were people
he encountered occasionally in meetings, but then whenever
he climbed up on the platform he tended to express what he
thought very freely. On several occasions, efforts were made by
their supporters to persuade him to join one of the parties, or
to help one or other of the leaders in the elections, in exchange
for a promotion. But he always refused any form of bribery. It
was his disposition, his forthright nature and also his religious
beliefs, and perhaps the fear of God's punishment. He dreamt of
an independent Egypt not ruled by foreigners, of a just system
that would defend the rights of poor people, of a different kind
of education in Al-Azhar and in the schools, and of religious
sheikhs who would think and believe in a different way. He
was fond of repeating what his mother said about God: 'God is
justice and people have come to know him through their reason.'
He established a modern school for children in the province of
Giza next to Cairo. To set it up, he organized a conference of
educators belonging to his generation which drafted a plan for

the school and then started to collect money for it. In one year there were enough funds to start it.

My father wrote poetry but made no effort to get it published. He read it to us as we sat on the verandah, nodding his head to the musical rhythm of the words. He liked to recite the poetry of Aboul Alla' Al-Ma'ari, Abou Nawas, Bashar ibn Burd and Al-Deeb. Abou Nawas was a poet who rebelled against established norms, loved wine and revelry. Al-Deeb said of himself: 'I am the wall on which is written, Here, O man with a full bladder, piss!'

I was happy listening to my father reading poetry or telling us about different things, but I was happiest when he took us children to the cinema, or the theatre or the circus.

In Menouf, there was only one cinema house. Amongst other films, it ran the films of Abdel Wahab.* One of these films was entitled *Tears of Love*: the only song I remember from it was called 'Too Often Have I Built a Palace of Hopes', and the only line of the song I can still remember says, 'Nawal, where are your eyes?'

The theatre was not like the cinema, which ran all the year round. It opened its doors only when there was a holiday or a festival, just like the circus. At the circus, one of the performers was a girl my age. She rode on the back of the lion and the tiger, walked the tightrope, danced, sang, and soared in the air like a bird. Her graceful body was so flexible that she could move it any way she wanted, as though she had no bones. Her image still lives in my memory, her voice as she sang, her movements light as a feather. I can hear her, see her in front of me in flesh and blood, as I sit in the circus on a narrow wooden bench. Her soprano voice soars beyond the big tent, out into space.

Hundreds of eyes are fixed on her as she walks the tightrope. I hold my breath. I can feel the audience hold its breath, feel my father and my brothers hold their breath as she springs off the

* A famous male composer and singer who started to be known in the 1940s.

Tante Ni'mat, my mother's sister.

rope and is suspended between the earth and the sky. I feel dizzy, on the verge of fainting and my lips part to let out a gasp. The image of her profile chiseled in precious stone bathes in a sacred light in the light of my enchantment.

The circus had come to Menouf in the Eid. The tent was there standing in its usual place, and I keep urging my father to hurry, to take us right away, but he insists on putting it off, keeps postponing it to another day. He is expecting his relatives and the visitors that come in the Eid. These maternal and paternal aunts are such a nuisance! During the Eid nothing is more annoying than the visitors. My heart is as heavy as a stone. I retreat to my room, try desperately to think of a way out, so that the joys of the Eid are not lost. All I can do is wait in my room, biting nervously at my nails, straining my ears to catch my father's voice as he calls out for us to go. Instead I hear him say: 'Nawal, come and greet your Aunt Ni'mat and your Aunt Rokaya.' The world goes all dark. The faces of my aunts Ni'mat and Rokaya seem the ugliest faces in the whole wide world. I go out of my room to meet them, obey my father to make sure that he will be pleased with me.

The circus opened its doors on the first day of the Eid and continued until the festival was over. My father always took us to it on the last day. I would be dressed and ready early in the morning but my father moved so slowly, tried my patience to the end, so that I could hardly bear to wait any more.

'Father! The circus!'

'What circus? What nonsense are you talking about. Stay here to help your mother in the kitchen', chorused Aunt Ni'mat and Aunt Rokaya or two or three of the women sitting around.

My heart dropped to the bottom of my shoes. I looked at my father. He seemed nonplussed, as though he would end up by taking my brothers and leaving me out. He was worried lest my mother be overburdened.

But it was my mother's voice that always came to the rescue. 'Take Nawal with you, Sayed. I don't need any help.'

My father tried to curry favour with my mother, at my expense. His tone would be all tenderness as he said: 'Let her stay here to give you a hand Zaynab. The Eid is too much for you.'

My heart plunged once more to the bottom of my shoes. I stood stock still in the parlour staring in turn at the faces of my mother and my father as they exchanged an infuriating smile. My father turned to her and said: 'Let her stay with you in the kitchen, Zaynab.'

I would keep turning this way and that, looking into their eyes, trying to find out what they really thought. Was father playing games with me, just joking? He knew I could not stand the word 'kitchen'.

Finally, after I was all bathed in sweat, my father smiled and said: 'We'll let you off this time. You can come with us.'

My heart leaped so high that it seemed as though my head was going to hit the ceiling. I was on the verge of hugging my father. Yet he lived and died without our ever embracing. Embracing in middle-class families was something that traditionally was not done. My peasant grandmother used to hug me and almost smother me in kisses, whereas my mother Zaynab Hanem, the daughter of Shoukri Bey, just like my father died without having kissed me or embraced me throughout her life.

I leaped up in the air with joy, dashed out of the house ahead of my father. My arms and legs moved with a vigour born of some internal impulsion, my heart overflowed with happiness. But happiness always breeds anxiety. Fears kept running through my mind. Had the circus already shut down? Were we too late for it? Would my father change his mind at the last moment, and order me back to help my mother?

My father could easily sense the state I was in. Maybe he was trying to have some fun teasing me. He would stop on the way and exclaim suddenly: 'That's bad. We've left your mother all alone in the kitchen. What do you think we should do, Nawal?' Or he would slow down to greet one of his friends on the street, or stop to buy a box of cigarettes, and start chatting with the owner of the store about the Second World War. O God, I whispered under my breath, calling on Him to come to my aid, as I stamped impatiently on the ground. My brother Tala'at stood next to me, moving from one foot to the other. But all our fretting seemed in vain. My father was now engrossed in a heated argument over the British and the Germans, and our anxiety kept growing. My brother tugged at father's hand complaining: 'Father, we're going to be late', and I wailed, 'The show has ended and the circus must have left. What a pity!'

At this father would glance at his wristwatch and say, 'It's still very early.' It was awful, and at that moment I hated him to death for he had a heart made of stone, hard enough to break my heart. But as soon as he took me with one hand, and my brother with the other, and we started to walk again my hatred was transformed to overwhelming love.

As we approached the circus I began to hear the roar of the lions, the snarl of the tigers, and the neighing of the horses. There was a big crowd of people standing around the entrance, and the only seats we were able to find were on the upper-level, third-class benches. In addition we had missed some of the acrobatic turns, as well as the dance of the horses, the lions, the tigers and the elephant.

Fortunately the dancing girl who walked the tightrope was the final act. Throughout, my heart did not stop pounding under my ribs, my chest rising and falling in gasps. I could not keep still, my arms and legs moving to her movements as she danced.

At the end of her turn she bowed, and the audience applauded wildly, clapping and shouting, and whistling, as she passed down the rows carrying a tambourine in her hand. She was coming nearer and nearer to where I sat, until she was only two or three rows away from me, and at one moment she was so close that my head began to spin. I felt like doing something extraordinary, jumping out of my seat in one bound that would land me where she stood, or throwing my arms around her in a warm embrace, then flying back to my seat in the wink of an eye, to sit once more wedged in between my father and my brother, as though crucified, or condemned to death. I kept trembling where I sat, fearful lest I actually leap out towards her, my face buried in my hands, the tears ready to drop from my eyes.

On the way back home I walked in silence, my head bent, my eyes glued to the ground. I could see nothing waiting for me except the gloomy house with my small gloomy room, days filled with an unchanging dreariness, with the gloomy faces of my aunts crowding in on me. There was no chance of seeing the circus again. They had already started to pull the stakes out of the ground and the space where it once stood was rapidly becoming a vast wasteland.

Before I went to bed that night I whispered into the ear of my brother, 'There's something very important I want to tell you.'

'What is it?'

'But you mustn't tell mother or father or anyone.'

'What is it?'

'Swear by God that you won't tell anyone.'

'What is it now you want to tell me?'

'No. Swear by God first.'

'I swear by God almighty that I won't tell anyone.'

'Swear by God three times.'

'Once is enough.'

'Either three times, or forget it.'

'Then forget it.'

In the morning I saw Al-Hajj Mahmoud standing in the parlour with my father. He had come to borrow some money until the first of the month. My father handed it to him in a small envelope.

'By the first of the month Sayed Bey, your excellency will have got back all I owe you', said Al-Hajj Mahmoud, as he held out a receipt to my father.

Father took the receipt and tore it up. 'I would never think of binding you with a slip of paper, Hajj Mahmoud. Your word is all I need. A man's word is binding. It's his honour.'

The servant-girl came in carrying a tray with coffee, biscuits and small cakes. In front of the house stood the she-ass carrying bolts of cloth on her back. My brother Tala'at kept calling out teasingly to her in an imitation of Al-Hajj Mahmoud's voice: 'Never mind, never mind, Aziza, shee! shee!'

The wolf-dog ran up to him. He patted him on the head and threw a quick glance at the girls gathered around the water pump. He noticed me standing in the parlour, came close up to me, and whispered in my ear: 'So what's the secret you wanted to tell me yesterday?'

'Swear by God three times that you won't tell anyone.'

My brother finally gave in and swore three times by Allah the Almighty. I brought my lips close up to his ear and whispered.

'I've decided what I'm going to be when I grow up.'

'What are you going to be?'

'A dancer like the girl in the circus.'

My brother Tala'at gazed at me with shining eyes. In turn he brought his lips close to my ear and whispered: 'I'll play the *ood* [lute] when you dance and together we'll make a film called *Tears of Love* like Abdel Wahab.' The secrets we had now exchanged had created a bond between us, and our friendship grew.

Tala'at had many hobbies and he flitted from one to the other. He began to share some of them with me, taught me how to play the *ood* and sing, and how to talk to the homing pigeons. He used to tie a message to the leg of one of the pigeons, bring his mouth close to her beak and whisper something. The pigeon flew off and returned after sometime with another message tied to its leg.

He had a girlfriend named Elena. She was the daughter of Zakhary, the owner of the grocery store on Al-Kenissa Street. She too was very fond of carrier pigeons. She sat next to me in class and she told me that she understood their language.

I too tried to learn pigeon language but despite all the efforts I made I never succeeded. I kept straining my ears to catch the sounds that a pigeon made when it put its beak close up to that of another pigeon. All I could hear was a lot of cooing but nothing that sounded like letters or words. I felt that Tala'at and his girlfriend Elena must be more intelligent than me.

My brother was the silent type. He always kept things to himself, was always closing the door of his room on himself and opening the window that overlooked the water pump. He stood there staring at the girls as they filled up their water jars. One day I saw a girl climb over the wall, hold on to the iron bars and take something from him. I wondered what he could be giving to her. On another day I saw him hanging black ribbons from his window, and thought one of his girlfriends had died. But my mother said to him 'It looks as though you take after Uncle Yehia when it comes to chasing after girls.' Before she went to bed, my mother locked the door on the servant-girl Sa'adeya to prevent my brother from sneaking in to her during the night.

During the summer holidays, I joined my brother in one of his new hobbies: that of sawing plywood and making figures out of it. We spent the summer months cutting into the wood with a long narrow saw in order to carve out different animals, people and birds. We set up a circus with a lion, a tiger, elephants and horses. We created a graceful dancer who kept her balance on one toe, a man who resembled Ismail Effendi and held a bamboo stick in his hand, a Miss Hamer with thick-soled shoes, a Tante Ni'mat and an Aunt Rokaya, an Um Muhammad and a Hajj Mahmoud riding on his she-ass.

We set up an exhibition in the cellar and mounted each of the different figures on a wooden stand. When everything was ready we invited mother and father to the inauguration of our show.

Over fifty years have gone by since that day but everything remains engraved in my memory in all its details. My mother and father descended the stairs to the sound of music played by my brother on the *ood*. My father cut the ribbon and we raised the big white sheet we had transformed into a curtain. My mother sat next to my father in the front row. The rest of the audience was composed of my brothers, my sisters and a small group of our relatives, neighbours and some classmates from the schools to which we went.

In my hand I held a slender wooden stick which I moved in the air to the music of the *ood*. I played the role of maestro. With the tip of my baton I pointed to the different characters and told stories which I had created for each of them. I could see the eyes of the audience following the movements of my hand as though tied to it by invisible threads.

The characters were real-life characters, and the stories were real too. The carrier pigeons spoke human language and even Hajj Mahmoud's she-ass said all sorts of things and sang to the melody that my brother played on the lute.

> From early morning I carry cloth on my back.
> Bolt upon bolt, upon bolt.
> And on top of the pile rides Al-Hajj Mahmoud.
> Dangling his legs on either side of my flanks.
> All day long through the lanes.
> Round and round I go.
> To come home at the end of the day.
> All the day long I walk and he rides.
> Never mind Aziza. Shee, shee.

My brother and I sang the refrain together to the rhythm of the lute.

> Never mind, Aziza, never mind.
> Shee, shee.
> Shee, shee.

The guests in the audience tapped the ground with their feet and sang the refrain with us. The carrier pigeon flew up and circled round, winging its way to the tune. Hanging from its leg was a love-letter fluttering like a small white flag. The lion, the tiger, the elephant and the horses danced up and down on their wooden stands, and the dancing girl kept leaping higher and higher into the air. Ismail Effendi followed her around, beating her on her rounded buttocks so zealously that his fez fell off his head, Miss Hamer tapped on the ground with her thick-heeled shoes, Tante Ni'mat pulled on the thick sticky paste of *halawa* as she peeled the hair off her legs, Aunt Rokaya tossed her long hair around her head as she danced a frenzied *zar*, and Um Muhammad chased the girls away from the water pump muttering all the time 'Brazen hussies of these times!'

At the end of the show my brother played a closing tune and applause broke out loudly in the cellar. Father and mother stood up, their eyes shining, and father for the first time ever in his life went up to my brother and shook hands warmly with him. In the midst of laughter I heard him say to Tala'at, 'If you fail at school, you can become a musician like Abdel Wahab.' Then he turned to me and shook my hand, which was also something he had never done before, and said: 'Your stories show imagination.' My mother, too, was overjoyed, bubbling with laughter: 'If they fire your father from government service we can form a theatre group like that of Al-Rihani.'*

After that, I began to have confidence in my imagination and in my talent as a story-teller. The cellar was now for me the most beautiful place in the world. Everything there seemed to dance,

---

* A famous Egyptian comedian of the 1940s renowned for his satires about the upper class.

even the spiders as they spun their webs on the ceiling danced, or applauded with their hands and feet, even the cockroaches and the beetles.

The applause of that day continues to echo in my ears. I can see my father's and my mother's hands clapping, see their eyes shining with happiness. Tears spring to my eyes, sparkle in the light. I feel deep inside the repressed, imprisoned energy, the vitality seeking to be freed, seeking to find its way, still shrouded in shadows.

15

The Singing Man

I felt an energy, a vitality imprisoned in my body somewhere just below the heart, in that deep groove between my ribs. What was it made of? Joy, sorrow, anger, a dream of freedom, of soaring beyond the walls of the kitchen, of our house, of school. But to where?

It was an ancient dream, more ancient than memory, than history. The truest of my dreams was born with childhood, was my childhood dream. It had no link with time or place, grew more true, more genuine no matter where, no matter the seasons and the years. It is reborn as they go by, gives birth to itself, for like the gods it is self-creating.

I clasp this dream of childhood to my bosom, and rock it gently. It is my sacred child, and around it floats a halo of innocence. As I sleep it becomes a warm body and its arms enfold me like the arms of my mother used to do. When it abandons me, my strength drains away. Then I yearn for it, as though it were the warmth in my heart, the energy that moves my body. If it swells, grows too big, it turns into a torrent of anger, sweeps through me, almost destroys me, then the torrent subsides, becomes a peaceful, gentle river, or a flow of warm sunlight.

In the morning, at the moment of awakening, I used to look into the eyes of my sister Leila, or my other sisters, search for the thing, for the dream that troubled me at night. Their eyes were always calm and clear, revealed no sign of anxiety, of anything that could have disturbed their sleep. At school too I used to look into the eyes of the girls trying to discover any of these signs, then later at the university in medical school I kept searching for them in the eyes of the young women who were my colleagues, or who had become doctors. Wherever I went I continued this search, continued to look for this dream in their eyes, hoping to find it.

Perhaps it is my imagination. Perhaps what I feel is not real, but for me my dreams always seemed to be a reality, a part of the real world. When I slept my subconscious mind woke up, moved around in my head, made me fly far away, hover high up in the sky, or plunge deep into the sea, or into the earth, and die there buried in a grave.

My subconscious mind was like a store-house, or a well. Things that weighed heavily on my heart penetrated me, sunk to the bottom. The lighter things floated to the surface to be swept away. When I opened my eyes in the morning they shone as though bathed in sunlight, and my heart beat with a new warmth for the new day. It was as though sleep had washed away the sorrows of the previous day, as though there had been no yesterday. Each day it was the same, yet I never understood how this came to be.

That morning, in the early autumn of 1941, I opened my window to let in the first breath of a gentle cold after the heat of summer. The fields stretched out before my eyes like green carpeting. A huge tree in the adjoining garden had taken on the multiple colours of autumn, red, blue, yellow, green, orange, silver and gold, its leaves fluttering, or falling to the ground with a last tremble of life.

My heart is beating quickly under my ribs. I am awaiting an important encounter, an extraordinary event. Today seems different to all other days, unique, goes far beyond the ordinary. My body echoes the tremble of the leaves. My eyes are wide open to observe every movement, my ears strained to pick up the sound of a voice... of that voice.

When I hear it I wonder. Is it a voice descending from the heavens? No, it comes from the balcony above me on the second floor. But it's not like any other voice. It's unique, caresses my ear, flows down my neck to my breast, to my belly and continues down as far as my feet, then rises up again to my heart and my head as though circulating with the blood in my body.

The voice sings to the music of a lute. It sings for me, for no-one else. No other ears than mine are capable of picking up its waves from amidst the myriads of waves that sweep through the universe, from the whispers of the leaves, and the music of their rustle in the wind, from the song of birds.

Khadija, the daughter of Al-Hajj Mahmoud, told me one evening that he was a relative of theirs, that he was studying fine arts in Cairo, and only came to Menouf during the summer holidays, or the Eid. During those periods his voice came to me, carried on the breeze. It floated in with the early morning light and at the end of the day when the sun set, and when the sky, just before dusk, became a flaming red dissolving slowly into hues of pink, orange and gold flowing into one another, lighting the edges of the clouds so that they became like the wings of butterflies.

I used to sit alone on the verandah gazing at the sky, wondering at the vast world, at its hidden depths pulsing with a perpetual movement hidden beneath what seemed a total stillness, as the colours of the sky disappeared to become a total black. Suddenly, the stars started to shine as though born in the underbelly of the sky, million of stars like millions of eyes shining with a gleam of madness as they looked down on me.

I was attracted by one particular star in a corner of the vast blackness. It stared at me from a distance. This was my star. It was born with me and would cease to shine when I died.

As I sit there on the verandah gazing at the sky, his voice wafts down to me from the balcony above singing to the rhythm of the lute:

> When night falls and the stars scatter over its darkness,
> Ask, O night, where is my star. When will it shine?

I often heard this song on the radio. People said that the man who sang it had the most beautiful voice in Egypt. Yet his voice never moved me, never made my heart beat. But the man upstairs was singing for me, and for no-one else. My heart beat strongly with the beat of his fingers on the lute. My eyes swept over the skies searching for his star amidst the millions of other stars, wondering when it would come out.

He seemed to be no more than a phantom born of my dreams. His voice came to me from somewhere beyond the universe. Yet the day came when I actually saw him in flesh and blood, standing in front of a wooden easel in the middle of a green field. In his hand he was holding a paint brush which he moved over a canvas.

His back was turned towards me so he did not see me, although the field where he stood was just in front of our house. It belonged to a peasant named Am Saber and the name of the peasant's wife was Sabireen.* She had a son the same age as me called Ábd Al-Mon'im, shortened to Min'im by those around him. He resembled Galal, the son of my paternal aunt Nefissa. I used to join in irrigating the crops and often played with Min'im and the neighbours' children in the fields in the same way as I used to do with the sons and daughters of my paternal aunts in Kafr Tahla.

As soon as Sabireen saw me she would smile, cough like my aunt Baheya, and pronouncing the words in the same way as she did, say happily to me: 'You bring a radiance with you when you come to our field, Sitt† Nawal.' Then she would break off a ripe

---

* Uncle ('Am') used as a form of respect. *Saber* means 'he who is patient'; the plural is Sabireen.
† A term of respect when addressing a female of a higher rank, meaning 'lady'.

corn cob, or a dark purple eggplant for me, or fill my two hands with the pods of fava beans.

Min'im wore a *gallabeya* which was always covered in mud. His skin was dark, his eyes black, his lips always parted in a broad smile, his teeth blackened through munching raw aubergines (egg plants). He was always clambering over our wall, grasping the iron bars of our window to look into our house and exclaim with a gasp: 'Oh my! You have lots of beautiful furniture, more beautiful than that of the king. God has been bountiful to you, but he does not seem to be pleased with peasants like us, Sitt Nawal.'

When he said Sitt Nawal it resounded in my ears, made the blood rush up to them, for he was accustomed to address me just as Nawal. Why had he started to give me the unpleasant title of Sitt? In his eyes had I become similar to women like Tante Ni'mat? Had Sittil Hajja given away my secret? Ever since I had started to menstruate she had not stopped saying 'Nawal has reached the age of reason. She is now as ripe as a fig ready to be plucked by a bridegroom.'

I wished that the earth would open up and swallow me. I yearned to move my legs and run as I had always done.

When I saw him standing there all I could do was to remain stock still, my feet nailed to the ground. His back was turned towards me, his face towards the canvas. In his hand he held a brush which he moved as he painted Am Saber irrigating his field, his arms and legs plunged in water, his head wrapped in a grey scarf with black dots, his deep set eyes gleaming under the sunlight, alive, looking at me as though they were his real eyes.

I started to retreat trying to disappear before he turned round and saw me there. But at that precise moment Min'im had already pronounced 'Sitt Nawal.' He turned round, and when he saw me his eyes widened in a kind of wonder, as though he were discovering my existence for the first time.

I looked at him in astonishment for now I realized that he was a real being, not a phantom.

This single moment of mutual discovery linked us to one another like a secret binds people together with a kind of magic.

I heard Am Saber's voice echo in the open space as he said, 'O my, am I as handsome as all that Oustaz* Fathy.'

So now I had found out his name! It was a name with four† letters. FATHY. A single letter of his name was enough to make my heart miss a beat, to disturb the regular movement of blood flowing through my heart, enough to turn the whole world topsy-turvy. I did not dare pronounce his name. The letter *F* alone was enough to create the chaos which his name had created in me.

I never mentioned his name in front of anyone. I was afraid people would detect the tremble in my voice, or hear the beat of my heart, or notice the blood rushing to my face, see my high cheeks turn the colour of red tomatoes, or carrots.

At the age of ten before I knew what consciousness was, I had already become conscious of the fact that love was *haram*, or forbidden, sacreligious, sinful. Yet the radio never stopped blaring out love songs. Day and night Um Koulsoum‡ would sing: 'Since you are in love why deny. Love shows in your eyes.' Abdel Wahab never stopped beseeching his beloved to come back: 'Nawal where are your eyes?' Fareed-Al-Atrash expressed his yearning for his beloved in one song after another, while his sister Asmahan's husky voice spoke of the lover who had departed and left her to suffer. Leila Mourad repeated unendingly: 'My love, come see what's happening to me.' Plastered over the walls everywhere were posters advertising films called *Long Live Love* or *Tears of Love*, or *Passion and Vengeance*, or displaying semi-naked women throwing their arms around men.

My mother went around singing with Um Koulsoum: 'Since you are in love, why deny?' Tante Ni'mat hummed an

---

* A term used to address learned people, meaning 'he who teaches us'.

† Four in Arabic, since the vowel a does not exist and is replaced by a sign on the *F*.

‡ Um Koulsoum: a very prestigious Egyptian singer who became the idol of all Arabs. Fareed and Asmahan Al-Atrash: Syrian Druze singers. Leila Mourad: a Jewish Egyptian singer.

accompaniment to love songs broadcast over radio. Tante Fahima (Oustaza Fahima Shoukry), whom my father had nicknamed the night watchman, stamped her iron heels on the ground, and sang in a subdued voice: 'Since you are in love, why deny?' Curled up on her prayer rug close to the radio, Sittil Hajja repeated Um Koulsoum's songs with her. When she lifted her legs to sit down or to stand up, her *gallabeya* mounted up over them, uncovering the lower half of her belly, and I would get a glimpse of a big, sagging pouch of skin.

I wondered how my father with his huge body had been lying inside that shrunken belly. My mother had given birth to one child after another through an opening between her thighs. Did Sittil Hajja have the same opening or had it been blocked up by the wrinkles of her sagging belly?

'Since you are in love, why deny? For when one is in love, love shows in one's eyes.' I hear the voice of Sittil Hajja accompany the radio after she is over with her prayers. Her dark wrinkled face is turned to the window. Her eyes are lost somewhere in the distant horizon, in some memory from the distant past. Could it be a memory of love?

'Our Lord Muhammad said, "One day for your heart, and one day for your God. Do in life as if you will live forever, and prepare for the after-life as though you will die tomorrow."'

After she said that I asked her, 'Sittil Hajja, have you ever known what it is to be in love?' She looked at me with her narrow deep-set eyes and smiled. Her eyes became full of light.

'Of course I have, daughter of my son. I have loved the most high and Almighty God and our Lord Muhammad, a thousand prayers be on him. And I have loved the Imam Al-Shafei,* and our Lady Zaynab, and our Lord Al-Badawi, and my son Al-Sayed, may God protect him, and all my five daughters, especially

---

* Imam Al-Shafei: the leader of one of the four principal Sunni sects in Islam. Lady Zaynab: wife of the Prophet Muhammad. Lord Al-Badawi: A Muslim saint whose memorial is located in the city of Tantah (Middle Delta).

Zaynab. But the dearest of all was your father, Al-Sayed, may
God protect him and prolong his days.'

'Sittil Hajja, I mean the other kind of love.'

'What other kind of love, daughter of my son?'

'The one that Um Koulsoum sings about.'

'That's radio talk, daughter of my son. Here in our village
we have no radio, neither do we have any of that thing called
love that you have in mind. A girl in our village, as soon as she
reaches puberty, hop, is married off at once. Next month is the
wedding of Zaynab, the daughter of your Aunt Baheya. You and
she were born about the same time and your bridegroom, God
willing, is certainly on his way so that we will be able to rejoice
during the Eid.' Her words sounded in my ears as though she
were saying, 'and will sacrifice you during the Eid.'

My first love was the first secret I had in my life. No creature,
whether human or a jinni, ever came to know about it. In the
Qur'an there is a verse which talks about jinnis. So I could not
possibly deny the existence of these hidden spirits. I feared that
one of them might come up to me and touch me as I stood on the
verandah, so I kept my eyes fastened on him as he stood in front
of his easel. At night, as I lay in bed, I was afraid to pronounce
his name. The spirits were capable of hearing everything.

No matter how hard I try I cannot remember what he looked
like. All I can remember is the shine in his eyes. I never found
out what colour they were. Black, or blue, or green like clover in
the fields. Their colour seemed to change with the movement of
the sun or the colours in the sky. His shirt was loose around his
body and it blew up with air. He seemed like a spirit hovering
over waves of green, without a body, or a belly, without thighs
or organs, especially that organ in my brother's body from which
the urine shot out. I could not imagine him urinating like my
brother, or like other human beings, or that he had an anal opening from which were expelled the remains of food, or gases.

I used to pass my examinations with distinction. My teachers said I was very intelligent, yet somehow all my intelligence

evaporated into thin air as soon as I caught sight of him. I lost
my voice, was unable to pronounce a single word.

'Welcome, Nawal.' That's all he said when we met. Just two
very ordinary words that I kept hearing from people around
me. Welcome was the habitual greeting used by everyone, yet
coming from him it sounded extraordinary. Nawal, too, seemed
to become a new name, which gave birth to a new girl, a Cin-
derella riding on a horse that flew up with her into the air like a
dove. Was this the unbridled imagination of a young child? Or
the songs and fabricated stories about love? Or was it the true
love that happens only at the age of ten?

My heart has never beaten as strongly as it did when I was
a child of ten. I used to wake up before dawn to the sound of
something like silent weeping. I did not know who it was that
was weeping. Was it just my deep breathing which sounded like
sobbing? Had the sound been enough to wake me up? Or was it
just a dream?

I curled up in bed wondering what I had been dreaming about.
I tried to remember, calling on all the powers of mind I possessed, mobilizing every single cell in my body. But the dream
slipped away from me like water through a sieve, or a mirage
evaporating when I came closer to it.

A month went by. We traveled to Kafr Tahla to attend the
wedding of Zaynab, the daughter of my aunt Baheya. It was
the first wedding I had attended in Kafr Tahla. Zaynab was a
little older than I was. Her height was the same as mine, and
her complexion the same colour. At school she used to hold the
pen between her fingers and write her name on the cover of her
notebooks: Zaynab Abd Al-Halim Al-Saadawi.

Zaynab had dreams. She saw herself becoming a teacher like
her uncle, Sayed Bey (my father), and the cousin of her father.
Her father wore a long, faded *gallabeya*, and a skull cap, the kind
with a lot of holes in it. The skin over his fingers was cracked, his
nails were black and his thumbnail had been broken by a blow
from a hoe. When he noticed my father approaching he would

jump to his feet, offer him the chair on which be was sitting, and
squat on the ground. I used to hear Zaynab say: 'I will never be
like my father. I must go to school and learn, so that I can follow
in the steps of my uncle Bey, and so that people will point to me
and say "There goes Al-Oustaza Zaynab Al-Sa'adawi."'

My Aunt Baheya's house was like a cave, its walls plastered
with dark mud. I squatted in the murky parlour on a mat laid
on the ground, and the fleas kept biting me. A large number of
men and women had crowded into the house. All of them were
peasants, dressed in long flowing *gallabeyas* which smelt of dust
and sweat. In the middle, a group of young girls in colourfully
embroidered robes were holding on to one another's tails as they
danced around singing a refrain:

> Walk on the earth with pride, O beautiful one, O rose from the
> garden.
> Be blessed with your light-hearted bridegroom, O bride.
> O ornament adorning the wedding procession, may you be blessed
> on this happy day.
> O bridegroom see how lovely she is
> And you too handsome youth of the procession, may you also be
> blessed.

Through the open door of the animal pen I glimpsed the cow
as she lowered her head and chewed dry fodder. She lifted it and
stared at me, her eyes filled with a silent sadness. Zaynab, the
bride, sat in the midst of the girls enveloped in her embroidered
wedding gown, her head lowered to the ground, wiping off her
tears with the edge of her sleeve. Our eyes met and she smiled,
then I saw her eyes fill with tears again. The mother of the bride,
my aunt Baheya, sat in a corner surrounded by other women
coughing nervously, and dabbing her eyes with the edge of her
tarha. Beneath the smiles of the women I could detect the sadness, the tears that had dried over the years, the gloom which
enveloped memories of their wedding night.

The bridegroom was Zaynab's cousin. Like most members of
the Al-Saadawi family he was tall, and now he walked around

with a proud swagger, dressed in his new *gallabeya*. The young men were gathered around him, beating on their *tablas*,* stamping on the ground as they danced and sang and waved their long staffs in the air like swords.

> We snatched her away from right inside her home.
> There sat her father not pleased at all.
> We took her at the point of the sword for her father did not want
>   her to go.†

Suddenly the *daya* was in our midst like an angel of death. She took Zaynab by the arm and led her into the inner room. I tried to go in with her but the door was shut in my face. The beat of the drums went faster, and the 'yoo-yoos' rose to a higher pitch, as though the women wanted to conceal the crime that was now being perpetrated inside. The next moment Zaynab's shriek penetrated through the closed door, a sharp prolonged shriek that rose high up to the heavens before it choked to an end in what seemed a final gasp.

I thought she had died. Then the door opened and Um Muhammad came out yoo-yooing at the top of her voice as she lifted the white towel, soaked with blood, above her head. The women burst out in a chorus of sharp, shrilling 'yoo-yoos' very much like the shrieks they were accustomed to emit at funerals. The father of Zaynab, Am Abd Al-Aleem, stood up and started to move with a new pride amongst the men. My aunt Baheya, Zaynab's mother, got to her feet, tied her *tarha* around her buttocks and joined the girls as they danced. The bridegroom, too, began to dance, lifting his long pointed staff high in the air.

The bridegroom's stick was destined to land on Zaynab's back later in the evening as she got ready to prepare his dinner. Custom had it that she must sample the sting of his stick before she could sample the taste of food brought home by him. This was to make sure that she realized that Allah ruled over all

---

* Deep conically shaped drums on which the drummer beats with his hands.
† This song is a relic of tribal days when tradition often required that the would-be bridegroom kidnap his bride to prove his prowess.

things from his place, high up in the heavens, and that her husband ruled over her here on earth, that to obey him was linked to her obedience to God.

After it was all over, I lay down on the ground with the mat under me and the covers pulled over my head, blocking my ears with both hands. Zaynab's screams still echoed in my ears. In a nearby room I could hear Sittil Hajja's voice as she whispered into the ears of one of my aunts. 'It's now the turn of the daughter of my son Al-Sayed. The bridegroom is all set. He's the son of her uncle Al-Hajj Afifi, who owns fourteen feddans, each feddan as good as the other. That's apart from the shop he owns. He will indeed be a bridegroom who will bring her happiness, and I pray God that he will make it so that everything works out for the best.'

Zaynab's screams must have affected my hearing, or reduced my ability to understand, since I thought that the daughter of Al-Sayed Bey was not me but someone else. Then I realized that Sittil Hajja was talking about me, that the bridegroom in question was ready for me. But who was this bridegroom? I hardly knew him at all, had seen him just once sitting on a wooden bench inside his father's shop. Then I slowly recalled a peasant with a lean body and a pale face. His eyes small, deep set, shining like the eyes of a hawk, black whiskers that stretched from ear to ear, his nose long and curved like a beak. He had been married before, but his wife had died while giving birth to her second child.

All through the night, my eyes remained wide open. The walls around me with their dark, muddy surface seemed to close in, and the low ceiling looked as though it were ready to collapse on me at any moment, despite the thick beams of wood which held it up. In the corners of the parlour stretched spider webs, and the beams were cracked where the worms had eaten their way through the wood. In the cracks had settled layers of black soot from the mud oven, and the beams kept making a squeaking sound like the faint mewing of cats, or a moan of eternal suffering. On the roof of the mud-house were stored earthenware jars filled with pickles, or salted cheese, piles of dry maize and cotton stalks, cakes of dung left to dry in the sun. Through all this crawled lizards, beetles, cockroaches and other insects, while around it jumped cats and frogs.

More than half of a century has gone by since that night but it is still alive in me. The sounds of the night reach me as I lie there, in the middle of that small village, its houses huddled close to the banks of the Nile, the howling of hungry wolves in the open spaces, the breathing of my sister Leila, lying beside me, her eyes half-closed, her mouth open, the saliva dribbling down her chin, her hands moving nervously as she scratches her belly and her back, where the flea bites would show in the morning after they had left scores of red marks over her milk-white skin.

The moaning sounds made by the wooden beams in the ceiling echo in my ears, and bring back the feel of tears trickling down my throat, their salty taste on my tongue. I swallow them as I lie on the mat, hold my breath to avoid anyone from noticing that I am still awake, hide myself under the covers wondering what I should do, whether I should surrender like my cousin Zaynab. But deep down inside, a voice says 'Never, never.' I see myself running as fast as I can into the darkness, hiding under the bank of the Nile, or throwing myself into its waters. Behind me runs the bridegroom, his mouth open, ready to swallow me up like the whale swallowed up Jonas. Inside the belly of the whale I make a hole, digging with the tip of my finger, then wriggle through it into the sea, and start to swim like a fish up to the surface. There I flap my fins in the sunshine until they turn into wings with feathers so that I now fly up like a bird into the sky, hover over green fields rolling out to the horizon, and there in the middle of a green field I see him standing in front of his easel, making a portrait of me, of a girl whose eyes are black and shining.

I hear him say, 'Welcome, Nawal', and his voice invades me from under the covers. My heart flutters like a feather in the wind and the sound of his singing comes to me from the balcony above:

> When the night falls and the stars scatter over the night,
> Ask the night when will my star come out.

The music he plays on the lute wafts through the night, soft like my skin, invades me under the covers, has the odour of green fields. I can smell it, touch it, feel it on my arm naked under the moonlight, as I lie here rolled up in the covers.

I open my eyes in the dark, glimpse the beams of black wood up in the ceiling, hear the whine of mosquitoes, the hissing noise made by the cow as she breathes in the animal pen, the snoring of Sittil Hajja in the adjoining room. I close my eyes, try to fall asleep, to go back to my dream, but the dream is gone. In its place is a nightmare, the face of a stranger with the eyes of a hawk, a nose like the beak of a bird of prey, with black whiskers like a beetle resting on his upper lip, its legs long, spider-like. I hated the sight of whiskers on a man's face. My father had a moustache, but it was not like the whiskers of males. My father was not a male. Fatherhood and maleness for me never went together.

16

The Whiskered Peasant

So the first would-be bridegroom in my life was a peasant with whiskers. In my imagination I saw myself looking like my cousin Zaynab, after she had become a peasant woman with rough, cracked feet, a peasant woman who can no longer read or write, has forgotten even the letters of her name, lies down to sleep in winter on the mud-oven with swollen legs, coughs like her mother and calls out to her daughter in hoarse, broken tones, 'You girl, yes you, Sodfa, get up, I said get up, and go milk the buffalo, then sweep the ground under the cow.'

Her grand-daughter is now ten years old. She has been taken out of school to work at home and in the fields, and to be prepared for marriage with her cousin. Zaynab has done to her daughters and her grand-daughters what her father did to her. When I remind her of her youthful dreams she laughs and says:

That was a very long time ago, Dr Nawal. Nowadays life is difficult, schools are expensive, and there's a lot of work to be done in the fields, and at home. And what have those who went to school and university done? Here they are sitting around in the village with no work, no jobs. It's not like it was before. Even those who went to Saudi Arabia or Kuwait have come back. And those who went to Libya or Iraq often never came home. Some of them died in the war, some were brought home naked bodies* lying in a wooden box, and many ran away to another country. God knows how many of our hearts were broken over our boys, Dr Nawal.

That was how my cousin answered my question, when I visited her home in Kafr Tahla during the summer of 1991 after the Gulf War.

In those distant days after Zaynab was married off, I was being pushed towards marriage, towards a disaster similar to hers, towards a marriage with the son of my uncle Al-Hajj Afifi. He would have built me a red-brick house next to the family shop. His mother would have taught me how to knead dough and bake bread, how to milk the buffalo, make strained cheese by rolling it in a mat, fill an earthenware jar with water from the river, and how to mix straw with cattle dung to make fuel cakes. But his mother never had the opportunity to do that. Every time she visited us and tried to get anywhere near me, I turned on her like a mad dog. So after a while, my first bridegroom evaporated into thin air like wisps of cloud in the summer. After that, rumours began to spread around in my mother's and my father's families about the hasty disappearance of the would-be bridegroom.

Oustaza Fahima Shoukry led the campaign in the family of Shoukry Bey. She hit the ground with the iron heel of her shoe, lifted the nose she had inherited from her father even higher in the air, and exclaimed: 'Can anyone possibly imagine the daughter of Zaynab Hanem being married off to a clumsy peasant?' The word clumsy echoed in my ears like music. Of course, Tante Fahima never used this description when my father and Sittil Hajja were there.

In the Al-Saadawi family it was my aunt Fatima who took the lead. She wound the black *tarha* around her head, hid her mouth with her big rough hand and whispered in my father's ear: 'I said to him, now lad, remember she's the daughter of Al-Sayed Bey and you know he's no ordinary man, and he said, auntie I don't

---

* Meaning without the shroud that is considered a mark of respect to the dead, who should not be left naked when they die.

want to hear that kind of talk. She's nothing but a town girl. She doesn't know how to make dough, or bake bread, or milk the buffalo. I said, lad, she's been to school, knows how to read and write. He said, auntie shut up, will you. What will she do with all her reading and writing. Her reading is not something I can eat, and her writing is not something I can drink!'

This clumsy peasant could have become my husband. It was reading and writing that saved me. It was reading and writing that saved me from other men, from other potential husbands who arrived later on carrying with them higher degrees from Cairo University, or the Sorbonne, or Oxford. One by one they discovered that I loved the touch of the pen in my hand much more than the feel of the ladle or the handle of a broom, and so one by one they disappeared like the whiff of a gentle breeze in the night.

In the summer of 1942, I passed the examinations of my primary certificate with distinction. No-one either in my mother's or my father's family rejoiced. Sadness over my brother's failures overcame any joy they felt at my success. Sittil Hajja kept staring at the two breasts that now stood out over my chest, and whispering in my mother's ear: 'The girl has grown, Sitti Zaynab, and I'm afraid the day will come when she'll be barren. May God send your daughter Nawal a bridegroom so that you can rejoice and be able to marry all your daughters while I'm still here on earth.'

I no longer went out of the house to play with other children, or to ride a bicycle. Whenever I asked my father or my mother if I could go out for a while the answer was always, 'You're grown up now. The house needs a cleaning! There's a bowl of onions in the kitchen which have to be peeled! The bathroom floor needs to be scrubbed!'

I kneel over the floor and scrub the tiles so hard that they shine, and I can see my face in them. It's a face full of sadness, full of tears. Yet the eyes of the people around me are full of happiness. They feel much more happy when I scrub the floor than when I do well at school.

When they lay down to rest in the afternoon I used to creep into my father's study. Among the books I discovered Taha Hussayn's *Al-Ayam* (The Days). I started to be afraid that I might lose my eyesight like Taha Hussayn because I cried so much at night, or my mother might make a mistake and put iodine in my eyes instead of eye-drops like his mother had done.

In Menouf and Kafr Tahla I often saw children who were blind, or with one eye open and the other closed, or with a white spot creeping over the black pupil, or with swollen eyelids exuding pus and with flies all over their faces.

'Chase the flies away from your face, Nawal', my mother always said as soon as she spotted a fly on my face. She called flies Al-Teir ('that which flies'). She was always getting hold of the fly-sprayer painted bright red, with a huge black fly drawn on it, filling its drum with Tox, or a solution of DDT, and going around spraying the whole house after she had closed the windows. The flies would fall like black raindrops, while I coughed and sneezed, tears running from my eyes.

Before we went to sleep my mother put white or red eye-drops in our eyes, or an ointment, or a kind of white paste called *shishm* (zinc oxide). It was supposed to prevent inflammations which could lead to blindness.

One of Al-Hajj Mahmoud's daughters was blind. She was a little older than her sister Khadija. Her name was Ni'matallah (a blessing, something good sent by God). Her mother had made a mistake and put ground red pepper instead of *shism* in her eyes. She used to stay imprisoned in the house, sitting on the ground reciting the Qur'an in a loud voice. Her *gallabeya* was torn, dirty, covered with dust, and her mother beat her on the back with a stick. I could hear her shouting at her: 'Get up girl, may your day of reckoning come soon. Get up and go wash the pots at the pump.'

I used to see her from between the iron bars of the window, bent over the pots, rubbing them with earth or with a stone. Her back would be turned towards me, but almost immediately she would turn around to face me as though she had seen me at the window, as though she had an additional hidden sense which had developed in her body to compensate for her blindness.

I could see her gazing with her eyes at my window, their black lashes trembling in a kind of rapid vibration. They looked like the eye-lashes of sugar dolls sold during the Moulid. Her pale lips parted in a smile, before she said: 'Good morning, Nawal.'

I could not look at her eyes without my head going around. I could not imagine that they were sightless. They were so wide-open. The whites were pure and their irises black and shining. How could she possibly be unable to see, and how had she lost her sight? I could not bring myself to ask her. Ground red pepper was red, and *shishm* was white. Her mother must have mistaken them in the dark, for in their house they had no electricity.

One day I went down to her carrying Taha Hussein's *Al-Ayam* with me. I wanted to read out parts of it to her. Maybe she could win the battle against darkness just as he had done. But when I sat down near her she brought her lips close to my ear and whispered: 'Fathy is coming tomorrow.'

The book fell out of my hand onto the ground. How had Ni'matallah discovered my secret? God was the only one who could know about it! Sittil Hajja said that God often put the secret of his power into the bodies of his weakest creatures. The fortune-teller in Kafr Tahla was a blind woman but she could read the future. And there was a blind sheikh who had the ability to know what no-one else was capable of knowing. He could tell whether the child in a woman's womb was a male or a female. A barren woman, once she had visited him, became pregnant. When she went to him he took her into a dark room and there he hung an amulet containing a verse of the Qur'an around her neck. So when I was a child I thought that the greater the loss of sight with which a woman or a man could be afflicted, the greater her or his knowledge of God and the greater her or his ability to reveal the secrets of the future.

I stood up in front of Ni'matallah trembling. It was as though my clothes had been ripped from my body leaving me completely naked, completely exposed to her eyes. The name Fathy coming from her was explosive enough to shatter the equilibrium in the whole world, to create chaos in the movement of the planets and the stars, to destroy balance on earth. The earth had been stable under my feet, unmoving, and now it was revolving around itself, or circling around the sun. The book I had been carrying too had not remained still. It had moved, shot out of my hand and fallen on the ground.

At first, I thought that chaos had swept only through the outer world. But after a moment I felt it inside me also, sweeping through me from the top of my head to the tip of my toes. Sweat poured from my body, wetting my clothes. I could feel it under my armpits, trickling on my back, down to my legs and my shoes and into my socks.

I bent down quickly to the ground trying to hide my face as I picked up the book. I avoided looking at Ni'matallah. Her ability to sense was more acute than the five senses of ordinary people combined. The four letters of Fathy's name seemed to be engraved on my forehead for her to read as though from a book. Her eyes were akin to those of a jinni capable of reading Al-Maktoub,* the destiny Allah inscribes on people's foreheads before they emerge from their mothers' wombs.

I held Taha Hussayn's book tightly in my hand and ran back to the house as fast as I could. I no longer remembered my intention to read to Ni'matallah some of the things he had written. Maybe the realization dawned on me that this girl was in no need for books, that she had surpassed Taha Hussayn in triumphing over the darkness which surrounded her.

I jumped into bed quickly and hid my head under the covers. Had Ni'matallah revealed my secret to anyone? I closed my eyes tight as though this way I could avoid anyone seeing me,

---

* What God has written, that is what he has inscribed to be fulfilled (ordained).

disappear from people's sight to seek refuge in sleep, but sleep refused to come to my aid, left me alone with my burden.

But what was this burden? Was it the burden of concealing something, of this secret? But was it really a secret to be concealed? My body was replete with things that I hid, things that were like weights that I carried around with me, was full of imprisoned feelings that I could not understand, of words I did not know how to express, unspoken words that no tongue, no language could pronounce.

Was it language, was it words which stood between me and my love? Was it the letters improvised, evolved by human tongues, then written or printed on sheets of papers. Was it fear? Was I just full of different fears? I feared God, but my fear of people's tongues, of what they might say, was even greater. God had no tongue, no mouth and lips. God would not say bad things about me, but people's tongues would smear my reputation, smear that of my parents too.

'What will people say about us?' This was a sentence I kept hearing from all the members of my mother's and my father's families. I never heard anyone say, 'What will God say about us?' Tante Fahima did not mind if I laughed out loudly when I was alone in my room and no-one except God could hear me. She scolded me only if this happened in front of people. 'People will say you are a girl with bad manners.' My Aunt Ni'mat did not care if a louse bit me in my scalp. All that mattered to her was that Miss Hamer would say 'that we were dirty people and had lice in our hair'. When my brother failed in his exams, father's comment would be, 'People will say the inspector of education does not know how to educate.' When the milk boiled over on the stove in front of me mother would exclaim, 'Now people will say that you don't even know how to boil a little milk.'

That night, when everyone was asleep, I crept out of bed and sat on the verandah all alone. The moonlight was reflected in the water canal, making it cut through the fields like a long thread of silver. The moon hung high up in the dark sky, a full circle of pure white with two black eyes which stared down at me. Somewhere, a voice like a gentle breeze whispered: 'Fathy will be here tomorrow.'

A shiver went through my body. The hair on my arms stood up, fine black hairs like tiny thorns under the white moonlight, and the pores on my skin opened wide to imbibe its rays. My eyes remained fixed on its silver disc, taking in its liquid silver to the last drop.

But at one moment I was seized with a sudden fear which made me quickly turn my eyes away from the moon. People said that staring at the full moon with both eyes could make one lose one's sight. My body started to shiver even more. Was it the sudden fear of going blind, or the air getting colder as I sat there on the verandah on the cane chair with a small cushion encased in a white cover underneath me?

As I moved the chair back a little out of the breeze I noticed a red spot on the cover. I felt as though my heart had dropped quickly down to my feet. Only two weeks had elapsed since my last period, and here it was again. A month or at least three weeks should have gone by. There must be some relationship between the cycle of the moon in the sky and the menstrual cycle in women. My grandmother used to say that the full moon burning with light was capable of making the menstrual blood burst out.

But the menstrual period in my body never followed the cycle of the moon. It had its own laws unrelated to the laws of the universe. Four weeks might pass without my seeing the sacrilegious stain. My heart would be light, happiness would invade me. It seemed to me that God had heard my supplications, and stopped the 'offence'* from afflicting me. But after a few days, there it was once more appearing in my knickers, a sign of my fate, my destiny in the form of a red stain changing into a flow of blood which broke my heart. It would last one day, or two, or ten, then

---

* From the Arabic word *aza*, used in the Qur'an to describe the menstruation of women.

stop only to return, sometimes after a week or two. It increased if I jumped high in the air, or coughed, or sneezed, or was sad or happy or emotionally moved more than usual.

'Fathy is coming tomorrow.' The news made me full of a great happi-ness, but with the happiness came unsuspected pain. In the morning I could not get up. Severe pains kept shooting through my body. I had a rasping cough and my chest hurt. Then I got cramps in my stomach and intestines, vomited and was overwhelmed with feelings of being impure, of humiliation, and a desire to hide away from people.

I exaggerated the degree of my suffering, coughed loudly so that my mother would hear, and leave me lying there in bed, not ask me to do anything in the kitchen. But in fact my cough got worse and my father began to think that I might have tuberculo-sis, like my aunt Baheya. I was made to swallow medicine which was bitter and smelled like iodine. My mother put poultices of anti-phlogistine on my back. She heated the greyish paste in its tin, then smeared it on my skin. But the paste had no effect except to leave me with burns and blisters. So my mother tried replacing it with small rounded glass cups which she heated to expel the air, then planted their open mouths on my back. The idea was that the cup pulled on the flesh to fill up the vacuum, and at the same time this pulled out the cold from the body. However, with all this I did not get better. Instead my skin was burnt in several places, and peeled off, leaving raw patches. But I preferred going through all this rather than being obliged to get out of bed and wash dishes, or scrub the floor of the kitchen or the toilet.

I slept in an iron bed painted white. It looked like a hospital bed and under the mattress the wires were stretched long and taut. When I lay down on the bed they sagged under the weight of my body. If I was sad, or had my period, my heart grew heavy and the wires sagged under me even more. When I moved they made a whining noise like a cat suffering from distemper, or a small and lonesome child.

My room had a window covered with iron bars like the other windows in the house. I thought the iron bars were there to prevent girls from going out of the house, and not to stop thieves from getting in. But at one moment as I lay there a ray of light shone through between the bars and with it came a sound that seemed like singing, a voice which said: 'Welcome, Nawal.'

I saw him standing under the window. When I looked out I saw nothing else, only him, the sudden presence, the materialization of what I had thought was only imagination. I could see him only from the waist upwards, or maybe I saw only his eyes, how they were shining, saw only the light that came from them, or the sun was in my eyes and prevented me from seeing, or his sudden presence made me blind, unable to see that he was present, that he was actually there.

I used to bring him back, make him present as I lay under the covers, make him materialize. When he was absent it was always sweeter. I could make him materialize in the form I desired and wanted most. And when he appeared, I vanished so that I could imagine his presence, create it myself although he was not there, give it the form I longed for. The imaginary form had become more beautiful than the real.

'Welcome, Nawal.'

'Welcome', I said.

I never spoke his name. When I said 'Welcome', I saw him smile, saw his face radiate. The light in his eyes was so strong I could not look into them. A moment later he departed on his way, went off to wherever he was going carrying a black leather bag in one hand, and his lute enveloped in a sack of white calico in the other, and suddenly the wind was blowing in gusts around his body and the ray of light had vanished behind the clouds.

I stood at the window holding on to the iron bars with my two hands. The rough rusty iron hurt their palms, but I held on with all my might not wanting to let go. They were the only solid, stable thing in a world which had lost all stability. I hid behind the window, concealing my face. My cheeks were on fire, my hands were raw with cold. The scratches made by the iron bars had roughened their skin. I pressed them to my flaming cheeks. Was I ill with a fever, perhaps afflicted with a tuberculosis of the lungs?

Suddenly, in less than a moment, all my illness disappeared. I shot out of my room like a locomotive under high pressure steam. Now I could do anything. Bring down the walls of the house, twist the iron bars with a single hand, break the front door with one kick and rush out into the road to catch up with him before he reached the street leading to the railway station.

I stood on the verandah for a moment to take my breath. The trees were swaying under gusts of wind, a hot strong wind loaded with desert sand. The world had gone yellow, and the clouds were the colour of sand. The heavens thundered and drops of rain were falling on the dusty ground below the verandah.

I rushed down the stairs in one leap. Inside me was a force driving me to break into open space. A strange powerful force springing from I knew not where. From the turbulent yellow leaves? From the blowing winds? From the noise of thunder? From the drops of rain falling on the dusty ground and the sharp smell of earth wetted with water?

I pushed the outer door open with my hand, and looked out. The rain was now pouring down. The holes in the ground filled up with water, forming small pools. I stood on the step holding the open door and all of a sudden my body collapsed weakly. I felt tired, sick, confused. Why had I rushed down to the door? Did I intend to go out into the road, and where would I then go?

After a while I regained my calm. The world became solid, stable again. I no longer wanted to go out of the house. I could not understand why everything had changed in a moment. Was my going out into the street no longer necessary, no longer reasonable?

I climbed the stairs back to the verandah, saw my mother covering the table with a new tablecloth which she had embroidered with a crochet needle. The drawing-room door was open.

I went to my room, hid myself once more under the bedcovers. No longer was I pretending to be ill, for what I had now was a real sickness, something like a pain in the heart, or regret, or a guilty conscience, or all of them combined. I had intended to catch up with him before he left, but the rain had flooded the streets, and I could not have waded through mud and water. But I kept asking myself again and again... Was that all?

17

Uncles, Suitors and Other Bloodsuckers

Next day the sun was shining brightly. The rain had washed the dust and the sand off the trees. I opened my eyes in the morning to the voice of Um Koulsoum singing on the radio: 'O evenings of the Eid you have brought us pleasurable company and renewed our hopes. O evenings of the Eid.' It was the last day of the Eid, or perhaps it was the day after. The parlour in our house was still filled with relatives from the two families.

The drawing-room had been opened and there were visitors inside. The radio was singing at the top of its voice, so that neighbours would know that we had a radio. Neither Um Koulsoum's voice nor that of Abdel Wahab was capable of moving me. I appreciated their voices but their songs stirred nothing in me. Their songs, their voices, were for everyone, were neutral as far as I was concerned.

The word 'everyone' gave me a feeling of emptiness. I wanted to be someone. I could not imagine that I would live and die like everyone else, without anything happening during my life. But what was it that I expected, that I wanted to happen? All I had were vague feelings but they never left me. Yet a voice deep down inside me insisted that I would not be like other girls, not like my grandmother or my mother, or my aunts, or other women in the family. Nor did I want to be like my grandfather, or my father, or my uncles or the other men in the family.

I rolled myself up in bed like a hedgehog, concentrated all my senses into the single sense of hearing, so that I could follow what was being said that day in the parlour. The women of both my father's and my mother's families, for some reason, had all gathered in the parlour, and there was much whispering going on between them. It sounded like the rustle of leaves. Something was being plotted in the dark, something that had to do with me in particular. Something that could wreck my life and destroy my dreams.

'Put on your silk dress, Nawal. We want you to bring in the coffee to the guests in the drawing-room.'

There was something different in the way my mother looked at me that day. Something that was not my mother's way of looking. The eyes that looked at me were not her eyes. They were the eyes of Tante Ni'mat, or Tante Fahima, or Tante Hanem. It was a look full of ambivalence. On the surface it expressed happiness but in its depths there was a sadness. There was truth mingled with deception, love with hatred.

At one time I often used to take a tray with cups of coffee and glasses of water in to visitors. But since I had reached the age of puberty, my younger sister became the one who took in the coffee, or if it was not her it was the servant-girl, Sa'adeya.

But this time why did they want me to take in the coffee, rather than my sister Leila or the servant-girl? The visitor must be no ordinary visitor. If they were planning something, I would see to it that their plans were upset. The women gathered in the parlour would not have the better of me. Their laughing echoed in my ears. Why were they laughing so obscenely? Why was Tante Ni'mat giggling in such a vulgar way? Even Tante Fahima kept bursting out in peals of prolonged almost licentious feminine laughter. However, my mother's laugh was not to be heard amidst their repeated laughter. I felt somewhat reassured. Was my mother taking sides with me against them?

The laughter stopped suddenly, to be replaced by whispering that sounded more like a hissing noise, and which sounded to me more obscene than the laughter which had preceded it. I could see them through the crack in the door huddled close together on the chairs and the sofas. The voice of my father or of some other man rang out in the drawing room and they trembled like hens frightened by a cock who was pursuing them in the chicken coop intent on ravishing one of them, afraid of him, yet competing for his favours, enticing him to come closer with one gesture only to hold back from him with another.

Was this a reflection of some kind of schizophrenia or was it the dream of being ravished that each of them hid inside her, like an embryo born of fornication, a dream which each one of them embraced in her arms when she slept, which looked out of her eyes when she awoke like the embers of a fire buried under ashes, yet ready to burst into flame at any moment?

In their cold, grey bilious eyes I could see the fine tortuous arteries almost bursting with blood. Would my eyes one day resemble theirs, have the same colour, the same ambivalent look which hid a burning fire under the white mask of their faces, under the layers of a white powder like lime, or plaster mixed with water?

I used to flee from their eyes for I could not bear to look into them, as though they carried some contagious disease like leprosy which would be transmitted to me no sooner than their look so much as fell on me.

In the midst of all the hissing I had caught the word bridegroom. And the night before the visitor was supposed to come I did not sleep a minute, sat out on the verandah wide awake. My face was hot and flushed, the touch of my hand on my cheeks was rough where the iron bars had left their marks. Once more I could see him standing below my window. His voice floated to my ears, carried on the breeze. 'Welcome, Nawal', he said. His voice was sweeter, more gentle now that he had gone. Sadness had ennobled it, rid it of everything that could have spoilt its beauty, cleared it even of the sorrow which I felt. It had become like crystal, like transparent drops of rain, like millions of radiant particles that swept away the sound, and smoke and dust, and made the cool night breeze caress my face.

Sadness invaded me, went deep into my body. The tender yearning that I felt kept telling me that I was now abandoned by tenderness itself, that I would never know again the tenderness I'd felt.

My eyes searched for the distant lonely star, for its strong and steady light. Could that be my star up there, the one that seemed to weep? My father used to point it out to me and say, 'That is the planet Venus, that the Arabs before Islam called Al-Uzza and worshipped as their goddess.' She was a goddess who sometimes changed into a harlot with a big head of flaming tousled hair which made her look like a monster. Then she went about seducing men and driving God out of their hearts, by competing with him for their affections. According to the New Testament she succeeded in seducing two men named Gog and Magog, who are referred to in the Qur'an as Majuj and Yajuj. After she had seduced both of them she tried to climb up to Heaven. But God stopped her from reaching her destination and she remained suspended half-way between heaven and earth, ended up as a solitary star stripped of her strength and her power with a name different to the one she had carried before.

The heavens by night were frightening, full of secrets. The eyes of Allah watched me as I sat there on the verandah. The eyes of Satan and those of the jinnis mentioned in the Qur'an watched me too.

I used to be afraid of sitting in the dark alone, for one of those spirits hidden in the night could pounce on me. But that night I sat there in the pitch dark all alone. My mind was occupied with something so fraught with danger that I forgot everything that could have something to do with devils or jinnis. Why not slip out of the house and flee before morning came? The idea grew so much on me, became so real, that I started to shiver. Could I venture into the night all alone? The hungry wolves howling out there in the dark could easily eat me up, and the thieves prowling through the streets while everyone slept could pounce on me and steal whatever I might have.

I sat there on the cane chair with a cushion under me, trembling with fear. But all the dangers that surrounded me seemed to shrink, to become trivial, in comparison with the terrible threat that lay in wait, ready to pounce on me the next day at half-past six in the evening.

Behind my back, in secret, everyone was preparing for that particular moment. New things suddenly made their appearance in our house. Coffee cups with colourful designs I had never seen before. Glasses that scintillated in the light like crystal. Napkins to put on the tables, curtains to hang on the windows. The white covers draped over the armchair and sofas were taken off to be washed then pressed under a hot iron. The big Persian carpet in the drawing-room was pulled out on to the verandah and hung over the balustrade in the sunshine, then the last speck of dust was beaten out of it with a bamboo beater wielded in turn by my mother and the other women of the family. Under the blows, the carpet kept scraping against the stone of the balustrade, emitting a repeated sound that resembled the moaning of someone undergoing torture.

This Persian carpet accompanied my mother in life from the night of her wedding to the day of her death. It kept moving with us from house to house, and from one town or city to the other, wherever the government saw fit to send my father. The feet of our visitors or guests were always treading on it as they came and went. It witnessed my birth, and that of my eight sisters and brothers. Over the years, its bright colours faded. Dust brought by stormy winds or accumulated through the inertia born of sadness gathered between its knots. Little by little, its wool was worn away, until a hole visible to everyone had been worn through it.

Whenever my mother beat the carpet she would close her eyes, tighten her lips, lift the carpet beater as high up in the air as she could, defying the heavens, then bring it down on the carpet with all her might, as though beating the life out of it. She became another woman, as though she was not my mother, no longer the refined sensitive lady with the gentle voice, the silky skin, and the honey-coloured eyes I knew. Everything about her seemed to change, even the colour of her eyes. Over them descended a dark grey mist which made them resemble the eyes of my grandmother Amna. She was in the habit of beating the servant-girl in the same way, with all her might, with all the anger accumulated in her body since the day her mother had given birth to her, lifting the beater high up in the air, flailing at the heavens with the rage that had built up deep in her over the years.

I used to think that the heavens and Allah were one thing. Then later I discovered that in the Arabic language the word heaven is feminine whereas the word Allah is masculine. Allah in all his majesty, as we say, is a masculine being. That is what the teacher explained to us during the classes on grammar and syntax. My mother did not seem to be as afraid of the heavens as she was of Allah, and flailed them with her carpet beater in the same unflinching way as she slammed down on the carpet, or the body of the servant-girl.

That day, Tante Ni'mat did not participate in the beating of the carpet. Hers was another role shared by Aunt Rokaya. Together they got hold of me in the bathroom. One of them imprisoned my hands. The other smeared sticky *halawa* over my skin and then started to rip the hair off my body. My screams rose higher and higher in the air. I kicked at them with my feet, hit into them with my knees. Hearing all the noise, Sittil Hajja came into the bathroom and started to pat me on the shoulder. 'It's all to your best interest, apple of your mother's eye', she said.

How could ripping the hair off my body be to my best interest? Instinct told me that it was against my dignity, that hair was power. What would I gain if my skin became smooth and hairless like a snake's? What kind of desire or passion other than the urge to violate, or humiliate would be aroused in a man seeking a body like that?

Sitting on the verandah, I swore under my breath to flee before dawn, brushed aside what remained of hesitation, and tiptoed down the stairs, opened the front door and looked out. Then, closing my eyes, I prepared to plunge into the night as though into a dark sea from which I might never come back.

But the next moment I was running back to where I had been on the verandah, sat down on the chair, my chest heaving. It would be much easier to cut the veins on my wrist than to go out into the pitch-black night. I looked for the razor-blade with which I sharpened my pencils, took it out of the drawer of my desk and went into the bathroom. It was an old razor-blade with which my father shaved his beard. Slowly I brought it close to the skin of my wrist with a hand that was shaking so much that I cut my finger. I saw the red blood, was seized with panic like a mouse that had been cornered, and almost unable to take my breath began to choke. The air seemed no longer air, but viscous black water drowning me under it, and I was barely able to stagger back to where I had been sitting on the verandah. The night was long and I still had plenty of alternatives, plenty of time to escape, or to commit suicide, or to jump over the balustrade and break my bones as I landed on the ground, or to scream at the top of my voice as though I was having a fit, or to light a match in a tin of kerosene and burn down the house.

After due thought, all these solutions appeared no more than mere acts of cowardice. My life was certainly too precious to be sacrificed as easily as all that. My bones were too precious to be broken by throwing myself from on high. Besides, the height of the balcony was not great enough to ensure that if I threw myself from it I would die. It might only break the bones of my legs and then I would have to walk on wooden crutches like my school friend Khadija. And why burn the house down with everyone in it? The fire might easily spread to the room where my small sisters were sleeping. They were all so innocent and had never committed any sin. I had a baby sister who was still suckling at the breast. Why light the fire that would burn her to death? All this was cowardly and mean.

My finger by now had stopped bleeding from the cut made in it by the razor-blade. Mosquitoes started to buzz around me, and one of them settled on my arm. The arm was white and smooth and without any hair on it at all like Tante Ni'mat's arm or like that of my mother. The mosquito was big, much bigger that the small mosquitoes which bite without causing any sickness. Its rear legs were longer than the front ones so that the posterior part of its body was raised, and its head lowered to approach my skin. Out of its mouth jutted a long needle-like protrusion which plunged into my flesh, so as to suck from my blood.

I felt no discomfort, no pain. On the contrary the bite gave me a feeling of pleasure. I wished the mosquito would go on sucking my blood until my veins were emptied, until it had injected all its poison into my veins. I watched as it filled up with blood, its belly swelling like a pregnant female. It stuck to my arm, seemed no longer able to fly, to have fallen asleep, or even to be dead. I felt as though it had sucked up all my poisoned blood to the last drop, like a leech placed behind the ear of an ill person by the village barber sucks out the bad blood. I felt relaxed, cured, and sleep started to weigh on my eyelids.

The first streaks of dawn spread over the horizon. I tucked myself up in bed, felt a pleasurable sensation like someone recovering from illness, a sensation of rest after a long night of exhaustion, a complete abandonment to my fate, and a complete freeing of myself from any fear of whatever awaited me. Other possibilities had opened up before me. With the first light of day my head had become as clear as crystal and a plan, a very simple plan much easier than the one of suicide, started to emerge in my mind.

'Come on, Nawal, get up and put on your new dress.' I got out of bed obediently. The arms of the women gathered in the house stretched out towards me, holding the dress. First Tante Fahima busying herself with arranging the pleats in my bodice after I had put on the dress, tweaking my breast with her fingers as her hand stroked over it, followed a few moments later by those of Tante Ni'mat pinching my other breast as she exclaimed: 'This so that God may bring me a husband straight away.' Her pinch squeezed my nipple so hard it felt like the sting of a scorpion, or the bite of a snake. They were doing all this because of the popular notion that pinching a bride in her breast, or her thigh, or her arm attracts suitors, brings milk to dry breasts or bestows offspring on barren women.

It seemed as though the women of both my father's and my mother's families had been waiting to waylay me, as though these spinsters, or divorcees, or widows or barren females, these women who had never married, or become pregnant, or found a man to extinguish the fire smoldering in them beneath a cold surface, had found in me a victim, a piece of flesh in which they could dig their hard cruel fingers seeking to wrench out of it some unlived pleasure buried deep in them, to bring to life some repressed desire hidden in the secret recesses of their bodies, like a soil so parched, so thirsty for water that it cracks open to imbibe, to devour whatever drop of moisture it can get.

I stood there abandoning myself passively to their roving hands, to the fingers that kept sinking themselves voraciously in my belly, my breasts, my thighs, my neck and other parts of my body. I left myself to them completely, put up not the slightest resistance, intent on reserving all my energy for the execution of the plan I was concealing from them. But in my nightmares I saw myself lying completely naked, pinned to the floor, while sharp pointed fingers like iron pincers tore at my body. I tried to get up and flee but was unable to move, since my arms and legs were attached to pegs, and all the doors were closed.

One of the habitual procedures meant to make me more beautiful in the eyes of my husband was to ensure that my teeth would be white and shiny by rubbing them with salt. My teeth were not considered as white as they should be since, like Min'im I was fond of eating raw eggplant in the fields. This left a blackish coating over them which the ordinary toothbrush was unable to remove.

Tante Fahima was the one who undertook to do this task. She grabbed hold of me, peered at my teeth and said: 'The groom will take to his heels the moment he sees those black teeth of yours', and, insensitive to my screams, took some salt out of a small jar and, holding my head by the neck, started to rub my front teeth with salt so that the following day, when I looked into the mirror, my gums were red and swollen and bled at the slightest touch.

My maternal aunts were also not happy with my hair, since it was not silky and flowing like theirs. It had frizzy curls which Tante Ni'mat felt were ugly. 'The groom will disappear the moment he sees your kinky hair, slave girl that you are, Warwar.' She then proceeded to straighten out my hair with an iron rod heated on a flame until it was almost red, around which she wound and then slowly unwound my hair, all the while pulling at its tresses, To my nose rose the smell of singeing hair, smoke filled my nostrils, almost choking me, and at one point she burnt the tip of my ear with the hot iron.

Near the door leading to the drawing-room was a coat-stand made of cane, with a tall mirror in which guests could see themselves as they took off their fezzes, scarves and overcoats to hang them on the brass hooks before they went in. The coat-stand was placed in a small square-shaped vestibule, through which I would have to pass with the coffee tray before taking it inside to where the bridegroom would be sitting. Under the bottom shelf of the coat-stand I hid an eggplant, its skin as black as the face of the devil.

As I passed through the vestibule with the tray, I stopped in front of the mirror. The girl who looked out at me was a stranger in a silk dress that revealed two white arms on which there was not a single hair. The hair around her head was straight, and flowed down over her shoulders in waves. Her lips were full and red, her cheeks painted, and her eyes looked out from under thin arched eyebrows plucked thin with tweezers. Her feet were arched over high, narrow, pointed heels which swayed under her as she walked.

I laid the tray on the floor for a moment, wiped the red off my lips quickly on the palm of my hand, bit into the black eggplant, tousled my hair, then picked up the tray and walked in on silent feet, looking like a well-behaved girl, with my head bowed to the ground, and my eyelids lowered over my eyes like a blind kitten.

Just before walking in, I had stood for a brief moment behind the door which was lightly ajar, to throw a quick glance around the brightly lit room, and listen to what was being said. My father was engrossed in a conversation with the bridegroom about the world war, the English and the Germans, the king and Al-Nahas Pasha and did not look at me as I entered. I heard him say: 'The king is siding with the Germans and Al-Nahas must support the British, but the British want us to enter the war and fight with them. What concern is this war of ours? Why should we fight on the side of the British and the allies? In all fairness, how could we possibly consider them allies of ours? Or what do you think, Abdel Maksoud Effendi?'

'Oh, I agree with you completely, Sayed Bey.'

The bridegroom, Abdel Maksoud Effendi spotted me the moment I entered the room. I advanced towards him with my back turned towards my father, and my face bent over the tray, walking with slow teetering steps. It was the first time I had ever worn shoes with these high, narrow, pointed heels. The bridegroom examined me with his small beady eyes like the eyes of a hawk. On his head he was wearing a red fez, tilted to one side with a black tassel which swayed back and forth over his ear. His suit was tight, dark coloured, and he wore a tight waistcoat, and a red neck-tie pulled tight around his neck. In his hand, he held a bushy fly whisk, and he sat sunken in his arm-chair, his mouth wide open as though he was no longer able to close it for some reason or other, leaving the spittle to form a white drop at the corners, like Ismail Effendi.

As I came nearer to him, I pressed my lips together in a bad-tempered pout, then when I was close enough, opened them wide in a broad smile so that he could take a good look at my teeth. He emitted a loud sneeze, 'atchoo', and I answered with an even louder one as though I had caught some contagious disease from him. The tray I was holding shook in my hands, spilling the frothy surface of the coffee which my mother had been at great pains to create, from the cup into the saucer. Into my nose rose the smell of ground roasted coffee mixed with cardamom and there it mingled with that of raw egg-plant, a mixture no doubt conducive to another fit of sneezing which made the tray I was carrying shake more violently, spilling more coffee into the saucer. Sweat poured down my body, feeling like cold water under my silken dress. I was now perspiring profusely as though fast asleep in summer in a warm bed, and it seemed to me that the odor of my sweat permeated the whole room. My body movements were wooden and I advanced with slow steps as though bound by something, or confined in space. If my father had looked my way he would not have recognized me, but he seemed to be still engrossed in the conversation and, besides, he could not see my face. Maybe he was trying to escape from the situation I was putting him in, trying to say that he was in no way responsible for it, leaving me to face the consequences all by myself, but a moment later I realized that it was much better for me if our eyes did not meet, that this neglect of his was more judicious, more wise.

Meanwhile the bridegroom continued to examine me with a searching stare. His narrow eyes kept shifting from one part of my body to another, and I caught him giving my breasts a long sideways glance. The electric lamp was shedding a strong light in the room, and helped to reveal the traces of black eggplant that covered my front teeth as I parted my lips in a smile. At that very moment my father suddenly decided to take notice of my presence, and I heard him say: 'This is Nawal, the eldest of my daughters.'

'God's will ... atchoo. God's will has indeed been fulfilled', commented Abdel Maksoud Effendi.*

He continued to repeat the same phrase, interrupted by sneezes. Maybe he was concealing the shock he had experienced at seeing me by sneezing. I stepped closer to where he sat, bent over him with the tray I was holding. There was a sudden frightening silence. All I could hear was the shriek of the flourmill on Railway Station Street. It sounded very much like the shriek of a living person, and my hands shook. As I took another step, the pointed spike of my heel caught in the hole which had gone through the carpet, and the tray tipped over with all the cups of hot coffee, and all the glasses of cold water on to the chest of my suitor.

It was like one of nature's terrible catastrophes, like a volcano or an earthquake turning all things upside down. An earthquake or a volcano, however, lasts only for a matter of seconds or minutes. This catastrophe lasted for several weeks. One of its consequences was a sound thrashing, but this was not something that bothered me much. What mattered was that my bridegroom had disappeared like a wispy summer cloud in the wind.

The following day I started a diary. My diary was a cheap notebook with a blue cover that I hid carefully from everyone else. The first lines I wrote were as follows:

I wonder what it is that saved me? Was it the sound of the flourmill like the shrieks of a human being in pain? Was it that sudden moment of silence, or the glare of the electric light on my face? For less than a minute everything seemed to come to a sudden stop in order to witness a moment outside time and space, that frightening moment when the tray slid out of my hands and overturned everything it had on it. Could that be all there was to it?

Menouf, 30 August 1941

---

* Meaning that I was a beautiful, striking creation of God.

18

A Stove for My Mother

In the summer of 1942 I obtained a primary-school certificate. My grades were excellent yet the faces of those around me exhibited no joy. Their lips continued to be pursed with dissatisfaction, and among the women the whispering went on: 'What's the use of a certificate if she's destined to be married?! What's the use of her cleverness at school if she's a dunce in the kitchen, and frightens away every suitor who happens to come along?'

I was no longer allowed to go out of the house. I was now eleven years old, was almost a spinster, to use the words of Tante Ni'mat. I was tall, taller even than my elder brother Tala'at, and my breasts stood out on my chest, round and full. Anyone seeing me as I was would have thought I was fifteen years old, not eleven. I no longer played with other children in the fields. I now specialized in cooking *mulukheya*,* in scrubbing the tiles until they shone like a mirror. Through the walls of the bathroom I could hear the cries of the children as they played. Their laughter hit my eardrums like the painful thrust of a needle. I remembered my own laughter as though it belonged

---

* A green viscous leafy plant cooked to make a thick soup with garlic and chicken, rabbit or meat stock and eaten usually with rice.

to another, faraway life. Through the iron bars of the window I could see my brother Tala'at running and jumping through the green fields, or riding a bicycle and flying away into open spaces that stretched as far as the horizon, breathing in the clean fresh air under a bright sunlight, while I stood in the dark kitchen swallowing the smoke rising from the primus stove.

Between me and the primus stove there was a visceral feeling of enmity. It was such a strange, moody creature with a will of its own that always seemed to conflict with mine, as though it represented some strange, antagonistic power on earth, or in the heavens. If I wanted it to burn, it went out. If I wanted it to go out, a tongue of fire would flare up from it in my face. It taunted me like the whims of fate or destiny.

It was a creature with a square head called a *tarboush* (a fez) which was black from the soot that accumulated on it. Below the head was a black neck with a hole like the eye of a needle in the middle. It was always getting blocked with soot, and whenever it got blocked my mother would put on her eye-glasses and start cleaning it with a special needle. Tante Ni'mat, however, had a round magnifying lens which she held in her left hand, then brought slowly up to her right eye upon which she would see the small hole magnified to the size of a walnut.

As soon as I had reached the age of seven my mother started to teach me how to light the primus stove, and my father began to show me how to pray. Was there some relationship between the primus stove and praying? I soon discovered that there was. The body movements were similar. To light the stove I had to bend my back in a movement which resembled bowing down in prayer. When I cleaned the blocked hole with a needle sometimes it broke inside, then in order to extract it with the help of another needle I would have to bend even more so that my nose almost touched the *tarboush* in a movement very much like prostration.

The hole was always getting blocked, either with a small particle of smoke or soot, or some impurity in the kerosene.

The kerosene was adulterated, and at the bottom of the tin there settled a dark sticky sediment like tar, or pitch. The kerosene vendor went round from house to house driving a donkey or mule cart with a huge barrel on it and calling out in a loud voice, 'Gas! Gas!'

'Your gas is adulterated, Uncle Uthman', my mother often said to him.

'I swear by Allah this is the best gas in the world', he would maintain.

'Why swear by Allah to something which is not true, Uncle Uthman.'

'I swear a triple oath* to divorce my wife if this is not the best gas in the world.'

'Shame on you, man! How can you swear to divorce your wife over a little bit of gas?'

'What should I swear by, lady?'

'You mean that you can only think of Allah or your wife to swear by. Can't you think of someone else?'

The gas vendor had a lean face and its skin was covered with blackheads. His eyes kept blinking as though he could not look my mother in the face. But once she disappeared from the window he would stare at the servant-girl Sa'adeya with wide-open eyes, wink at her, pinch her in the arm and declare emphatically, 'This gas is like milk, girl, and one can drink it on an empty stomach.'

The smell of kerosene gave me nausea. If my mother discovered a louse or nit in my hair she washed my head with kerosene. When I stood over the kerosene stove to light it, a flame would often shoot up in my face, making me take a quick step backwards as I had seen my mother do, to prevent it burning the ends of my hair, and filling my nose with its smell and that of singed hair which made me vomit.

Little by little I trained myself to light the stove without breaking the needle, to clean the hole when it became blocked

---

* A definitive divorce from which there is no return.

without bending down or stooping, to stand in front of it with an upright back and with my head held up. My eyesight was so keen that, as people said, I could see the stars in broad daylight, just like that woman Zarq'a Al-Yamama,* who was known for her capacity to spot the approach of enemy armies before anyone else.

'Nawal's become really clever,' they began to say in the family. I was awarded the title of *shatra*, meaning sharp or skilful. It was a term bestowed on girls who were clever in the kitchen, at washing clothes, rubbing floors, and lighting stoves without breaking the needle. I became accustomed to hear them say 'Nawal *shatra*' (Nawal is sharp and clever). It made me both joyful and sad, but the joy was greater than the sorrow, and increased my zeal for cooking, washing, and scouring the floor tiles until I could see my face in them.

My mother now left the task of lighting the primus stove to me. Every night when I went to sleep I would dream that the stove had exploded, see my mother in the midst of the flames, and rush to save her, but too late, for she had already burned to death. They would wrap her in a white silk shroud and lay her body down on the brass bed. In my dream, the shroud was her white silk wedding gown.

The dream kept repeating itself in different forms and accompanied me throughout the years of my childhood and youth. It left me only after I graduated from medical college and became a 'distinction'† resident doctor in the university hospital of Kasr Al-Aini. At the beginning of April 1955, for the first time in my life I cashed a monthly salary. It was nine pounds, each pound as big as the other, to use Sittil Hajja's expression.

In the month of April the flowers open their petals. I walked down the street, my head held up to the sky, my bag clutched tightly under my arm. Thieves' eyes were capable of penetrat-

---

* An Arab woman who lived before Islam and became famous as a scout during the battles fought by her tribe.

† Medical students who graduated with honours were assigned as resident doctors in the university hospital.

ing anything, their noses able to detect the aroma of banknotes kilometres away. I walked into a big store called Shaher on Fouad Al-Awal Street,* next to the Rivoli cinema. I was looking for only one thing, a butane gas stove with an oven and four burners of the make known at that time as Master Flame. The first instalment I had to pay was five pounds, and the monthly payments would last for another thirty-six months.

The day I became a medical doctor my mother looked like a flower in bloom. She recovered her childlike laugh, the sparkle in her honey-coloured eyes. I could see them shine as she read through my certificate of graduation.

'May it be a blessing to you Nawal, Dr Nawal.'

'I owe it all to you, Mama.'

The word 'mama' burst out of my lips in a gush of suppressed love. The conventions running in my mother's family did not permit expressions of love, even if it were love for one's mother. Children once they were weaned were no longer kissed. This was the tradition in middle- or upper-class Turkish families, in which not to express warm feelings, to be cold, was considered a sign of distinction.

In my mother's eyes I could see maternal love burning like a flame but held back, surrounded by a barrier like an iron cast through which it could not break. I, too, behaved in the same way, put up the same barrier like a partition of glass behind which smouldered my emotion.

That day in the first week of April I slipped into the house accompanied by three men from the store carrying the butane stove. They crept into the kitchen, placed the stove under the window next to the pantry, then tiptoed out. Rays of afternoon sunlight fell between the walls of the houses and penetrated through the iron bars on the window into the kitchen. They landed on the butane stove as though guided by some celestial will to make its white surface radiant with light.

---

* The first king of Egypt who ascended to the throne in 1922 under British occupation.

My mother walked into the kitchen. Her eyes opened wide in amazement. 'Where did this butane stove come from?', she asked.

'From heaven', I said.

Her eyes shone with the joy that belongs only to children. Like me, from her earliest years she had dreamed of the day when the primus stove would disappear. Like me, she had looked at the shops and stores, seen the butane gas stoves which burned with a pure blue flame, were lighted with a single strike of the match, needed no needle to clear away particles of smoke or soot. She would gaze at the price fastened on the stove, heave a sigh, and walk on.

I wanted to put my arms around her, lay my head on her breast, and cry. I wanted to let out the tears suppressed within me ever since I had been born. She, too, wanted to put her arms around me to free the feelings of motherhood imprisoned within her for so long. But we stood there unable to embrace one another, to exchange a single kiss, separated by barely a finger's breadth of air yet which seemed like a vast ocean, like a thousand years of time which neither of us could cross.

My mother lived for thirty-four months after that day. She died two months before I paid the last instalment.

19

Coming to Cairo

Abdel Maksoud Effendi was not the last of my suitors. Others followed, but none of them ever came back after I had served them with coffee. The coffee tray did not need to be upset after that first time. Something else seemed to happen. Perhaps it was the whistle of the flourmill, or the croaking of frogs in the fields, or the shrilling of the cockroaches, or the hoot of an owl at the top of a tree – for the hoot of an owl is enough to fill people, especially if they are potential bridegrooms, with foreboding. I now had a reputation in both my mother's and father's families for making suitors take to their heels. People wondered why, and busied themselves trying to fathom the mystery. Opinions and theories were many and varied, and included my dark complexion, the signs of poverty in our family, my tall stature, my big mouth, my protruding front teeth and my developed muscles, undesirable in a female body.

My protruding front teeth were an inheritance from Shoukry Bey's family and resembled those of my maternal aunts. My paternal aunt Rokaya therefore insisted that it was the only reason why suitors ran away. Sittil Hajja disagreed. She said her son Al-Sayed Bey had been given the evil eye by someone and so his eldest daughter, which was me, was destined to become barren, and after her the younger daughters would follow suit. The solution was for Sittil Hajja to cast a spell and destroy the evil eye.

At school I had a different reputation, that of being a very intelligent girl. But intelligence in girls was not considered a quality. When my brother's school reports arrived exhibiting a red circle which was the sign indicating failure, a deep silence settled over our home as though someone had recently died. My father said nothing when he left, and said nothing when he came home. If he did open his mouth it was to reprimand my brother by saying: 'Your sister, the girl succeeded in her examinations, and you go on failing? The son of the shopkeeper who sells notebooks and nibs succeeds, and the son of the inspector of education fails again! How can anybody imagine such a thing?'

The sorrow over my brother's failures overshadowed any joy at my success. At night I could hear my father whisper to my mother: 'I wish she had been born the boy and he the girl. This must be a sign of God's wrath descending upon us, Zaynab.' So my intelligence, my achievements, were no more than the result of Allah's anger against my father and my mother. It was a kind of sin, something to be concealed, just like my down-trodden shoes, or the hole in the Persian carpet.

There was no secondary school for girls in Menouf, so my father suggested to my mother that I stay at home to help her, and reduce the heavy burden she was carrying in order to take care of an increasing number of children. But my mother refused. My performance at school encouraged her to insist that I continue my education, or maybe it was her feeling that I would not make a success out of marriage, not submit like other girls.

My mother was not like her sisters, for deep down inside her were the seeds of rebellion. At school she had shown intelligence and did well in class. She had dreams of a different life to that of her mother, and the unquestioned authority of her father at home had led her to avoid exercising the same kind of authority on her children.

My father, too, was not at all like my grandfather Shoukry Bey. He never drank, never stayed out late at night, never had relations with a woman other than my mother. Law and the jurisprudence of Allah gave him the absolute right to divorce and to marry four women, but he had never used this right, was a devoted husband, helped my mother with the chores of the house, and carried the burden of providing for the family alone. In many ways he was a model father, rarely beat his children as other fathers did, played games with them, and gave them space to discuss and agree even in religious matters.

Not once did I see my father and my mother quarrel, or maybe it happened just once, when my mother dreamt she saw my father with another woman. When she woke up in the morning, her eyes were red, and she spoke to him about her dream with anger. For the first time in my life I heard my father raise his voice to her: 'Does all this nonsense mean that I am responsible even for what you dream, Zaynab?'

Father's voice never rose higher than that of my mother. Between them was a mutual respect, for each of them had come to know the strength of character in the other. My father was the sole breadwinner in our family so that the only influence which my mother exercised was the influence which stemmed from her personality, from her refusal to accept humiliation of any kind, her readiness to pack her bags if necessary, and return to her father's house.

Class differences played a role in the balance of power at home. Mother was conscious of the fact that she came from a higher-class family than my father. She never said so much, but her behaviour gave the impression that she belonged to the nobility.

Both my father and my mother realized the importance of education. Were it not for education, my father would not have risen from the class of poor peasants to become a middle-class intellectual. He felt that my future as an educated woman would be better assured than if I became just a wife. Thus arose the question of sending me to a secondary school in Cairo over which my father hesitated for some time. During the night I could hear my father and mother whispering to each other.

'You want Nawal to live on her own in Cairo, Zaynab?'

'She can stay in her aunt Hanem's house.'

'Living in her aunt's house is not the same as living in her father's and her mother's house.'

'Nawal knows what she must do. Don't worry about that, Sayed.'

'But Cairo is not like Menouf Zaynab.'

'Nawal has her wits about her. I trust her. You can throw her in the midst of fire and she'll come out unscathed.'

My mother's words lifted me to the heavens in the same way as her arms used to carry me up high above the waves. I could see myself walking through flames without getting burnt, plunging into the sea and riding over the waves without ever drowning. My mother, not the outer gentle woman but the real one, would always be there. I might be far away, in some distant place, but she would appear at the right moment to save me, exactly how I did not know.

That clear autumn morning I walked to the station carrying my bag. My father walked by my side, stood on the platform until the train started to move. It was the first time I was boarding a train alone. My father's eyes looked at me full of anxiety, full also of something else like imprisoned tears which surfaced to form a transparent film, but which he quickly swallowed so that I would not see them flow. I wanted to hug him but my arms would not move, so I stood at the carriage window, looking down at him, hiding my tears and showing my teeth in a broad smile. The train whistle echoed in my ears and the air was suddenly full of smoke. My father who was holding on to the window sill, started to walk, then to run with the train.

'Keep your wits about you, and mind you don't drop the ticket. You can ride a taxi from Misr station to your aunt Hanem's house. Take care of yourself and peace be with you, Nawal.'

I wanted to reach out to him, to hold his hand. I was afraid he might fall under the train, lose both legs and end up walking on crutches. He held on to the window sill until the end of the platform, let go of it suddenly and started to wave as he and the station receded into the distance. I stood at the window, waving back, smiling with the tears flowing down my face.

I loved travelling, loved riding in trains but that day I sat on the seat wiping away the tears. The journey before me seemed so long, so lonely. Eyes kept staring at me as I sat there alone, a young girl barely eleven years old, left to travel all alone. My clothes bag lay on the seat beside me, and I rested my hand on it lest someone steal it. I kept my school-bag on my knees. Inside it I carried my purse, my ticket, and my diary, a cheap notebook with a blue cover. I took the blue notebook out of my bag, opened it and wrote:

> Today is 9 September 1942. I feel sad at leaving father and mother, am full of regret and a sense of guilt, for there was a time when I wished they would die, so that I could go out into the street without permission, and play like my brother, or ride a bicycle. My heart is full of love for them, as though love for them was born in my heart when I left them behind. Does one have to be separated from people in order to love them?

I was dragged out of my thoughts by the voice of a man. He was sitting on the seat opposite me and kept shooting sidelong glances at my bag. Is it me he wants to kidnap or is he after my money purse, I wondered.

'Are you going to Cairo on your own, child?' he asked. I did not answer. I never spoke to strangers I might meet on the way. His features resembled those of Abdel Maksoud Effendi, and he had the same beady eyes that went directly for my breasts. I put the blue notebook back into my bag and held my arms tight around it. Through the window I watched the telegraph poles moving backwards. The green fields, too, were beginning to disappear, to be replaced by dreary walls and falling houses covered by smoke. I glimpsed a thin pale woman hanging out washing on one of the balconies, then her face and the white sheets of washing disappeared into the smoke.

The sun was setting when I arrived at Cairo station, and as the train slowed down the colourless houses and buildings huddling under the grey sky seemed to close in on it, surrounded by a kind of mist created by the smoke hanging over everything.

I walked through the crowded station carrying a bag in each hand. My clothes were of cheap wool, and over them I wore a thin faded pullover through which the cold penetrated to my body. As I walked I kept turning round, afraid that the man in the train might be following me. I passed through a huge portico to find myself in Bab Al-Hadeed Square, caught up in a sea of bodies that kept colliding like waves hitting against each other, and a whirlpool of cars, tramcars, carts and motor cycles. I steadied my feet on the tarmac pavement, and plunged into the sea like someone who has never swum. Crossing over the huge square I was almost run over by a car and fell to the ground. Hands stretched out and pulled me to my feet. There were a number of taxis waiting around the station but the passengers who had just arrived quickly got into them and they drove away. I spotted one remaining taxi. It was rickety and had no mud-guards, but before I could make a move a tall man jumped into it.

It was getting dark and the street lights were coming on, so I decided to walk to Tante Hanem's house. I had to ask the way and chose an old woman whose features looked kindly and asked her how I could get to Al-Daher Street. To show me the way she pointed with her finger and said: 'D'you see that road over there? That is Fagalla Road. Walk straight down it all the way following the tram line and you'll find yourself in Al-Daher Street.'

That was my first walk down Fagalla Road where all the bookshops are. As I walk I can see the books arranged behind the glass windows. Hundreds of volumes, hundreds of titles and authors, amongst which I read the name of Taha Hussayn.*

---

* A well-known liberal writer who lived in the first half of the twentieth century, was blind and became Minister of Education.

A Daughter of Isis

At the crossing between Fagalla Road and Al-Daher Street there was a big building. On it was inscribed School of Sewing Skills for Girls. I noticed a girl, about my age, carrying her bag and walking down the street alone. She hit the tarmac with the heels of her leather shoes, self-confident, unafraid. I felt ashamed of myself. Was this girl more courageous than me? I felt ashamed, too, of my old torn shoes covered with dust from the streets of Menouf, for the streets of Menouf were not made of tarmac. I bent down, wiped off the dust, pulled my shoulders up and strode over the tarmac with a firm, steady step.

Al-Daher Street shone with cleanliness under the street lamps. The buildings on either side were new and had a gleam as though built of some precious stone. The entrances to the buildings had transparent glass doors and tall marble pillars. In my dreams I often saw doors like these. Above one of them was a big board on which was written Secondary School for Girls. I could see myself emerging from the door carrying my secondary-school certificate, entering with it through the gates of the university. The word university made my heart jump. I had only heard people talk about the School of Literature in the university. That was where I would graduate, become a learned scholar and after that they would put my books in the windows of the bookstores on Fagalla Road.

The lamp posts of Al-Daher Street looked down as though they had eyes that gazed at me, brimming with happiness. The street stretched out in front of me, and as I walked along it I felt it welcoming, opening its arms to receive me, proud of this young girl, this scholar of the future.

I finally reached the building owned by my aunt's husband, but when I saw his face all my happiness evaporated, and Tante Hanem, too, received me with all the coldness, all the lack of feeling, traditional in the family of Shoukry Bey. She took me to the bathroom, made me take off my shoes, gave the hole in my sock a haughty stare, sat me down in the bath tub and began to scrub me with a *lifa* (loofah). As I crouched in the white shiny tub

I felt humiliated. To me it resembled a huge soup plate made out of mother of pearl. There was nothing like it in Menouf. There we used to bathe in a big copper tub. Tante Hanem submerged me in the water and I swallowed the humiliation and the soap. I felt like Sa'adeya, the servant-girl. My mother used to sink her in the tub, and wash her hair with kerosene, or shave it off.

Tante Hanem did not look like my mother. Her skin was dark, and her hair was thick and black. She was fond of showing off her jewels or the furniture in her drawing-room to visitors. The outer hall she called the *entrée*, a French word which means the room into which you first enter. She liked to display a knowledge of French in front of others.

I used to see her sitting among her visitors in the drawing-room. She was in the habit of calling the gilt furniture covered in silk *Aubusson*. Her silk dress rose above her knees when she crossed one leg over the other, then lit a cigarette. However, when she was alone she did not smoke. She would call the *suffragui*,* and say to him: 'Am Uthman, please bring me *un verre d'eau.*'

Am Uthman understood that much. So he would bring her a glass of water. He also liked to show that he understood French (at that time spoken by the aristocracy). But his knowledge, like that of his mistress, did not go beyond as many words as could be counted on the fingers of one hand.

Hind, Tante Hanem's daughter, was a little younger than I was. But she was like a child to whom I played the role of mother. Her room was crowded with dolls, and her bed was the colour pink. A school bus painted bright red carried her and her bag every day to school.

Hind sat with me at the breakfast table everyday in the early morning. Tante Hanem would give her a big glass of milk, then ask me coldly: 'Do you want milk?'

'No', I always answered.

---

* Usually a black Nubian or Sudanese manservant dressed in flowing white robes with a broad red belt at the waist and wearing a white turban or a fez on his head, employed in rich households. The word is Turkish.

I loved milk, but I pronounced the word 'No' as though I hated it. My father paid her for the milk, and for all my expenses, including the washing, the ironing, the electricity, and everything else. But the way she asked me could elicit only one answer, that of no.

After the milk, she proceeded to fill up her daughter's plate with large amounts of food, but for me she reserved a smaller plate with little on it. Feeling the bite of hunger I got into the habit of buying a loaf of bread and a piece of cheese, out of my meagre pocket money.

I slept on a narrow bed made out of metal sheeting which my father had bought, and Tante Hanem set it up for me in the distant corner of an unused room. My father also bought me a small table to study on and a table lamp.

Tante Hanem never encouraged me to study. Every time she saw my lamp burning at night she would come into my room, put it out and say: 'Study during the day. Electricity's expensive.'

At the beginning of each month she sent the various items of my expenditure to my father, including milk and electricity. I never drank the milk but she always listed it as an item. I thought of telling my mother or my father, but I was afraid that they would take me back home, and in Menouf there was no school to which I could go.

In Cairo I had been admitted to the Nabaweya Moussa Secondary School in Abbassieh district. It was the nearest school to Tante Hanem's house in Al-Daher Street. I used to catch a tramcar opposite the door of our house and it dropped me right in front of the school gate. I spent the whole year of 1943 without getting to know anything about Cairo, other than the tramcar from the door of Tante Hanem's house to the door of the Nabaweya Moussa Secondary School for Girls.

At school the girls had nicknamed Nabaweya Moussa 'Bo'o Bo'o Effendi'.* During the morning parade I used to see her walking in front of us in exactly the same way as Miss Hamer had

---

* The equivalent of a witch or wolf, evoked to frighten children.

done, dressed in a black jacket and skirt and black stockings, her black eyes looking out at us with a solid blackness.

She insisted that the girls dress in the same black from the top of their heads to the tips of their toes. My father gave Tante Hanem money to buy me the necessary apparel and from then on I started to wear a black skirt, long thick black stockings that showed nothing of my legs, and a black taffeta ribbon tied around my hair.

In the mirror, I could see myself looking like a black crow. Tante Hanem tightened her lips as she examined me and said: 'Nabaweya Moussa must be a spinster like Tante Fahima and wants all the girls to end up spinsters like her.'

I knew nothing about Nabaweya Moussa. People said she was a pioneer in women's education. But what pioneer and for what education? For me she was never a pioneer or a model. Her face was always scowling, angry and looked even more forbidding than that of my grandfather. I never saw her smile, even once. I never heard her say good morning. She imitated English head-mistresses, or German headmistresses under Hitler, or French headmistresses in schools run by nuns. And she hated the girls. When our eyes met I could read the hate in her look, read hate for the self she carried around dressed in black. School under her had become for me like a funeral where everything was the colour of mourning.

Tante Hanem was two years younger than my mother. My grandfather had sent her to a nun's school just as he had done with my mother. He took her out of school to marry her to a tradesman, who owned a shop in Al-Mouski Street* and a few buildings, including the building in Al-Daher Street.

In wartime, traders, including Tante Hanem's husband, had made money. My father disliked traders, described them as people not to be trusted, who cared for nothing but money

---

* An old street in Cairo in the district of Al-Hussayn near Al-Azhar religious university, where artisans and traders had set up their workshops and businesses many years ago.

and profit. According to him they put one millime on top of the other until they accumulated millions. He said they did not read books, did not even read newspapers, never participated in patriotic demonstrations. No matter how rich they became, they continued to be miserly, to count every penny. Half a millime was enough to make a fight break out between them.

Sittil Hajja, using one of her expressions, said they were even afraid to empty their bowels lest they became hungry and be obliged to eat again. That's why they suffered from constipation. She said miserliness was a contagious disease passed on from husband to wife, and the wife became even more miserly in order to please her husband and avoid his wrath.

Tante Hanem feared her husband, although I heard from my mother that he was unfaithful to her. He spent his nights in bars and taverns and came back at dawn. She often detected traces of the women he frequented on his clothes: lipstick on his handkerchiefs or the scent of perfume on his underwear. But she was afraid to open her mouth, said nothing because he threatened her with divorce. The richer he grew, the more overbearing he became and the more freedoms he allowed himself.

I used to address him as Am Abd Al-Halim. He was tall with a flat elongated face and narrow deep-set eyes like a crocodile. His lips were always closed tight because he never said anything. He came home at dawn when I was still asleep and went out around noon before I came back from school. I saw him only on Sundays, for that was the day when he closed his shop on Al-Mouski Street. That day I would come home from school to find him sitting at the table having his morning meal. When I came in he did not lift his face from the plate, his eyes remained closed as though he were half-asleep, but a moment later he would give me a quick look from the corner of his eyes, and let out a short, unchanging 'How are you?', to which I would answer 'Fine' and go off to my room, followed by a stare which seemed to say that I was treading on his head and not on the floor.

On the eve of Eid vacations I travelled back to Menouf. I took the train from Bab Al-Hadeed station, my heart fluttering with happiness. I was going to see mother and father, my brothers and my sisters. For the first time in my life I had lived away from them.

They welcomed me with joy, with shining eyes. No hugs, no kisses but their eyes expressed what they felt more eloquently than anything else could have done. My mother asked me: 'Are you happy in Tante Hanem's house?'

'Yes, mother', I said. I was afraid to tell her the truth, for the only alternative was for me to stay back in Menouf, to be deprived of the chance to continue my schooling. But the day came when Tante Hanem sent a sudden message to my mother, a message which said: 'Send her back to her uncle's house.'

One Sunday I was getting ready to put on my black Nabaweya Moussa outfit before going to school. I looked around the room searching for the black skirt and jacket but they had disappeared, and I had only one set. How was I going to go to school without my uniform!

Tante Hanem by oversight had hung my uniform in the cupboard of the room where her husband slept. No one was allowed to open the door of his room until he woke up of his own accord around noon.

The red school bus came along and picked up her daughter Hind. I was left there alone to puzzle over what I should do. How could I be absent from school for such a ridiculous reason? Mother used to open the door of the room in which my father was sleeping without any problems. Was Tante Hanem so afraid of her husband?

She left me to bite my nails in frustration, and went off to another room. She cared little whether I went to school or not. The seriousness with which I took my schooling used to irritate her. Whenever she saw me doing my reading she would say to her daughter Hind: 'See how your cousin studies all the time while you spend your days playing with your dolls.'

Anger kept growing within me, rising up like compressed steam. I never stayed away from school even when I was ill. Every moment that went by made me feel the same way as I did when I was obliged to rest in bed because of some illness. Anger had never stopped accumulating in me since the day I was born, and now it was ready to burst. Through the window I looked up at the sky. It was empty, without meaning. The cars raced down the street aimlessly. The present moment seemed endless, without past or future, and the future was dark and gloomy. To stay away from school was like withdrawing from life, my world going to pieces, everything in it ruined. This was not a momentary suspension in my life, it was something that could last for ever, a holiday with no rest, no respite, as it had been ever since the day my mother bore me.

I hated vacations. I felt exhausted, drained when I had a holiday. Vacations had always meant staying at home, the four walls, the kitchen, the primus stove with its smoke, the dissipation of all dreams.

But school was not just a matter of leaving the house. It was a release from the things which bound me. It was freedom. It was putting a distance between me and the earth, moving up to the heavens.

The window was open on the heavens. They looked down on the earth, on the street. It was six floors above the ground. One leap through it into space, and I could fly on wings as I did in my dreams, or fall to the ground and break my head! My feet moved closer to the window, then stopped their movement. I did not want to go further. I was afraid of death but also of being absent from school, and the two fears mingled together were making the ground unsteady under my feet. It seemed to lean under me, to take me towards the window again. Was it easier for me to face death than to face one day away from school? But easier than these two alternatives was to move in another direction, to move towards the door, the door that was closed on my uniform. I edged towards it. My fear increased the nearer I got.

I was experiencing a new fear which was being added to all the fears that had started with the beginning of life. But suddenly I found myself leaping to the door like a locomotive racing under steam, leaning against it with all the weight of my body, with all the force I could muster in it, to find myself inside the room sunk deep in dark shadows, heavy with stagnant air, as though in it lay a dead crocodile. I rushed to the cupboard, wrenched it open and pulled out my uniform from the depths, before escaping back through the open door, impelled by the strength of my fear.

I was shaking all over as I put on my uniform. I pulled the jacket around me to close the buttons, but one of them had been torn off. All the primitive elements of fear seemed to have invaded my body, to weigh heavy on the air, to make the curtains on the windows shake with fear so that I could hear the sound of their thick silk drapery hitting against the wall like chattering teeth. I heard a noise like that of a storm approaching. Was that Tante Hanem's voice? Was it her husband's? Or was it the sound of the wind blowing through the open window? I grasped my bag, leapt down the stairs, leapt into the morning tramcar as it gathered speed, leapt off it in front of the school, and was almost run over by a car as I crossed the street before rushing through the gates of the school just as they were being closed.

The bell had already rung. It was examination day, the yard was empty, the girls in class. I sat on a bench, my head bent to the ground, the tears running down my face. If I did not sit for the examinations it meant I would be failed. Father had always warned me against failure. He would point to the pail and the scrubbing brush and say: 'If you fail just once, all that will be left to you is scrubbing floors.' I got up from the wooden bench quickly. A thought ran through my head insistently: to go to the office of the headmistress, tell her what had happened with my uniform and ask her to let me sit for the examinations.

It was to be the first and the last time I would meet face to face with Oustaza Nabaweya Moussa. She had a face capable of cutting off yeast from the house,* to use another of Sittil Hajja's favourite sayings, and I ended up by hating all faces which resembled hers. In those days she made me hate school, education and almost everything else in the world. My father when he wanted to frighten or scold me used to say: 'I should send you back to Nabaweya Moussa.' All I can see whenever I remember her is a face contracted in an ugly scowl, and big black eyes, big enough to absorb all the dark gloom in the world.

I stood in front of her, trembling as she sat there in her office like an old lion in its den, crouching, ready to jump on me. Before I even opened my mouth, she burst out: 'I know the stupid excuses of spoilt girls like you. You must have spent an hour in front of the mirror putting on eyebrow pencil.'

I had no mirror in my room. I never saw myself in a mirror except at the moment when I opened the front door of the house. There was a tall mirror in the vestibule and in it I could get a glimpse of a long dark shadow carrying a head which looked like mine, of a tall, lean girl with a pale face, dressed in black mourning. And I was certainly not spoilt. I walked like a black trooper, my body upright. Tante Hanem was fond of calling me Al-Ghaffeer, the village night watchman.

But Nabaweya Moussa did not see me. Her eyes seemed to look inwards, or they were two globular spheres looking outwards to wander faraway in the sky. She was angry with the heavens, harboured a smouldering anger against the female species. Her anger showed itself in the ugly frown which resembled that of Tante Fahima.

'Go to your exams immediately', she said, 'and if you're ever late again you'll be expelled once and for all from school, do you understand?'

Her voice pierced through my eardrums as she chased me out of her office. I ran as fast as I could to the examination hall.

---

* Yeast is a necessity in all peasant houses which used to bake their own bread. No bread means no life, means death. A scowling ugly face in a woman would make people refuse to sell, or to give her yeast. It's an anti-life face.

20

The Long, Strong Bones
of a Horse

I passed my examinations without difficulty and was moved up to second year in secondary (high) school. My father transferred me to the Saneya girls' school after Tante Hanem had written to mother saying that she no longer wanted me to stay in her house, and at the same time moved me to the house of my uncle Sheikh Muhammad Al-Saadawi in the district of Anbari near the Citadel. I spent two years, 1944-45, in the Saneya Secondary School for Girls.

The name Saneya School for Girls was surrounded by awe, by a feeling of grandeur. It was a prestigious institution, with a history. The first pioneers of female education had graduated from there. Tante Fahima pronounced the name Saneya through the tip of her nose. 'In Saneya I met Abla* Nazeera', she would say.

The name Abla Nazeera echoed in my ears, filling me with an even greater awe than the name Saneya. I wondered who she could be. Was she a pioneer like Nabaweya Moussa? I used to hear her voice coming out of that magical apparatus called a radio, out of the wooden box with small holes in it leading to

---

* Title given to an older woman, for example an elder sister, a tutor or a teacher, as a sign of respect. Means 'elder sister' in Turkish.

something inside, with magical eyes that were open to other worlds, and magical voices that came from somewhere in the heavens.

Tante Fahima, addressed as Oustaza Fahima Shoukry, was considered of great importance among the men and women members of my mother's and my father's families, for she was acquainted with one of those magical beings who spoke on the radio and had met her at the Saneya school.

I sat in the taxi between my father and my brother as it raced towards the house of my uncle Sheikh Muhammad. My father was explaining to my brother that he had managed to get him accepted in the Banbakaden Boys' Secondary School, then he turned to tell me that I would be going to the Saneya Girls' Secondary School.

My heart beat so violently that I felt as though the taxi was shaking. Its wheels hit the tarmac road with a loud smack, and my body jumped up and down. My father's body, too, kept jumping up and down making his fez hit against the roof. He put his hand on either side of it to hold it down but it fell off his head, so he put it on his knees, then looked out of the window and said: 'This is Muhammad Ali Street.'

On either side, I could see pillars holding up the arches of arcades, under which people walked, and there were many small shops. A tramcar clanged behind us and almost ran over the taxi. The two drivers started to quarrel, shouting at one another in loud voices and insulting one another's mothers, then followed with the fathers and the grandfathers of their mothers all the way back, after which both of them drove off swearing away at the world, at every thing sacred, at Muhammad Ali Street with its brothels, and its prostitutes, and at whatever occurred to them.

My uncle's house was in a narrow dusty lane. Its ground was not covered in tarmac and everywhere there were pot-holes and piles of rubbish. The taxi driver muttered angrily as we drove into the lane, and stopped the taxi before we had reached the house near a small muddy pool of water from which rose the smell of an open sewer. What a difference between this lane and Al-Daher Street, between Tante Fahima's house and that of Sheikh Muhammad, I thought.

My uncle Sheikh Muhammad bore the title of Oustaz of Religious Jurisprudence in the holy university of Al-Azhar. I imagined his house would be much better than that of the trader in Mouski Street, but I found a cramped, gloomy flat on the fourth floor of an old house which looked as though it would collapse at any moment The entrance to the house was narrow and dark and we could see hardly anything. I was carrying a big bag and kept stumbling on the stairs as I climbed behind my father and my brother. Each of them was carrying a bag in one hand, and holding up a lighted match in the other. My father stopped at every floor to take his breath and light another match, while my brother and I panted noisily behind.

The name Saneya, with all the grandeur attached to it, evaporated. My heart was dropping with every step I climbed to my uncle's house. My father kept up a conversation as though trying to soften the blow, or relieve the guilt he was feeling at having brought us to this place, or perhaps he found it a suitable opportunity to express his political views in a place where they could carry weight.

'The government is just corrupt. It neither respects learning, nor men of learning. It's a corrupt system. Only ignorant people, only Mouski street traders who buy and sell old car parts, can make money.' Father's words had their effect on my thoughts and reduced my feeling of humiliation. Was it not poverty that deprived people of their dignity, filled their noses with the smell of bursting sewers every morning, forced them to feed on lentils and fava beans, and made their bodies let out ugly noises from behind the doors of their latrines?

The latrine was next door to the room which had become ours (my brother's and mine). The room was like an icebox in winter, very cold and damp. In summer it was burning hot like a tin box on the surface of the sun. A single small window looked out at a blackened wall. Through it crept the smell of stale food being heated on a stove. A second small door opened from it onto the outer staircase.

This second door was a blessing sent to us by God. It avoided our passing through the parlour when we went out. The parlour was a long and narrow tunnel-like room. In it was placed a kind of sofa on which sat my uncle, his wife and on many occasions relatives from her family, the Al-Akbawis.

Somehow the sound of the name Al-Akbawi evokes other names or words in my mind, names like Al-Akkad[*] or Al-Ala'a[†] or Al-Anbary, or Banbakaden, or words like rheumatism of the spinal column. In my memory they remain names and words linked by a single chain to the gloomy lane in the district of Al-Anbari near Al-Ala'a, to the damp room with a damp tiled floor which made me develop severe pain in my spinal column, to Banbakaden, the secondary school where my brother failed year after year, to Al-Akkad, mentioned repeatedly in the conversations between my uncle Sheikh Muhammad and Al-Akbawi, to the Qur'an chanted by my uncle before he fell asleep, and the call to prayer shooting out at dawn from the nearby mosque with a sound like cannon fire. In my mind, Saneya school is transformed into something more like a fortress, or a huge prison surrounded by a high stone wall near the mosque of Sayeda Zaynab where the beggars, the cripples and the infirm gathered whining, supplicating, panting in front of the main door.

I walked from my uncle's house to school every day carrying a bag full of copy books and texts. My body began to lean on one side, and I felt pain in the lower part of my back, and in my left leg. I often stopped half-way to rest, and sometimes reached school after the bell had rung to find the door closed. It was a huge door made of wood, more like a prison door and it was

---

[*] A conservative, misogynist Egyptian writer, in the first half of the twentieth century.
[†] The citadel. A palace and fortress built by Salah Al-Dine Al-Ayoubi.

guarded by a giant porter with a fearsome frown that seemed as though it had been carved into the flesh of his forehead. I banged on the door with my fist. On cold days my fingers would swell and the weight of my bag would cut a line deep into the palm of my hand. Pains kept shooting up my arm to my shoulder, and then down from my shoulder to the lower part of my spinal column, and the back of my left leg. I banged at the door again and again until my swollen fingers bled, stood there in the street swallowing my tears, the taste of salt mixing with the saliva in my mouth. For me, now, Tante Hanem had become a fair angel in paradise lost.

But no-one opened the door, and I walked all the way back to my gloomy room, slid under the blankets into my cold iron bed to study my lessons, or sat on a chair with rickety legs bending over the low table, a seventy-watt lamp shedding its pale light, paler during the day than in the night, over my books.

Sometimes if my banging were hard enough, or if Allah had mercy on me and wanted to lighten my burden, I would hear the rheumatic joints of the door screech as it opened, and the black face of the giant would look out, his big white teeth making a grinding noise that resembled the screeching of the door. 'You're not allowed to enter the school now. Those are the instructions of the headmistress. Is that clear?'

'I want to meet the headmistress, Am Abdallah.'

'You're not allowed to meet the headmistress. Is that clear?'

The door screeched again and closed with a bang.

During the holiday of the Eid I returned to Menouf with my brother. In the morning, when I woke up I was coughing. I walked with a bent back and my body was leaning to one side. My father took me off to his old friend, Dr Hanna. He examined me in less then a minute, pinched my cheek, and said:

'Your daughter's health is as strong as that of a horse, Sayed Bey. She just needs to take some iron and arsenic. She's grown very quickly. She's now even taller than I am. God's will is doing fine!'

I was indeed taller than Dr Hanna, taller than my elder brother Tala'at and taller than all my school-mates. I wondered when I had grown so quickly! When I woke up one morning I discovered that if I stretched out my arm my fingers could reach the buttons of the radio as it lay on the uppermost shelf to one side of the bed. It seemed to me that only yesterday I could not have reached that high. Did my bones grow longer during the night when I slept with my body stretched out? I decided from then on to sleep curled up like an embryo. During the day-time I got into the habit of bending forwards with my back, and my head, for in one of our school-books, entitled *Thoughtful Readings*, it said: 'A tall stature is a characteristic of men, and of manliness. A short stature is characteristic of women, is feminine.' So it appeared to me then that a beautiful woman should have small soft bones, like a dove, or a chick, bones that would break when someone put his arms around her.

But my bones were long and strong like those of a horse, and they were not liable to break. Every day I was accustomed to walk for two whole hours carrying my heavy bag. Now my gait was slower than it used to be, but still I continued to walk on and on until I arrived at the door of the school, for this door was my salvation. It was the only opening in the closed walls of my life, the only opening through which I could escape to another life, a life other than the one I led in the gloomy room in my uncle's house in which I lived as though buried in a tomb.

Despite the iron and the arsenic my pains got worse, so my father took me to a doctor in a huge square in Cairo called Ismaileya Square. Tante Fahima had told us that he was the most renowned of all doctors specialized in the treatment of bone diseases. Since the day I went to Dr Hanna in Menouf I had started to hate doctors. I could not forget his hard, bony fingers tapping on my chest as though it were a box made of wood, his quick, panting breath smelling of iodine, or Lysol, or methylated spirits, his metallic voice and mechanical laugh devoid of any mirth, his stuck-up nose unrelated to any real dignity.

For the first time I rode in that box surrounded by iron bars which carries people up to higher floors in a building. Tante Hanem referred to it as the *ascenseur*, which is French for the word lift. The pains in my back disappeared with this ride in the lift to the ninth floor. I felt as though I were flying in a plane. I was being freed of the earth's gravity, my body felt light, my laughter rang out as I closed my eyes and flew up.

My joy abandoned me when I entered the big waiting room. It was crowded with patients, wooden crutches, wan, yellow faces. There was a broken look in people's eyes, a total passivity, as though they were expecting death while they sat waiting to go in to the doctor. And I was going to become like them, to lean on a crutch and spend the hours of my life in this waiting room.

I have never been able to stand waiting. For me waiting is death. I got up from my chair, went outside and started to walk up and down in the corridor, hitting the floor with my heels. I was saying to myself that I was able to walk without crutches, that I was not sick, had no need for a doctor, did not need to wait.

The male nurse finally came up to us wearing a white coat and glass spectacles like those worn by doctors. His eyes were small, deep-set with a gleam in them like the eyes of a hawk. He had a black mustache hanging over his upper lip. I wondered from where he had emerged so suddenly. He must have been hiding in some inner room, noting down the fees patients had paid during the day in a special register. Now he was pouncing on my father, speaking to him in a voice that croaked like a frog: 'Do you want a first priority* examination, Bey?'

On the wall hung a small board with the fees of the doctor, like the price list I had seen posted in the 'One Thousand and One Items' store in Menouf. Near it hung a doctorate degree in a gilt frame, and a graduation photograph of students from medical college. Some of the students were standing in line, others were

---

* In Egypt, famous doctors who are usually overwhelmed with patients charge higher fees for an immediate examination and lower fees for appointments fixed several days, or even weeks in advance.

sitting on chairs in front wearing dark suits with a serious stony
expression on their faces, their noses lifted up as though sniffing
the air, their legs crossed one over the other.

My father paid for a first priority examination and after a few
moments we were ushered into the doctor's room. He reminded
me of Dr. Hanna: the same voice, the same way of pronouncing
his words, of mixing Arabic with English, the same mechanical
laugh. Did medical school mint them like coins, beat them into
the same shape with a sledgehammer?

He made me lie down on the examination table half-naked,
shivering with cold, while he engaged in a long telephone conversation as though he had forgotten all about me, then came
back holding something long and black in his mouth, something
I remembered Tante Hanem called a pipe. He blew out some
smoke towards the ceiling and proceeded to examine my bones,
twisting my spinal column and making it crack with a loud
noise. I thought he had broken something and let out a loud
scream.

This visit to the bone specialist failed to cure me. In fact
what I think he did was to make me worse, to pave the way for a
prolapsed disc in the lower part of my spinal column with which
I have suffered for many long years. I came out of his clinic
limping, almost unable to walk. When I trod on the ground
I felt pain shooting down my back. My father was obliged to
support me until we reached the lift. Ismaileya Square seemed
more vast even than before. The tram station had moved further
away and the distance we had to walk was greater than before. I
was unable to go further than a few steps, so I sat down on the
pavement, and my father had to hire a taxi instead of taking me
home in the tramcar.

I was absent from school for a whole week. The doctor had
prescribed tablets for me but the pain increased. My father spoke
of taking me back with him to Menouf. I jumped out of bed, and
stood upright on my feet to prove to my father that I could go
to school, and not be absent for a single day more. Going back

to Menouf meant staying away from school for at least a month, meant staying away perhaps for ever. The siege would begin all over again, a new suitor would appear, a new plot would be weaved to push me into the trap destined for girls.

I insisted on staying on in my uncle's house until the end of the school year, but my father overruled this suggestion and decided to take me to my grandfather's house where I would be under the supervision of Tante Fahima. She had said to him that it was not reasonable for a boy and a girl to go on living together in a room like the one in which we had lived the past year. 'I am ready to take them under my care if they live in their grandfather's house' she said.

I succeeded in my examinations and was moved up to the third year in secondary school, but my brother failed and was obliged to repeat the school year. We had moved to my grandfather's house and were living in a big villa surrounded by a garden located on Zeitoun (Olive) Road. My grandfather had died two years before we moved in. He caught pneumonia after a cold winter's night of revelry, and returned home shivering with fever. He died a week later, and during that week he insisted on treating his fever with drink, developed hallucinations, and kept muttering 'cure me with that which is the cause of my ruin.'* At that time there was no penicillin in Egypt. No-one had heard about it, but Tante Fahima read an article about penicillin after he died and told us that it was extracted from a fungus. I began to eat bread which had started to rot, and had fungi on it, and after that my pains got better.

After my grandfather died my grandmother Amna sighed with relief. For the first time she opened the mouth she had always kept tightly shut and filled her lungs with air. But the air she inhaled apparently carried a mysterious germ with it, and the germ settled in her throat. The irony of fate wanted that the first time she should open her mouth after years of silence, the

---

* A popular saying used to describe people who hold on to something, and plunge further and further into it as though seeking their ruin.

first time she should ever say anything, ever speak was also the time when her throat was closed up by a malignant growth.

No-one dared, no-one could bear to pronounce the word cancer. Death was a word that was easier spoken. When people spoke about cancer they said, 'You know, that disease.'

My grandmother never heard the word. They told her she had influenza and inflamed tonsils. She lay in bed for a whole year. Suffering mixed with sorrow accumulated in her body. The 'specialist in malignant tumours' sunk needles in her neck. Her neck was pierced with needles and wound up in gauze, so she could not move her head, but her ash-grey eyes kept moving around her, filled with helpless pain, and her finger pale and ghostlike kept pointing to the needles in her neck. A blurry finger pointing to the blurry mass of white gauze asking the question she could not ask: 'What is it then that I have in my neck?' Her eyes looking at the ceiling seemed to pierce through to the heavens, seeking, asking God: 'Why? Why? O God, why?'

My ears did not hear the sound of her breathing, the sound of her voice. At the time I was in my uncle's house. But Tante Ni'mat used to wake up to a voice whispering in the night, 'O God.' She wondered, was it her own voice in a dream, or the voice of her mother next door. She could hear it say, 'O God what did I do to you?'

Tante Ni'mat's eyes were swollen with weeping as she called to God in the night. During the day she held back her tears, and they kept accumulating as though they were forming something which started to close her throat. Is a malignant tumour just a sac which over the years fills up with tears?

I spent the year 1945 in my grandfather's house. He was now called Al-Marhoum (the deceased who has been granted God's mercy). My grandmother Amna was now referred to in the feminine as Al-Marhouma. I was now in the third year of secondary school and slept in a big bed with Tante Fahima. My brother Tala'at had a separate room near that of Uncle Zakareya. Tante Ni'mat had her own room and so did Uncle Yehia. There were other rooms in the house which remained unoccupied, but Tante Fahima had become headmistress of a girls' school and did not want me to have a separate room, insisted on exercising a strict control over me while I slept, and while I dreamt. I could not understand why taking care of me meant nothing more than this continuous supervision.

She carried a ring of keys with her like a jailor. A key to the study of Al-Marhoum. A key to the room of Al-Marhouma. A key to the store-room where necessary victuals were kept. A key to the room of the *dada*,* a young servant-girl like Sa'adeya. A key to the store-room in the garden where she kept the gilt-framed family photographs. A key to the cupboard in which she kept valuables and important papers, which included an old faded document written by the Khedive Ismail in his own hand. She had come upon it in the study of Al-Marhoûm and was in the habit of bringing it out for visitors to see while she stared at it fixedly with eyes bulging behind thick glass spectacles, and her nose in the air, as she said: 'The Khedive Ismail took the lands which belonged to my deceased grandfather, God have mercy on him, and was supposed to pay for them. But he died without paying him anything and I will continue to insist on our rights until the government gives them back to us.'

My uncle Zakareya was a student in Fouad Al-Awal university. His eyes would glisten as he listened to her. He dreamt of the farm which would be restored to them, of the day in which he would wallow in riches, and grandeur. Like my brother Tala'at he hated books and studying, preferred going to the cinema, or the theatre, or to the horse races.

I used to leave the house early in the morning to go to school. The big clock in the hall would strike six chimes and Tante Fahima would open her eyes, and say: 'Wake up Nawal, it's six o'clock.' I got up, washed and dressed quickly, rushed out without breakfast, to walk down Zeitoun Road carrying my

---

* A Turkish word for a servant-girl or a wet-nurse who looks after the children.

bag, then after a little while broke into a run to make sure that I caught the train on time.

Sitting in the train I looked out of the window to keep track of the stations and their names. At Saray Al-Koubba station there was a huge red wall which surrounded the palace of the king, and there were gardens with expanses of green and beds of flowers. Later came Manchiet Al-Sadr station with old houses, covered in grime, on the verge of collapsing, and washing hanging on the balconies that quivered as the train went by.

I got down at Koubri Al-Lemoun (Lemon Bridge) station, and crossed over Bab Al-Hadeed (Door of Iron) Square. In the middle of the square stood the statue called Renaissance of Egypt. It was the work of Mahmoud Mokhtar, a sculptor who lived from 1891 to 1934. Later it was moved, to be placed in front of the university in Giza, and was replaced by the statue of Ramses II.

I rode a tramcar from Bab Al-Hadeed to Al-Sayeda Zaynab tram station, got down near the stone wall surrounding Al-Saneya Secondary School for Girls, just in time to walk in through the huge, cracked black, wooden door as the bell was ringing, and to rush up to the morning assembly and stand in line.

The distance from the house on Zeitoun Road to school by train and then tram took two hours. I left at 6.30 in the morning to arrive at 8.30. In winter when I left the house in the early morning, Zeitoun Road was still dark, and I used to run all the way to the train station without stopping. My legs were long and helped me to run fast, and I had regained my health living in this house where the sun came in through all the windows, and the air carried the scent of roses. The gloomy room in my uncle's house was forgotten, as I noted in the small notebook with the blue cover.

The first of January 1945. Yesterday we celebrated the New Year. Uncle Zakareya attended the big party in the house of his uncle Taher Bey in Malik Street, and my brother Tala'at went with him. Tante Ni'mat went off to the house of her aunt Boudour Hanem in Hadaik Al-Koubba (Koubba Gardens). Tante Fahima joined the teachers in her school at a party, and Uncle Yehia went out with some of his colleagues who were employed like him in the Department of Railways.

I did not accompany my brother to grand-uncle Taher's house. I didn't like going there, did not like Tante Yildiz, or Tante Dawlat or Uncle Mamdouh. I disliked the three of them. Tante Yildiz stuck her nose up at me, and stared me up and down with her green eyes. She pronounced words in French I did not understand. Tante Dawlat crossed her legs, asked me about my name, and the name of my school, as though she was speaking through the tip of her nose. Uncle Mamdouh opened my bag without asking me, searched through it and said in a voice that was more like a hiss, 'Girls are always hiding nice things in their bags.' I was afraid he would find my diary so I tried to pull it out of his hands, but he ran away with it to his room, and I followed, hoping to snatch it away before he had a chance to look through it. In his room he tried to kiss me, but I gave him a push and he almost fell over. My muscles and bones were strong and they saved me from him.

Uncle Mamdouh was a student in the university like Uncle Zakareya. He was thin and frail, with beady eyes, something like an ailing hawk or maybe a mouse. When he looked at me there was no love or admiration in his eyes. He was fond of showing off the things he had, the golden cigarette-lighter with the flame that shot up at one snap, the silver cigarette case which opened almost by itself for him to extract a cigarette and tap it delicately on its back, the golden chain with his keys dangling from it as he let it run through his fingers like a rosary before he extracted the key to his car and showed it to me. And above all his small yellow car which he insisted on parking right in front of the entrance to the house as though intent on blocking the way, and on demonstrating to all those who came and went that he was the owner of this wonderful car, and not the neighbours.

Uncle Mamdouh could never carry on a conversation with me. He thought I was like other girls in the family of Shoukry

Bey, or in that of Taher Bey, who were dazzled by his car and the other things he had.

But I was immune to his riches for, like my father, I did not hold money and possessions in great esteem. My father's words continued to echo in my ears. 'He's just a sack full of money.'

My uncle Mamdouh was one of those sacks full of money. He was a student at the university, but he had never heard of Taha Hussayn. He did not read books, or write, or draw, or play the lute. He had no hobbies, no interest in anything except running after girls. He and my uncle Yehia were twin characters.

The clock on the wall struck midnight. No-one was yet back from the New Year's Eve celebrations. I stopped writing, sat motionless in the big hall. From the walls jutted out the nails on which the photographs once hung. Tante Fahima had taken them down. She wanted to forget her father. When he died she heaved a sigh of relief just like my grandmother Amna.

I seemed to hear a voice calling out from my grandmother's room: 'O God. Why are you so unjust?' My grandmother's spirit must have risen from her tomb! I glimpsed a dark shadow moving behind the door, sat motionless. The big house was frightening, peopled with the phantoms of the dead. I heard the spirit of my grandfather strike the ground with his stick, and his voice echoed in the silence: 'O God you are the power and the glory.' The door-bell clanged although no-one had come in or gone out. It could only be a spirit!

The small gloomy room in my uncle's house now seemed to me like a haven where I had nothing to fear, for the spirits of the dead did not inhabit it. The only phantom there was my uncle's wife moving through the parlour when she went to the latrine, but she was a living being, she was not dead like my grandfather and my grandmother. Yet in the shadowy parlour she looked like a spirit that had risen from the tomb, or like a strange phantom, as she leant on the wall with her hand, her legs bowing under her fat body, her breath panting when she stopped to take in a deep sighing inspiration, then resumed the slow, creeping movement of her feet encased in slippers, the heels tapping against the tiles as she advanced. Once inside the latrine her voice would whip through the air as she asked loudly: 'Who has blocked the *kaneef*?'

The word *kaneef* meant the latrine or the toilet, or 'the house of good manners' to use another of Sittil Hajja's terms. My uncle's wife was in the habit of rapping against the door of our room to ask in her croaking voice: 'Which of you two has blocked the *kaneef*?'

My brother Tala'at, choking with suppressed laughter, would open the door and shoot back at her: 'It must be my uncle, Sheikh Muhammad. He adores stuffed cabbage.'

My uncle's wife was accustomed to cook in her bedroom. She squatted on the floor and spent the whole day stuffing cabbage leaves and eggplant or preparing a *fetta** of lamb's feet with garlic, or stuffing tripe with onion and green peppers.

My uncle, Sheikh Muhammad, had another wife in Kafr Tahla called Um Fawzeya. Lean and quick, she never stopped casting spells on her rival in Cairo who was the younger, second wife. She would whisper in my ear 'Sheikh Muhammad's wife in Misr is the living image of an elephant with a trunk. She does nothing but stuff Sheikh Muhammad's belly until one of these days he'll burst and die. And all this is so he doesn't seek to marry another woman. You know he's nothing but a loose womanizer just like his father. But what's to be done if Sittil Hajja decided to give him an education, to spend her money and send him to Al-Azhar. Now he dresses in a kaftan and a turban, and so under the dome there's now a Sheikh Muhammad.'[†]

But in the house in Anbari district I heard a different story from my uncle's second wife. She would say to me: 'Your uncle Sheikh Muhammad left Um Fawzeya because she's nothing but

---

* A meat soup to which are added pieces of bread, and rice, topped with a sauce made of vinegar and fried garlic and sometimes tomatoes. Eaten with meat, or lambs' or calves' feet.

† A saying which means that appearances create the illusion that there's something underneath.

a madwoman. Her mind has snapped and all she does is gossip, and cast spells to try and get him back.'

Before Tante Fahima came home from her New Year's Eve party, I wrote in my diary: 'I am waiting impatiently for the holidays of the Eid when I can travel back to Menouf. I long to see mother and father, long for the letter F, for the lute playing in the quiet of the night, for the voice that sings, "When the night falls and the stars are scattered across the sky." I will go to the school of Fine Arts to meet him. But maybe he has graduated, and has married. I wonder if he still lives in Cairo? Perhaps I'll meet him by accident while he's on his way to school.'

The holidays came and we travelled to Menouf. My brother had bought a small camera. He loved taking pictures and used to enter the store-room where Tante Fahima kept the photographs of the family, and spend hours looking at them. There he came upon a photograph of my mother when she was a school-girl, and another one where she was holding him close to her breast. She looked like Queen Nazli carrying her son Farouk, or like the Virgin Mary with her baby son Jesus. Tala'at wanted to take these pictures with him to Menouf but Tante Fahima refused. So he went hungry, saved the money piastre by piastre, and bought the small camera, so that he could take pictures of mother in Menouf.

I liked photographs, the same as my brother, but I preferred reading. I read short stories and novels during recreation time, and while the girls played in the school-yard I sat on a bench reading. I also read during hours usually devoted to physical education. In my bag I was ready with a doctor's certificate written in a handwriting which resembled the scratches of a kitten and which said: 'The pupil, Nawal Al-Saadawi, suffers with rheumatism of the back and left leg and is to be exempted from physical education classes.' The certificate remained in my bag long after the rheumatic pains had disappeared. I used to produce it for the headmistress every time I was late for school, or absent from it for one or two days, and she gave orders to the gate-keeper to open the gate for me. Father's comment was: 'Maybe harm can be beneficial.'

My brother took lots of photographs in Menouf. In one of them, mother is walking across a field surrounded by my younger sisters and brothers. In another, I am chasing after a white butterfly. In a third, he put his arm through mine and my mother took the picture. Then my father happened to come along and there was a fourth of him standing in the fields wearing a fez, with a fly whisk in his hand.

21

Love and the Hideous Cat

In Al-Saneya school I had a school-mate called So'ad. She lived in a house near that of my uncle Sheikh Muhammad, But her house was much better than that of my uncle. Sunshine flowed in through the windows, and the toilet was clean. When I was in my uncle's house I used to visit her just to be able to enter the toilet. We walked together to school, and she gave me her exercise books to copy the lessons I had missed during the days I was absent.

So'ad was short and thin, and had a dark complexion. Her face was narrow and pale, her lips slightly blue and she always kept them tightly pressed together, as though she were very serious, and would accept no nonsense. When I looked at myself in the mirror, I noticed that my lips were always slightly apart, were never pressed tightly together. I thought maybe that I was not serious enough, not as firm as I ought to be, so I began to contract the muscles of my face, and to tighten my lips. I decided from then onwards never to smile, no matter what happened. Nothing in the world was going well enough for me to smile. But it did not last for long. My lips kept parting in a smile for the slightest of reasons. A kitten lifting its tail to urinate on the wall of a mosque. The headmistress standing on the platform with her nose stuck up in the air, then suddenly falling off it on to the ground. I would burst into peals of laughter, but I could see So'ad standing near me with her lips as tightly closed as ever.

My brother Tala'at was like me. He was always bursting into laughter. He kept imitating people. Tante Fahima striking the ground with her heels when she walked, or Sheikh Muhammad making raucous noises as he cleared his throat, or my uncle's wife when she let out one of her prolonged female moans.

Every Friday I went to Al-Ezbakeya, or Al-Andalous gardens with my brother. Sometimes we went to the zoo in Giza, and on the way we competed in an attempt to take the tramcar without paying a ticket. My brother was more hardy than I was, and succeeded in jumping off the tramcar before the ticket collector reached him. I immediately followed suit, but the ticket collector left him, and chased after me, for girls did not usually jump off the tramcar to avoid paying for a ticket. Riding the tramcar without paying for a ticket was one of the great thrills in our limited existence. The price of a ticket was six millimes but to us it seemed like six pounds.

Tala'at was only a year older than I was but to me it seemed as though he knew everything about the city of Cairo, about the Metro cinema, the Al-Rihani theatre and Casino Badia, the cabaret owned by a famous dancer named Badia. He disliked school, disliked studying. He used to take me to the public library in Bab Al-Khalk.* There we sat reading novels, or looking into old books. He loved poetry and music, loved to play the lute, to sing and to act, and he could have developed as a gifted artist were it not for what happened to him in Menouf when he was ten years old. A boy hit him with a bottle on the left side of his face, leaving him with a scar. Half a century went by and yet still he could not forget it. He could see it every day when he looked in

---

* One of the doors in the walls surrounding old Cairo. It means 'door of the people'. Khalk means creation, or those who have been created.

the mirror, the white scar which had healed on his left cheek, the
scar deep down inside him which had never healed.

'If it were not for Menouf, Nawal', he said to me that
evening.

'What could have happened, Tala'at?' I asked.

'I would have become a great musician.'

I can still hear the words he said to me a short while before I
left Egypt in 1992, I can still hear his voice. He came to my flat
in Giza. A childish gleam looked out of his eyes, or was it a thin
film of tears that had dried over the years, a fine cloud of ancient
sadness? He held out a doctor's report to me, a rise in his blood
urea, something in the left kidney.

'What's wrong with your left kidney?' I asked.

'O nothing. Just a slight fatigue', he said.

The word fatigue spoken in his voice sounded strange to me.
He had never felt tired, stayed awake all night practising on his
ood and singing. When he looked into the mirror he saw a great
musician, and when he rode his bicycle he flew off on it into
space, across the green fields, like a butterfly. He had a fair skin
with a rosy tint like my mother, had handsome regular features,
and a tall, slender body. Girls looked at him with admiration,
boys with envy, so one of them held a bottle by its neck and hit
him with it on the face. The blow cut his left cheek open. He
was still a child of ten, so perhaps the blow went through to his
heart, to his left kidney.

My father took him to a doctor in Menouf, then to a better
one in Cairo. The wound in his left cheek healed but it left a scar
which he used to see every day in the mirror.

'If it were not for the wound I would have become...'

'But it no longer shows, Tala'at.'

All he could see in the mirror was this wound, and ever
since he received this blow he held back his tears, for a man can
receive a blow but he must not cry. Crying is for girls, and my
brother had to become a man at the age of ten. From then on he
swallowed his tears. He swallowed his tears when my father hit

him for not studying, or because he had failed in his exams. My father was unable to see that he was gifted.

'You want to be a photographer?'

'You want to earn a living playing music?'

The arts were not valued. Certificates and diplomas were what was important. If you did not go to the university you were not an intellectual. If you were not a university graduate you could not qualify to become a bridegroom.

The word university had a magic ring. I was fourteen when I first saw its dome. I had gone to the zoo in Giza with my brother and my school-mate So'ad. We went in through the front entrance and came out through a back door which opened onto University Road. The dome looked grandiose as it shone under the sunlight with a copper glow, looked more grandiose than the disc of the sun itself. The clock in the high tower chimed out strokes that sounded more awe-inspiring than the roars of the lion in the zoo. Towering trees lined University Road on either side, and their green was greener than the green of any tree. The scent of jasmine flowers floated in the air, and the black tarmac of the road shone as though it had been washed clean with soap and water. The students walked over it, striking the ground with their solid leather shoes, dressed in grey woollen suits and carrying bags made of shining leather, their heads lifted high, their eyes looking at some distant horizon, or resting on us school-children with a rapid, haughty glance.

Would the day come when I would enter through the university gates, and sit beside these men? Graduate? Become a writer like Taha Hussayn? Taha Hussayn had once been a poor, blind child, but I was not blind, and my father was not as poor as his father had been.

My eyes kept feeding on the sights of University Road and the Orman Gardens, Badia Bridge (Evacuation Bridge) crossing over a branch of the Nile, the mainstream of the Nile, and Kasr Al-Nil Bridge with the twin granite lions at either end, their size much bigger than the lions in the zoo, the waters of the Nile rushing under the bridge with the lights reflected on their surface, expanses of water that seemed endless, another Nile, different to the Nile in Kafr Tahla with cars racing over it, making the bridge move under our feet, lifting our bodies up, then down, in a wave, making me wonder whether it could collapse under us.

We walked from the university, called Fouad Al-Awal after the king, as far as the huge square called Ismaileya Square after the Khedive Ismail, then on to Farouk Square to reach Al-Malika Nazli* Road, and Al-Malika Farida[†] Road, wandered back to the Palace of Muhammad Ali Pasha and continued to the school of Al-Amira Fawzeya and Al-Amira Fawkeya.[‡] All these names had an awesome ring to my ears, like the names of gods in the heavens, for little did I know that they would collapse, together with the pashas, after the revolution of 1952 led by Nasser.

My friend So'ad dreamt, like me, of going to the university, to the school of law, so that she could become a lawyer and defend the rights of the poor, but my brother wanted to enter the Institute of Music, and I thought of choosing the School of Fine Arts, or alternatively the School of Literature. I was not sure whether writers graduated from the School of Literature or not, but in my dreams I kept seeing myself as a literary scholar, or a writer, or as a musician playing the lute or the piano, or as a painter with a brush in my hand and a canvas stretched on a wooden easel in front of me.

This last image was always there in my mind. It was the image of the first love in my life, and I kept recalling it as I lay in bed next to Tante Fahima. Her bulging eyes stared at me as though she was trying to find out what I was dreaming about, but suddenly she would be fast asleep, her snores resounding in the silence. Then I would creep out of bed to the big verandah

---

* Queen, wife of King Fouad Al-Awal.
† Wife of King Farouk, the son of Fouad.
‡ Princesses, sisters of King Farouk.

and sit there gazing at the stars, trying to penetrate the future, remembering the past, writing things in my diary:

> The past seems to have something magical about it. Maybe when things no longer exist in the present, are no longer there within our reach, they gain a strange attraction. The manure in Am Saber's field has a smell of scent. The muddy pool of water becomes a lake reflecting the moon. The drops of rain on the window-pane are fingers strumming on a lute. The hee-haw of Al-Hajj Mahmoud's she-ass is more gentle than the snores of Tante Fahima.

I crossed out the last sentence. It would be a disaster if Tante Fahima came upon it. There were many things that I ended up dropping from my diary. I tore up pages and pages and threw them out of the window of the train, or put them in the toilet bowl and pulled the flush. I was afraid to throw them in the refuse bin below the kitchen sink for I had seen Tante Fahima searching its contents.

After my grandfather died Tante Fahima replaced the wolf-dog with a ferocious cat. In the dark of the night I would feel a large shadowy body jump over me and wake up panic-stricken, but Tante Fahima would reach out and cuddle him in her arms. There was a love relationship between them. When she was there, he nestled down quietly in her arms. When she was absent, he became restless, ready to pounce at any time on whoever was there. Something like a tongue of fire shot out of his eyes, but at night he mewed in her arms like a lover courting his loved one. She treated him with a much greater gentleness than she showed to anyone else in the house. I thought perhaps she preferred the company of animals to that of human beings, felt he had a right to be loved and cared for. Yet I was deprived of any kind of affection. She never once stretched out her hand and patted me on the shoulder. She never once held me in her arms, or put a plate of milk in front of me, but the cat's plate was always filled with milk.

> At night I sit on the verandah like I did in Menouf. In front of me stretches the garden, its tree leaves shining under the moon. I

gaze at a lonely distant star. It's my star, was born with me and will die with me. Beside it another star is scintillating in the dark.. He gazes at the stars with shining eyes as he stands on the balcony above me. He plays the lute and sings for me. Amongst the million of people who live on the earth he sings for me alone.

I close my eyes, imagine myself climbing the fence to the balcony above. Arrived at the second floor I stop and hold on to the balustrade. I find him there leaning with his elbows on it. I bring my hand up close to his. A sudden gust of wind blows up his loose shirt. He seems to float in the air like a spirit without body, then disappears behind the clouds. My eyes search everywhere but he is nowhere to be found on earth or in the heavens. His disappearance is sudden, unexpected, has never happened before. I stretch my hand out over the stone fence. It feels warm like human flesh, has the odour of a human body, yields under my touch as though it is his arm.

I wake up in bed with a start. Tante Fahima opens her eyes, and the black cat cuddled up in her arms also opens his eyes and stares at me angrily, for I am his rival in bed. He wants to be the only one who sleeps with her in it, like a husband who cannot bear sharing his wife with anybody else.

If Tante Fahima knew how I spent the best part of my nights cuddling into F's arms what would she say? Describe me as a loose girl with no morals! She used to do very bad things openly in broad daylight, behave in a very bad way towards me, her nose up in the air, not give me my milk in the morning and instead give it to that hideous cat. Should I tell her what I really think? Should I face people with the truth? At night I dream of facing the world openly, being myself as I really am. My mother brought me into this world, but I am not at home in it. This land is not my land, and heaven is not my heaven. My family is not a real family to me. I am living without a land of my own, without a heaven of my own, without a family. I dream of a different world, of a time when I will break through my shell, through the walls that hold me back, and prevent me from speaking, from saying what I want to say.

Why did I not pronounce his name? We meet face to face and yet my lips remain closed, do not open to let out the words 'I love you.' In my dream I whisper the word love, and he looks at me with surprise. How can a girl pronounce that word?! His eyes open wide with amazement, he smiles with scorn, and walks off on his way to the railway station with his bag in one hand and his *ood* in the other. And I wake up bathing in sweat, overwhelmed by a feeling of deep remorse, fearful lest his scornful smile be more than just a dream. If ever my diary fell into some one's hands what would they say of the serious and well-behaved girl?! That she was remembering her first love? Recreating it again and again? Resurrecting it time after time? Breathing it in like whiffs of fresh air in an atmosphere that suffocated her? Or was it a beautiful image in a world in which there was no beauty?

22

Art Thieves

One day my brother came up to me and whispered cautiously in my ear: 'I have an idea that not even the devil could have thought of.' He very often got ideas like that. An outing to the zoo in Giza, an excursion to Al-Kanatir Al-Khaireya,* a visit to the public library in Bab Al-Khalk, or spending a few hours at the cinema, or at a theatre. But this time it was none of these things. This time it was an adventure which sounded really dangerous. Nevertheless, I decided to join in. He was my only friend in the big desolate house and I couldn't risk losing him. Besides, like him, I adored photographs, hated Tante Fahima and wanted to take my revenge on her.

That day, apart from me and my brother there was no-one in the house. Everyone had left on vacation for two days.

My brother went down to the store-room in the garden. 'I have hired a donkey-cart to carry all the photographs inside', he said to me. I was shaking, but he did not give me a chance to protest, and started to carry the photographs from the store-room to the donkey-cart waiting in the street outside. I found myself

---

* A barrage on the Nile just north of Cairo. The name means barrage of plenty, bountiful.

helping, like an obedient servant. Some of the pictures were big and heavy, so I helped him carry them, or he loaded them on to my back as though I was a she-ass. The gilt-framed pictures were thick and weighty as though made of solid gold, or covered with a thick layer of it. There was a picture of my grandfather wearing his ceremonial uniform with all the medals on his breast which made him look like Saad Zaghloul. There were pictures of the Khedive Ismail and the Khedive Abbas, of King Fouad Al-Awal, and of the Emperor of Abyssinia Haile Selassie. There were pictures of Oustaza Fahima Shoukry receiving her certificate the day she graduated as a teacher, of mother and father on their wedding day, of Tante Ni'mat being betrothed to Muhammad Effendi Al-Shami. She was wearing a short lace dress for the occasion, but Tante Hanem's wedding dress was long, with a long tail which was left to trail on the ground. There was also a picture of Boudour Hanem, my grandfather's sister, cuddling her child and looking like Queen Nazli with her baby son, Prince Farouk, or the Virgin Mary holding the child Jesus. Other pictures were of Uncle Taher with his wife wearing a yashmak;* of three boys dressed very smartly, namely uncles Zakareya, Yehia and Mamdouh in their early youth; of Muhammad Ali Pasha, the Albanian founder of modern Egypt; the Khedive Tewfik, commander of the Turkish army; probably Tala'at Pasha one of Shoukry Bey's ancestors, my mother in an evening dress (*soirée*) on a New Year's Eve night; and again my mother carrying her first-born, Tala'at, like the goddess Isis carrying Horus. My brother held up the last picture. My mother looked so beautiful. 'Isn't it a pity to leave these pictures thrown like that, covered in dust', he commented.

For two whole hours we kept transporting the pictures from the store-room to the donkey-cart. My brother climbed on to the cart beside the driver to tie the ropes around the stacks of pictures loaded on the cart to which was attached the donkey, a

---

* A fine, usually white, veil worn by upper-class women over the lower part of the face, starting below the eyes. Turkish in origin.

white skinny animal that resembled Al-Hajj Mahmoud's she-ass in Menouf, and the owner kept muttering that the load was much heavier than he had expected and bargaining for more money. My brother was in a hurry and did not want to risk wasting more time so he agreed, without putting up any resistance.

We were all set to leave with my brother and I seated on the cart behind our precious booty when suddenly Tante Fahima appeared on the scene. It was as though the earth had split to let her through. My brother and I spotted her at the exact moment she was pushing the gate open. Her back was turned towards us, and we heard the bell hanging above the iron gate ring. She turned to close the gate behind her and heard a hee-haw. Strange! In Zeitoun Road there were no donkeys. As she was turning the movement of her head suddenly stopped short, and her bulging eyes flickered behind the spectacles. She was myopic and could not see well, but the donkey cart behind which my brother and I were now hidden had not started to move, because the donkey, feeling the full weight of the load, decided to dig its hooves into the tarmac of the road, and express its protest in a plaintive heehaw.

'Shee Aziza, shee', urged my brother. Tante Fahima's eyes were unable to see the cart. What they did see was the donkey and from the donkey they travelled back to the cart, to the stacks of pictutes piled up on it. She hesitated for a short moment, then turned round to go into the house. Her back was now towards us. We were saved, praise be to Allah!

But before going further she turned round to face us again. Why, I never understood. Before turning round to enter the house she must have caught a glimpse of our blessed deceased grandfather Al-Marhoum squatting on the donkey cart in a gilt frame, all dressed up in his ceremonial uniform, with the medals dangling on his breast. We heard her shriek. 'O my God, what a disaster.' Here was her father risen from the tomb sitting on a cart.

The disaster was later to become a scandal that spread from the house of Al-Marhoum in Zeitoun Road to the house of the grand sheikh near the Citadel, on to the tall building in Al-Daher Street to Menouf and Kafr Tahla, before it spread to the whole universe.

Al-Marhoum went back (with all the pictures) to the store-room in the back garden. The donkey went off at full speed taking its owner with it, and the owner of course went off with the money since he had had no time to return what he had been paid in advance. Tante Fahima hired a carpenter, and the door of the store-room was provided with a lock that even the jinnis could not have opened.

My brother puzzled for a long time over an explanation for the sudden appearance of Tante Fahima. To him it appeared even more complicated than the theorem of Pythagorus. If only Tante Fahima had arrived one minute later. If only the donkey had started to move one minute earlier, just one minute before Tante Fahima arrived on the scene!

But my brother Tala'at was an obstinate person. He disliked failing in his adventures much more than he disliked failing in his exams. One day, I entered his room to find the pictures, the very faces which I had carried out on my back from the rear store-room, hanging on the walls. Right in the middle hung my grandfather Al-Marhoum in the gilt frame, wearing his ceremonial uniform with the medals dangling down on his chest. How he managed to get hold of the pictures I was never able to find out.

23

Mad Aunts and
Abandoned Babies

During the year 1945 something occurred in Al-Saneya school which turned our whole world upside down. One of the female cleaners, a woman named Dada Um Ali, entered the latrines. A few moments later we heard a scream coming from behind the door, and after a few more moments she came out carrying a baby in her arms.

The headmistress imposed a state of emergency, closed all the doors and forbade any one to leave. I did not understand what it was that had happened. Was it that Dada Um Ali had given birth to her child in the toilets? But my school-mate So'ad whispered a word I had not heard before into my ears: 'Bastard.'

The headmistress resembled Tante Fahima and Nabaweya Moussa. She kept staring suspiciously at the girls with her bulging eyes, wore glass spectacles, struck the ground with her heels when she walked. Her prominent nose seen from the side twitched nervously all the time, and was always up in the air since she belonged to an aristocratic line, was the descendant of princes and pashas who belonged to the dynasty of Muhammad Ali.

Every single girl in the school was now under suspicion of an illegitimate pregnancy even though the headmistress was not able to prove any of them guilty of this crime. The word *sefah* (illegitimate) echoed in my ears, but when I heard it I though it was *saffah* (killer). Tante Hanem had once spoken to me about the killer who roamed around in the locality of Sakakini, near her house in Al-Daher Street, and carried a knife with which he butchered his victims. The plural of *sekin* (knife) was *sakakin* and so I never went near the locality of Sakakini because I thought that only those who carried knives, or were killers, lived there. 'But you're really a simpleton, Nawal' said Tante Hanem. They named the locality after a man called Sakakini Pasha. 'Was that his name because he made his fortune from selling knives?' I asked.

It was So'ad who enlightened me on the difference between *sefah* and *saffah*. *Sefah* had a special sign under the *S* that could only be followed by the sound *e*, and it meant a child born without a father. A child born without a father? That sounded to me like our Lord Jesus, peace be with him. 'Were there other people like him?' I asked, so So'ad went on explaining things to me while the supervisors walked up and down the lines, their eyes roaming over our faces like searchlights trying to discover some criminal sign. I wondered if an illegitimate pregnancy would show on a school-girl's face, or in the print of her hand.

Despite these efforts, not one of the girls was found to be guilty, so as a result all of them remained under suspicion, remained guilty, and our school became a school of bad repute.

'What school do you go to, Nawal?' I would be asked.

'To Al-Saneya school, auntie.'

'My God. Is that the school in which they found I don't know what in the toilets?'

The women of the house of my grandfather Al-Marhoum were seized with violent shudders and gasped 'O my God' in chorus. They kept repeating the same question: 'What school do you go to?' 'Al-Saneya school, auntie.' 'O, what a disaster', they gasped. But in their eyes I could detect nothing that expressed their feeling that it was a disaster. What seemed to be there looked more like a secret feeling of delight. I wondered if at night they dreamt of being impregnated with a bastard.

Boys from other schools began to walk behind us chanting: 'Girls of Al-Saneya, the way you walk on the earth pleases the eye.'*

Sometimes one of the boys would pick up a stone and throw it at us, or hit one of the girls on her breast with his bag, or get into the tramcar behind her and follow her home, muttering words to her in a low coarse voice, words which were even uglier than his voice.

One day a boy hit me on the breast with his elbow as I stood waiting for the tramcar. I lifted my bag full of books high up in the air and brought it down on his head. He staggered off onto the tram lines and was almost run over, but his friends dragged him up quickly out of the way. Not one of them dared to come anywhere near me. They stood at a distance, throwing hesitant glances in my direction. When one of them finally started to step towards me they called out to him, 'Look out for your head, son. She belongs to the Tarzan family!'

Uncle Yehia used to stand on the verandah and tease the girls passing by, and Uncle Mamdouh often joined him in this pastime, but Uncle Zakareya was well behaved. Tante Fahima had adopted the role of a father and kept warning him against following his brother Yehia, and his cousin Mamdouh. 'They are vagabonds', she repeatedly said to him 'and you must not follow after them.'

Tante Ni'mat, who was the eldest of the sisters, tended to mother the boys and spoil them, and so quarrels kept breaking out between her and Tante Fahima. She nicknamed Uncle Yehia endearingly, Touha, and Uncle Zakareya, Zika. I found it was probably her way of holding on to old-fashioned family traditions. The name Touha was suggestive of a child with smooth, soft cheeks which was not at all like uncle Yehia, who was short,

---

* Taken from a popular song which says, 'Girls of Alexandria, the way you walk on the sea shore pleases the eye.'

and thin, had a slight hunchback, a big head with a bulging forehead and frizzy hair which he greased with brilliantine and parted on one side. On his head he often wore a bright red fez, tilted to one side like his father. Behind his glass spectacles his eyes looked watery as though always bathed in tears, but he laughed all the time at jokes which no-one else laughed at. The black of his eyes was expressionless, dull, tinted with a shade of blue that reminded one of the blue which covered the glass window-panes during the war. His eyebrows were thick, arched upwards, expressing a wonder he did not feel, and his nose, thin and pointed, looked down on everything, a sign of the aristocratic blood which ran through his veins. He had big flaring nostrils which trembled all the time, and the hairs which jutted out of them had something inhuman about them. His lips were thin, and he was always moistening them with the tip of his tongue, swallowing his saliva noisily, or sucking his tongue and lips. When he laughed, his gums showed red; his teeth were pointed, serrated like a saw, stained yellow with nicotine. He wore narrow suits and waistcoats buttoned tight around his chest, smoked one cigarette after the other, holding them between his smoke-stained fingers, tapping them violently against the arm of his chair before he lit them, and his slender fingers exhibited a nervous tremor all the time.

He had not completed his schooling and worked as an employee in the railways, mending station clocks, had reached manhood but remained a perpetual child, seemingly cultured and yet, in fact, ignorant. An upper-class person who had fallen low in life, he always smelt of tobacco and female perfume. My father considered him an effeminate, spoilt youth, the product of an upper class which was quickly collapsing and destined to disappear.

One day I returned home from school to find Tante Fahima slapping her cheeks with both hands and shrieking, 'O my God, what a disaster, what a black disaster.'

The servant-girl Shalabeya was curled up on the floor sobbing. I thought somebody had died and went into Tante Ni'mat's room wondering if I would see her corpse stretched out on the bed. Instead I found her standing in front of the mirror wearing her black silk dress. She had tied her hair tightly with a big clasp, studded with shining stones, and forced her feet into a pair of shining black shoes with thin high heels. I watched her open the chest of drawers (*chiffonière*) and put on her bracelets, and small wristwatch with the tiny stones given to her as engagement presents by Muhammad Effendi Al-Shami. Then she sat down at the dressing table (*toilette*), powdered her face, put black *kohl* on her eyelashes, plunging the long black rod into the bottle of *kohl* and then drawing it between her eyelids. After that she painted her thin lips with lipstick, drew her upper lip over her lower lip, and pouted in the mirror, only to discover that I was standing there in the door to her bed-room, looking at her belly which was slightly raised under her silk dress, and thinking to myself that inside it she might be carrying an illegitimate child.

'Why are you staring at me like that, Warwar, you slave girl?' she exclaimed.

'What's the terrible disaster that has befallen us, Tante Ni'mat?' I asked, ignoring her question.

'That girl Shalabeya who needs to have her neck twisted has been flirting with the laundry boy. I'm going to go out now to drag him here by the back of his neck together with the *ma'azoun** and have them married off at once.'

The servant-girl Shalabeya looked younger than me, so how could she be carrying a child in her belly? Tante Ni'mat called her the 'dwarf', for her age could not be less than fifteen years. She was as thin as a stick, had no breasts, or buttocks, and was just skin and bone. She slept on a sofa in the maidservant's room and at night Tante Fahima locked the door on her, so how could she become pregnant?

---

* The sheikh or religious functionary who presides over the signing of the marriage contract. According to Islamic law (*shari'a*), there is no civil marriage in Egypt.

Tante Ni'mat said the culprit must be the laundry-boy, or the young grocer-boy who worked next door, or maybe one of the youths who went round in the neighbourhood buying old, discarded articles, or the boy who collected refuse, one of those people whom she described as 'the offspring of menials, lacking faith, or a conscience, or morals'. But Tante Fahima did not think it was one of the boys who belonged to these menial classes. Their kind would not have the effontery to violate the servant-girl of Al-Oustaza Fahima Shoukry. Every single person in Zeitoun Road was very careful in his or her dealing with Al-Oustaza. And to disrespect the servant-girl was a mark of disrespect for her employer. Tante Fahima firmly believed that it was one of those vagabond boys, Yehia Bey Shoukry or his brother Zakareya.

The features of Shalabeya resembled those of Zaynab, the daughter of my paternal aunt Baheya. She wore a wide, loose dress which could hide any rise in her belly, and squatted there on the floor, curled up on herself, pulling at the hem of her *gallabeya* to cover her knees, while Tante Ni'mat stood over her, giving her stinging hits with the cane stick over her body.

'Own up girl. Is it the laundry boy, or the dustman?'

'I swear by God I don't know, *ya sitti*.'

'You dare to lie and swear by God. May Allah burn you in hellfire.'

'Have mercy on me, *ya sitti*. I'm ready to kiss your feet.'

My aunt Ni'mat did not soften to her calls for mercy. Instead she became even more cruel, started to land more blows on her with the cane, beating whatever part of her body came within her reach. Shalabeya curled up on herself like a porcupine, shielding her head with her fleshless arms as thin as the stalks of bulrushes. But the cane kept landing on them with a sound like cane hitting against cane. Then I heard something snap and wondered whether it was the cane or her arm.

Tante Ni'mat was short and fat, and I was much taller than she was, and much stronger. I had hit the boy on the tram station with the full weight of my bag, and my arms had strong muscles, for in the morning I did exercises in the back garden on horizontal bars which Uncle Zakareya had installed, and on which he did all sorts of twists and turns. In addition, I competed with my uncle in carrying weights, and as a result my body grew stronger every day and my step lighter as though I had developed some new force which held me up, so that my feet no longer touched the ground when I walked, and I began to wonder whether the stronger the body is, the lighter it becomes, and the more gentle the spirit that it carries.

That sound of something snapping resounded in my ears. Was it the cane, or was it her arm? I reached out, snatched the cane from Tante Ni'mat, held it with both hands, closed my eyes tight, and prepared to hit with all my might. But when I opened my eyes I was still holding the cane in both my hands, still hesitating to bring it down on Tante Ni'mat.

That day I did not hit her despite all her cruelty. I was sorry for her. She was my mother's sister and a blood relationship bound us together. So I took the stick away from her, threw it into the garden and that was that.

Shalabeya's problem, however, remained unsolved. There was no-one from among the class of servants to marry her, for each one of them already had at least one wife. All Tante Ni'mat's efforts with them failed, just as she failed in everything else in her life. And from then on it became Shalabeya who was responsible for all her failures, Shalabeya alone. Shalabeya became the real cause of all the disasters that had befallen her, starting with her divorce, and ending with the cancer growth in the throat of Al-Marhouma, my grandmother.

When I was alone at night I remembered Shalabeya, and wept over her. She was a child, only fourteen years old, like me, a child who had become a victim, been made a scapegoat, transformed into the sacrificial lamb to be butchered in place of the Bey. There was nothing to prove his guilt. He had received some education, the knowledge necessary to commit his crime without leaving any fingerprints behind, and who, in any case, was going to look for his fingerprints? But the girl, the girl knew no-one in Cairo. Her parents were living in upper Egypt, and there a girl with a bastard child in her belly must be punished by death without question.

So the one that committed the crime went unpunished, free. It was the cruelty of our world, the cruelty of abandoned, frustrated women, like Tante Ni'mat and others like her. It was the cruelty that had grown in them through suppression, the steam held back under pressure until their bodies were filled with it to bursting point. It was a black cruelty under a smooth skin from which the hair had been ripped off to leave it with the smoothness of a snake. It was the cane stick held like a whip by soft fingers tapering into nails like claws. It was the short squat body full of flesh, and anger, and frustration, and sorrow, the body that quivers with every quiver of the girl servant being beaten, for the beater and the beaten, the punisher and the punished are only separated by the stick which links them.

Tante Ni'mat was beating herself into exhaustion until she collapsed with fatigue on the arm-chair, exhaling the air from her lungs, panting, choking, sobbing, the tears flowing from her eyes, the sweat pouring from her body, as though she was emptying it of the black stagnant water lying in her depth, its colour like that at the bottom of a cesspool.

Tante Fahima did not hit Shalabeya. She let out her energy elsewhere by going out of the house to school, and hitting the girls with the edge of a ruler, by passing down the lines of girls standing in the morning assembly, and landing her ruler on the tips of their outstretched fingers one after the other, just like Miss Hamer, and Nabaweya Moussa, just like the headmistress of Al-Saneya Girls' School, and all the other headmistresses who return at the end of each day drained of their energy.

My mother did not beat the servant-girl Sa'adeya as cruelly as Tante Ni'mat beat Shalabeya. She let out her energy beating the Persian carpet with a cane carpet-beater, or shredding the *mulukheya* with a special curved knife with a handle at each end, or mincing the meat in the mincer. She had nine children and their father to feed every day, the hand of her husband to caress her in the night, his body to warm her when it was cold and dark.

Tante Ni'mat lived and died without ever being pregnant, without giving birth to a child, or having someone to care for her. All she ever possessed in her life was the furniture and equipment brought for her wedding day – the gilt drawing-room chairs, the yellow brass bed, the big cupboard, the chest of drawers, the dining-room table and the *buffet*, the glass cupboard for the china and the crockery, and the silver, the bed tables, the dressing-table – that is, the same items of furniture that my mother also had.

Tante Ni'mat was never given a share in her father's pension after he died. The law deprived divorced women of their share. After she was divorced she received an alimony which lasted for one year, and after that she was left without any source of income, and so she got into the habit of dropping in at the houses of her relatives at mealtimes.

My paternal aunt Rokaya, who lived in the village, was in the same situation as Tante Ni'mat, and the poverty around her was harsher than it was in the city, but people's hearts in the city are harder than in the village, and so my aunt Rokaya lived and died under better circumstances than Tante Ni'mat.

Tante Fahima received a part of her father's pension and added it to her salary from the school. She therefore belonged to a higher category than that of Tante Ni'mat, and tended to look down on her. She did not want to lose her share of the pension so she refused to marry, since a married daughter, like a divorced daughter, is deprived by law of her share of the father's pension. She arranged to have what is called a marriage of custom, in which the marriage contract is not registered officially but is considered valid according to religious law. Thus she was able to preserve her share of the pension until the day she died.

Nevertheless, a marriage of custom is not looked upon with respect, although in religion it is legal! Only official marriages are considered fully respectable.

The image of Shalabeya carrying her clothes wrapped in a calico bundle and walking behind Tante Fahima has remained engraved in my memory. I wondered where she was taking her? Was she rescuing her from the hands of Tante Ni'mat, or trying to save the family reputation?

I never found out what happened to Shalabeya. Did Tante Fahima send her home to her family where the fate that awaited her was death at the hands of her father? Was she wandering in the streets begging for food, or selling her body in the prostitution market if it had somehow been able to put on some flesh? I never found out what happened to the child she carried in her belly. The law does not permit that children be named after their mothers, nor does Islam allow adoption, for there is a verse in the Qur'an which says, 'Bestow upon them the descent which is that of their fathers.' If the father of a child cannot be identified the child is considered illegitimate, and is punished for its father's sin. It becomes one more innocent victim to be sacrificed like the lamb which people sacrifice in the big Eid.

How could Tante Fahima have had the heart to chase Shalabeya out of the house? For Tante Ni'mat this was something much more cruel than beating her with a stick. Deep down inside her she nurtured a suppressed motherhood, a tenderness concealed at the bottom of her heart. I used to see her looking at Shalabeya almost on the verge of tears, see her swallow them before anyone noticed, but sometimes a tear would drop down and she would quickly wipe it away with her silk handkerchief.

Tante Ni'mat was ashamed to be seen crying. She might slap her cheeks with her hands as a sign of lamentation, but tears had to be held back. This was a characteristic of families who considered themselves of upper-class descent. My peasant aunts wept, unashamed of exhibiting their tears, or they were happy and yoo-yood loudly without restraint. When we arrived they welcomed us with a torrent of kisses and embraces, and when we left their tears flowed freely. At funerals they let out shrieks like yoo-yoos and they gathered together in the fields, or in the houses, or in the market to console one another whenever there was some disaster, or a cause for sadness. Each house was huddled up against the other, its women looked out at the women next door, neighbours gathered on the threshold or in front of the houses and every time a woman passed by through the lane she sat down among the other women. A woman was never lonely, there was no solitude, no hunger, for she just had to stretch out her hand and take a cob of maize from the field.

But Tante Ni'mat lived all alone in the big house surrounded by a large garden and an iron fence. The windows of the neighbours were at a distance. She could not sit on the threshold like Sittil Hajja, or my aunt Rokaya. She could not reach out in a bakery and just pick up a loaf of bread, or stretch out her hand in a field to take a cob of maize.

Tante Fahima, like Tante Ni'mat, slapped her cheeks in lamentation, but suppressed her tears. Yet I would wake up to the shudders of her body in the bed, to her voice emerging from between clenched grinding teeth, to words spoken while her eyes remained closed 'I beg forgiveness from God almighty for all almighty sins.' Suddenly I would cease to hear her voice, or even her breathing. Had she died, I wondered? But then she would let out a sentence in a prolonged harsh sigh: 'I seek refuge in thee Allah from the evil Satan', and her body would jerk up just once like a slaughtered chicken, after which she became quiet, her breathing once more deep and regular, accompanied by a gentle snore from time to time.

It seemed to me that she was having nightmares in her sleep. Maybe the phantom of Shalabeya visited her at night, the phantom of a child curled up on the floor with her bundle of clothes beside her, and the sound of her weeping piercing her ears like the whistle of the train to which she was leading her, as she held her little hand in a tight grasp, forced her to climb up the steps into the carriage, pushed her with her fist in her back, followed her up into the train, seated her on the wooden bench of a third-class compartment with the bundle of clothes tied by a string around its neck placed beside her.

I was not with Tante Fahima that day but I imagined her standing on the railway platform with Shalabeya sitting on the bench near the window, her thin hand on the window-sill, the other on her bundle, her face pale without a drop of blood, her eyes with the tears of the whole world in them.

Tante Fahima avoids looking at her. Her eyes are fixed on something else, the sky, or a telegraph pole. Then suddenly the train jerks, starts to move and the platform with Tante Fahima standing on it retreats, and a moment later Tante Fahima seems to be walking backwards, and Shalabeya's face seems as though it's now at the back of her head, so Tante Fahima raises her hand to her eyes to make sure they are in the right place, and it knocks off her spectacles, and they fall on the ground and their glass breaks into small pieces that fly in the air like drops of rain. Without glasses she is unable to see, cannot discern things, so how is she going to get back home?

Tante Fahima came back from the railway station without Shalabeya. She spoke to no-one, and no-one addressed a single word to her, and later whenever someone asked her a question about what she had done to Shalabeya she burst out savagely like her cat. But soon things returned to normal and no-one mentioned Shalabeya again. An ageing servant, about seventy years old, now served in the house. Tante Fahima became her old self again, but she kept having nightmares in her sleep. I used to wake up in the middle of the night to her body shaking in the bed, to her voice as she spoke to herself in choking, hoarse tones, to subdued sounds like sobs that were being suppressed. Her eyes would be wide open and bulging, as though they were lost in something terrible, and her hand would creep under the pillow searching for her Qur'an or for her ring of keys, then she would close her eyes and sink into a deep sleep.

She insisted on closing the door on the ageing servant as though she feared that he too would have an illegitimate pregnancy, and Tante Ni'mat made fun of her. But she was no longer secure about anything, even herself. She locked the door on us at night, kept reading the verse of Yasseen in the Qur'an to chase away evil spirits and jinnis. 'I take refuge in Allah against evil Satan' she kept muttering, and her voice now resembled that of Sittil Hajja or my aunt Rokaya. Her features also changed and began to resemble those of Tante Ni'mat, as though drained of all their strength and vitality, and resigned to an inevitable fate. But in the morning she underwent a transformation, put on the face of the arrogant headmistress together with her smart woollen skirt and jacket, and her solid leather shoes, sat at the dressing table to press red lipstick over her lips, threw back her head and laughed loudly.

This woman who has heard Shalabeya sobbing as she pushed her by force into the train, could she be the same woman that I now saw laughing as she painted her lips red with lipstick?

I was fourteen years old when I used to sleep in the same bed with her. I felt afraid of her, was scared when her hand moved over to cover me, and trembled with fear. Would her hand continue to move up until it reached my neck? Would she push me off the bed with her fist in my back?

24

The House of Desolation

I spent a whole year in this house where reigned only sadness and desolation. The nights were long, and seemed peopled with spirits and devils: the spirits of my grandfather and of my dead grandmother, and other spirits too. But the spirits of the dead did not frighten me as much as those of the living. Could Uncle Yehia's body shrink enough to let him slip under the closed door into my room?

Tante Fahima hated Uncle Yehia. She said he was stupid, had failed to finish school and had become just a 'repairer of clocks'. In my dreams the black cat changed into an evil spirit but Uncle Yehia seemed even more stupid than the black cat. He tiptoed into the room passing underneath the bottom of the closed door, crept up to the pillow on which rested Tante Fahima's head, slipped his hand under it and took the key of the door. In the dream I say to myself, 'How stupid. Why did he take the key if he can manage to get in without it?'

I never told my dreams to Tante Fahima. She would not stand my talking to her about nonsense like that. All she expected me to talk about was school, and my lessons. But Tante Ni'mat adored nonsense, adored these silly stories. They whiled away her empty hours. For her there was no better way of killing time. Her whole life was made up of empty time which she filled by talking about anything and nothing. She squatted on a carpet placed in the sunshine, with a cushion under her. At her side she placed a tray on which there was a small methylated-spirits wick burner which she lighted under a small pot of Turkish coffee. When it was ready she poured it out and started to take one slow sip after the other from the small painted coffee cup, all the while sucking in what remained on her lips, and telling stories which went back as far as the day she was born. When she had finished with the various stages of the past, she went on to the future, turned the coffee cup upside down on the saucer to empty it of its remaining contents, lifted it close up to her eyes and began to read what she could see of her future in the form of black twisted lines made by the coffee dregs.

Once she was over with the future, she went back to remembering the past, to the story of her bridegroom, Muhammad Al-Shami, and their wedding night, pouting her lips to say 'Nothing, nothing at all happened on that night', then to her recollections of her father Al-Marhoum. She would ask God to forgive him his sins, especially the biggest sin of all, that of having taken her out of school at a young age to marry her off, heave a deep sigh and say, 'May God forgive him and soften the stone that lies under his head.'

Tante Ni'mat was closer to me than Tante Fahima. Out of her escaped moments of tenderness. At night, when I remembered the sadness in her voice, tears sprang to my eyes. The big house was full of sadness, a sadness which transferred itself to me like a contagion, and which I breathed in with the air respired by its inmates.

I used to see my uncle Yehia sitting in the hall, gazing at nothing, or staring at the room of his dead father, or his dead mother, smoking cigarette after cigarette until his teeth and his fingers were all yellow. Despite his habit of bursting into laughter frequently, he seemed to carry a heavy weight of sadness on his back, a sadness which had made him develop a hump, like a camel. He would walk down the railway platform, his back all hunched over, hurrying on bandy legs hidden in his baggy trousers, climb up a long thin ladder to the big clock hanging in the station, move its motionless hands, and wink at the girls standing below through the corner of one eye. He was the man who restored movement to time.

But the sadness in this house later became a source of inspiration, awakened within me a sensitivity to art, made me write. The servant-girl Shalabeya is perhaps the heroine of my novel, *The Circling Song*. My uncle Yehia could be the old man in my short story 'She is not Virgin'. My aunt Rokaya might be the woman Zakeya in my novel, *God Dies by the Nile*. Maybe Tante Fahima is the school superintendent or the headmistress, and Tante Ni'mat one of those frustrated women who are often to be found in some of my works.

The day came when I moved out of the big, sad desolate house on Zeitoun Road and become a boarder at the Helwan Secondary School for Girls. The years passed, but I never went back to visit that house. I like to recall old memories, to bring back past images, to remember places. This house was an exception. I never went back, perhaps because sadness can burn out one's heart and destroy one's memory. When I used to ask my mother why she married, she would answer with one unchanging sentence: 'To get away from the house of your grandfather Shoukry.'

This was the house of sadness where eyes turned to the colour of grey ash, where death snatched one after the other from life, where tears accumulated in a cyst somewhere in the throat, or inside the chest, where my uncle Zakareya died a young man without children, without a son or a daughter, without leaving anything behind, where uncle Yehia died without anybody ever remembering him, where Tante Fahima lived buried in sadness with a husband who kept threatening her with divorce until the day she lay on her deathbed, where Tante Hanem passed away only to discover at the last moment that she could not take her property with her.

Was it my grandfather who caused the unhappiness which filled this house? Was it the army discipline he imposed on it? Patriarchal authority destroying those who are closest to us? The feudal class collapsing at the end of the Second World War? The patriarchal class system which rules over our world to this day? Was it a poison which runs in the blood, ran in my veins, in my arteries, a poison I used to breathe in with the air when I lived surrounded by the sadness and desolation of that house.

The last one of this family I saw was Tante Ni'mat. It was during the winter of 1959. I was in my clinic located in Giza Square. The telephone rang. A voice came to me over the wires.

'How are you, Dr Nawal' said the voice.

'Who is it?' I asked.

'Don't you remember me, Warwar the slave girl?'

'Tante Ni'mat! How are you Tante Ni'mat? Are you alright?'

'Thanks be to Him whom alone we can thank for whatever befalls us.'

'O my. So you still remember that, Tante Ni'mat.'

'I've no-one else to hold on to.'

'Whom are you talking about Tante Ni'mat?'

'Who else can it be besides God?'

'You sound rather tired, auntie.'

'I am tired, doctor, very tired.'

Her voice was weak, full of that old ring of sadness, and I was hearing the hoarse breathing of a chest full of death.

She gave me her address in the district of Helmeyat Al-Zeitoun. She was living in her brother's flat, together with him and his wife and children. I entered the gloomy room they had given her next to the toilet, remembered the room in my uncle's house in Anbari. There was a twenty-watt bulb hanging from the ceiling covered in black smoke. Her wedding furniture, or part of it, was piled up just anyhow looking like a funeral pyre.

In the middle was the yellow brass bed. She was lying between its bars as though crucified, her face white as the bed sheets, her eyes ash grey like the eyes of my dead grandmother, Amna. She opened her dry lips and said:

'Thank you for coming. There was always a lot of good in you, Dr Nawal.'

'I'm Warwar the slave girl, Tante Ni'mat.'

I heard her laugh, saw her eyes fight the darkness, saw her strain to open them, and let through the remains of an old light which had gone out years ago.

She pointed to her left breast. I rested my hand on the swelling, and my body went rigid. 'It's that illness, isn't it Dr Nawal? I knew I had to die this way like my mother, and like your late mother too.'

I walked out of her room. My hand felt its way to my breast. Perhaps I, too, had a malignant swelling in my left breast right over the heart. Perhaps I, too, would die within the three months I gave Tante Ni'mat to live.

I caught the train from Zeitoun station, remembered that fourteen years ago I used to take the train from the same station. Now it looked gloomy, the stairs and the walls were almost in ruins. The railway platform which in those days had seemed infinitely long had now grown so short that I walked down it from the beginning to the end in less than half a minute. I used to run along this platform panting, trying to catch the train before it left. Often I would miss it. In winter I shivered with cold, in summer poured with sweat. At times I jumped into the train before it had started moving. It was so crowded that the boys used to stand on the steps, or ride on the roof to avoid the crowding, or escape paying the price of a ticket, but sometimes the ticket collector used to climb up to them on the roof of the train, and then they would jump off on to the ground before he caught them.

One day one of the school-boys fell on to the railway line and the train ran over both his legs. I saw him bleeding on the platform of Saray Al-Koubba station. The picture of King Farouk looked down on him, on his body cut in two lying in a pool of red blood creeping slowly over the platform which shone white like marble. A shoe had flown off the foot of his amputated leg, the other remained on the foot of the other dying leg. He could not feel anything, did not realize that he had lost his legs, smiled innocently at the people around him and asked in a childish voice, 'Where is my other shoe?'

All he could think of, all he was worrying about was his shoe. Like me, he was in his second year in secondary school. Like me he had come from his village to go to school, and had been left by his parents to live in the huge city with relatives. My cousin Zaynab was fond of saying, *al arrayib, zarayib.* * Maybe like me he had a paternal or a maternal aunt who used to lay her hands on the piastres his father sent him, so he had no money to buy a train ticket, maybe he was dreaming of going to the university, of becoming a well-known scholar like Taha Hussayn.

In my sleep. I saw myself lying between the rails of the Zeitoun train or of the Sayeda Zaynab tramcar. People lifted my legless trunk and laid it on a marble platform while I searched vainly for my shoe, got up and walked barefoot, then hobbled on a pair of crutches. The face of Hamida Shakankiri appeared at some distance and I watched her walking towards me on a pair of crutches. When she came near I woke up, panic-stricken, bathed in sweat.

The Zeitoun train was known for the terrible accidents which happened all the time. I do not know why but perhaps it was because it started in the very poor suburb of Matareya or of Ain Shams, ending in Koubri Al-Lemoun or Bab Al-Hadeed stations. School-boys and -girls lived in these two suburbs with their families or with relatives who had emigrated from the countryside. Often they were just lone emigrants looking for a job, or for a chance to go to school or the university. The huge city swallowed

---

* Meaning that relatives are stables full of shit.

them up like an enormous drain sucking in cockroaches. A train or a tramcar could cut off one or two legs, so that they turned sometimes into pick-pockets, or hawkers jumping with a remaining leg on the step of a tramcar to sell razor-blades, or combs, or boxes of matches, then jumping off the other side after they had stolen someone's wallet or purse, or the sandwich that a girl was munching in the woman's compartment.

In those days there were special compartments for women on trains and in tramcars. I preferred sitting in them, rather than being crowded in amongst the men, for their eyes would gaze at my breasts, or a hard finger would be dug into my flesh, or sometimes it could be that other thing they had between their thighs, becoming erect and pushing itself into some part of my body, or between my buttocks as I stood crucified between them, my hand or both hands holding on to the bar which hung from the ceiling of the tramcar, or the bus, or the train.

Sometimes I would turn round suddenly and slap one of them in the face. From where I got the courage to do this, I do not know. I was a young girl of thirteen or fourteen, almost a child, but the anger of a child is the most powerful, the most pure, the most true of all angers. It accumulates in the body, multiplies over time, but it is like God, in that it gives birth only to itself.

I do not know how the child in me remained alive. Somehow it has escaped death. Maybe it taught itself to face death from the moment it was born and right from the start learnt not to fear it. Maybe it has built up what in our medical studies we call immunity. The body needs to be injected with germs all the time if it is to develop immunity. 'Cure me with that which is the cause of my disease.' Perhaps the saying I heard from my grandfather has some truth in it. Perhaps we need doses of death to develop immunity against it.

When I was in the second year of secondary school I was taught in a class on algebra that the negation of the negation gives us something positive, that if we add a negative sign to a negative sign it gives us a positive sign. It was the first lesson we were given in algebra and geometry which together with arithmetic we called *riyada*. But *riyada* also meant 'exercise', in the sense of sports or gymnastics, so at first I thought that sports was what they were referring to.

I learnt to enjoy the mental exercises involved in this *riyada*, and experienced great pleasure in solving different problems in algebra. The more difficult the problem, the greater was the pleasure I experienced. Sometimes a problem would appear to me insoluble, with one difficulty coming on top of another, like a series of complicated knots. The page would be covered in brackets, and cubes, and squares, in triangles and hexagonals, so that the formula looked like a huge structure, like a pyramid rising higher and higher, and then suddenly in the middle of my confusion, in the middle of the puzzle, like a mesh out of which I could not extricate myself, and just as I was negating a negation to reach a positive proof, the whole huge structure would suddenly collapse, the knot would be undone, the problem solved and the difficult formula ended by giving me a zero. My mind kept making leaps as though I was Pythagorus in person. Logarithms became my game. I would open my exercise book in the train, or in the tramcar, and amuse myself with solving problems, almost shrieking with pleasure.

At the end of the year, after the final examinations were over, I travelled back to Menouf for the summer vacations. My certificate said that I had passed with distinction, and was accompanied by a letter from the headmistress of Al-Saneya school to the trustee of the pupil Nawal El-Sayed El-Saadawi which read as follows: 'The pupil has been awarded top marks in algebra and geometry and thus is eligible for admission to the course line on mathematics and can be given a scholarship, and a monthly stipend. After she passes her secondary school certificate this can qualify her for admission into the teachers' institute to become a teacher of mathematics in secondary schools for girls, subject to the rules and regulations of the law which govern such matters.'

There was no boarding house in Al-Saneya School for Girls. I could not bring myself to go back to my grandfather's house and continue to be fed on sorrow. In addition, I disliked teachers profoundly, especially Tante Fahima and Nabaweya Moussa and other teachers and headmistresses of their kind. I also knew nothing about what was meant by the rules and regulations of the law. My father explained to me that the Ministry of Education needed teachers in mathematics, but that graduates from the Teachers' Institute had to continue teaching for a minimum period of four years, during which they were not allowed to marry. If the graduate at any time broke any of these rules she was required to refund the Ministry of Education for whatever had been spent on her education in the institute, as well as the stipend she had been paid during the years she had spent in it.

My father was hesitant about what it was best for me to do, but I very quickly took the decision to refuse, since I was not prepared to accept any conditions for the scholarship. They appeared to me as a form of servitude, as though the Ministry of Education were purchasing me at a price which was the expenses of my education and then calling that a scholarship. If they thought I was an exceptional student then a free education should be my right, with no strings attached.

When I explained my decision father stood up and shook my hands warmly. 'Bravo', he said, 'you have shown that you are really a daughter of mine.' It sounded to me as though he was saying that prior to that moment he had not considered me worthy to be his daughter, or that I was able to do whatever I did only because I was a daughter of his!

When he stood up and shook hands with me his grasp around my hand was firm and strong, yet at the same time gentle and loving. I felt that he had a strength which springs from gentleness and love, for he was a very gentle father. His black eyes shone with a tear ready to drop but he swallowed it quickly. I wondered: was my father at last feeling happy with my achievements?

My brother Tala'at failed again that year, but my father was no longer terribly sad at his failure. He just closed his eyes and his thoughts seemed to wander for some time. Was I beginning to have a place in his dreams? Was he seeing in me a famous teacher? An eminent professor? A skilled doctor? Were my achievements becoming a compensation for my brother's failures? Were his dreams shifting from the boy to the girl?

25

The Secret Communist

The year 1945 led me to a new stage of life: the stage we call adolescence. I was fourteen years old, my height was growing rapidly, and my dreams were multiplying. They were wild, reaching out to a sky without limits. The only difference between them and madness was that they were born of a desire to change things in the world, they had a reason.

At night I dreamt of myself riding a white horse like Joan of Arc, my eyes like the eyes of Zarq'a Al-Yamama* able to see what remained concealed from others, my lips reciting line after line of poetry as though I was Al-Khansa'a.†

I no longer wasted my energy fighting the battles I used to fight in the family. My father and mother took over this task. A suitor presented himself, sent by Tante Fahima. He carried a degree from the School of Law, the school from which graduated cabinet ministers and important personalities of state. Tante Fahima twisted her neck backwards like a turkey cock when she

---

* An Arab woman who lived in the Hejaz before Islam. Member of a warring tribe, she had such strong eyesight that she could spot the enemy before anyone else and was used as a scout by her tribe.
† A famous Arab woman poet who lived in Hejaz during the period immediately before Islam.

pronounced the word 'licence' (degree). He was a husband any girl would wish for, be she the king's daughter. Was there any escape from him, this man with a nose like a beak, who spoke as if the words were dropping out of it?

My father and mother stood by me against Tante Fahima and against the two tribes of Shoukry and Al-Saadawi. Their diligent daughter was capable of obtaining a 'licence' or a *baccalaureat* herself. Her future no longer lay in marriage like the submissive, idle girls waiting at home for a bridegroom to appear.

The image of me wearing a wedding dress had disappeared from the imagination of my parents, to be replaced by that of a tall, slender body enveloped in a lawyer's robe, or a doctor's white coat, or the clothes which eminent professors or writers might wear.

It was an unpheaval in their lives. My brother Tala'at had been their big dream, but his failure in school, time after time, had filled them with frustration. Now their frustration had been transformed into a new hope placed in their daughter. By a twist of fortune I was that daughter. I had to have a brother who was a failure to become an object of interest.

At that time I had reached the third year of secondary schooling and was living as a boarder in Helwan Secondary School for Girls. I slept in a big dormitory, and there were thirty schoolgirls living together in it. We slept in iron beds painted white, very much like in hospitals, and they were laid out in a long row on either side of the dormitory. Near each bed was a small niche in the wall covered by a panel which we could lock. The name of each girl was fixed to the panel with a drawing pin. Our blankets were coloured grey like army blankets, and around the school was a high wall very much like a prison wall. The superintendent used to walk into the dormitory to inspect our dreams as we slept, her bloodshot eyes glistening eerily. She held a pocket searchlight in her hand, and was wont to appear suddenly like the angel of death, only to disappear as suddenly as she came.

Nevertheless I was now liberated from the pressures of the family homes in which I had lived before. The image of the crocodile that was Tante Hanem's husband, or the gloomy room in the district of Al-Anbari, had vanished from my mind. At the beginning, I felt a deep longing for mother and father, for my sisters and my brothers, and at night I cried under the covers. In class I did not know the name of a single girl, and in the dormitory I went to bed without talking to anyone. Everybody here was a stranger to me, but above all it was the place which made me feel estranged.

In the bed on my right there was a girl called Fikreya. She had black eyes and seemed always to be looking at something far away. Her lower lip protruded below the upper one and she was in the habit of turning it over as though she was disdainful of everything. She would squat on her bed, spread a canvas on it and start to draw with colours. When the lights went out she remained seated upright in the bed staring into the darkness.

On the other side was the bed of a girl called Samia. Thin and short, she resembled So'ad, my previous friend in Al-Saneya School. Her complexion was dark and had a strange pallor, and she always kept her lips tightly pressed together. Her seriousness attracted me. I was not fond of girls who liked to play around, painted their lips red and whose mouths were always open, chattering, or gossiping or laughing over something or other.

After classes were over I used to spend my time reading in the library. It was an abandoned room showing signs of neglect and it opened on the school-yard next to the latrines. Its shelves were covered in dust and cobwebs, and the book covers were an ugly black. From the books exuded an odour of mummies or mouse excrement.

I used to search among the books for novels and short stories, whereas Samia chose to read books on history and politics. Fikreya was not fond of reading. She would turn her lower lip over in scorn when she saw a book, and Samia, when she saw the books I read, would glance at them and pout her mouth in disgust. 'Novels. There's nothing in them but nonsense, romantic nonsense.' It was the first time I had heard the word 'romantic'. Samia pronounced it through tightened lips as though it was some kind of an insult, as she held a book on the Crusades in her hands. I in turn disliked books on war, on the campaigns of Salah Al-Dine Al-Ayoubi* or Amr Ibn Al-Aas† and similar things.

The history classes bored me. History in them was nothing but a series of past invasions which we were supposed to learn by heart, beginning with the campaign of Badr‡ and ending with Napoleon's invasion of Egypt.

The history courses did not deal with modern Egypt. We were not told anything about the British invasion of 1882 because the British still occupied Egypt at that time, nor did we read anything that dealt with the corrupt rule of the king and the political parties. The classes we were given hid what was real history, made heroes out of the most corrupt rulers, separated one area from the other so that we could never see the connection, the continuity between them, made parrots out of us, parrots that were expected to repeat what they had memorized from the books given to them.

Fikreya could not bear listening to anything about modern or ancient history. She considered that all rulers were corrupt and all people ruled by them cowardly and submissive. She used to draw King Farouk in the form of a sheep ready to be slaughtered on the occasion of the big Eid and changed Al-Nahas Pasha§ into a cross-eyed clown in the circus. Ahmed Maher Pasha⁋ she portrayed as a sack of cotton riddled with holes.

---

* An Arab leader of Kurdish descent who fought a successful campaign against the Crusades and liberated Jerusalem.
† The Muslim Arab commander who invaded and occupied Egypt in the year 624 AD.
‡ The first battle fought by the Prophet Muhammad and his followers against the tribe of Kuraish that ruled over Mecca and controlled trade in the Arab peninsula.
§ Leader of the Wafdist Party after the death of Saad Zaghloul in 1927.
⁋ The prime minister of Egypt who declared war on the Axis in September 1945 and was assassinated as he was leaving Parliament House.

Like Fikreya, Samia was critical of everything but instead of a paintbrush she used her tongue. In her view Ahmed Pasha Maher deserved the bullets that were lodged in his body. Was he not the one who took the decision to declare war? Nahas Pasha was no more than a clown who vacillated between the king and the British, and the Wafd Party was not anywhere near a people's party, nor was Saad Zagloul the hero of the revolution of 1919. It was the Egyptian people who made the revolution, but the workers and the peasants gained nothing from it, and their martyrs shed their blood for nothing.

'Is your father from the working class, Samia?' I asked her.

'My father is a respected Oustaz', she answered angrily, clenching her teeth as she pronounced the word Oustaz. I realized that she had no respect for workers or for peasants although she never stopped talking about them.

'And what does your father do, Nawal?' she asked in return.

I blew myself up triumphantly like a peacock and replied that my father, just like her father, was a respected Oustaz. Then I started to tell her how my father had been one of the heroes of the 1919 revolution. A piece of metal from a bullet had lodged in his foot, and blood flowed from his wound over the pavement. Samia tightened her lips and asked me: 'What's the name of your father?'

The question seemed strange to me, but then I realized that my father's name had not gone down in history.

'Is your father in the Wafd Party, Nawal?'

'I don't know', I said.

'My God, you don't even know which party your father is in?'

'What about you, what party is your father in?'

She was silent for a long moment, and did not answer my question. The pallor in her face showed more than usual. Then she whispered in my ear: 'My father is in the Communist Party, and that's a secret party.'

It was the first time I had heard of some thing called a secret party. But when she said that I saw her lips open in a smile, or perhaps in what was more like the shadow of a smile. But after that she started to give me a newspaper rolled up in a cylinder, glancing around cautiously as she handed it to me, whispering: 'Read it immediately, and give it back to me, and don't let anyone see you with it.'

I did not like secretiveness and whispering. They were repugnant to me, made me feel suspicious. I thought it was only thieves who hide in the dark, but later I learnt that revolutionaries hide from the police.

The toilets were the only place in school where I could close the door on myself and read the newspaper without anyone seeing. It was called *Al-Gamaheer* (The Masses) and resembled other newspapers but was smaller in size, had fewer pages, was darker in colour. Its lines were black and closely printed, and in some places the letters were eaten away. Sometimes the black ink had spilled over some of the letters or words. The style was more difficult than that of *Al-Akkad*, or my uncle Sheikh Muhammad, or Ibn Al-Mokafa'a.* I was barely able to decipher what was written, or to understand it. I was so frustrated, or perhaps so frightened, that I used to tear it up into little pieces, throw it in the basin of the toilet and pull the flush on it.

Samia continued to thrust this newspaper on me. She would push it with a quick movement into my bag, as though it were a time-bomb. At night after all the girls in the dormitory were fast asleep, I got out of bed on tiptoe, went to the toilets and under the distant light of a street lamp tried to decipher the puzzle of the words huddled up against each other, to follow the meaning of the sentences flowing into one another without full stops or commas.

There were words and expressions which repeated themselves on every page. The workers, the peasants, the toiling classes, the proletariat, the bourgeoisie, the conspirators, the traitors, the class struggle, the ruling classes, the oppressed majority,

---

* An Arab literary figure, and linguist in the Abbassid period.

the minority of opportunists and the thieves who stole the daily bread of the people.

During the summer holidays when I went back to Menouf, Samia sent me the newspaper by post. It came in the form of a cylinder tied round with a piece of string. My father undid the knot with difficulty, wiped off the dust on it, and scanned the headlines printed in thick black ink on the front page, parts of which had come off with the dust.

'Who sends you this newspaper, Nawal?'

'A school-friend of mine called Samia.'

'This is the Communist Party's newspaper.'

'What's the Communist Party, father?'

My father knew nothing about the Communist Party apart from what he read in the government newspapers, or in the publications of the political parties like the Wafd. Communism for them was equivalent to atheism, moral corruption, sowing the seeds of hatred in the hearts of the people, conspiring to overthrow the ruling system by violence, allegiance to external powers in Moscow.

Father supported the Wafdist Party when it opposed the British or took measures in the interests of the majority of the poor. He never sympathized with the Muslim Brothers or their founder and leader Hassan Al-Banna, whom he considered as not differing from Al-Sheikh Al-Maraghi,* since both were men who used religion as a weapon in the political game.

'Politics, Nawal', he would say 'is a game without principles.'

'But you always took part in demonstrations, father.'

'Popular demonstrations are a different thing.'

My father's words engraved themselves in my mind. Politics is a game without principles, the news in the papers is all about war, massacres and party struggles.

I was always more attracted by art and literature. I devoured every novel I could put my hands on in the library. At night after the lights went off I brought out my secret diary and wrote under

---

* Grand Sheikh of Al-Azhar during the reign of King Farouk.

the light of the moon. The previous summer I had started a novel which I called *Memories of a Child called So'ad*. After classes were over I used to sit on a bench in the school-yard under a eucalyptus tree near the tennis court, hugging my pen and my blue notebook.

The winter sun in Helwan was strong and warm. Its rays penetrated into my body and my mind, as my pen covered the pages of my notebook with the novel I was writing, Sixty pages of my handwriting mingled with the tears I was shedding over what was happening to my heroine So'ad, as though So'ad were me.

One day the Arabic teacher gave our class a test. He asked us to write a piece from our imagination, so I gave in the novel which I had written. When he returned it to me the following week he kept examining me with narrowed eyes, before he blurted out, 'Stupid ass. The heavens cannot be described as tyrannical. You need to know your religion better.' He had given me a zero for my piece. On every page he had crossed out something, or made a sign, or a remark in red ink, like 'a sick imagination born of a lack of real faith', or 'strange distorted ideas which should never occur to a girl of your age'.

In my dreams I began to see a zero written in red ink as though it were a condemnation to death. When the sun rose, and I woke up, I would put the zero in front of me and stare at it until I felt a burning pain in the whites of my eyes, and the tears welling up under my lids, then drying like salt water under the heat of the sun.

During the summer holidays, I took my notebook back to Menouf, and hid it between the other ones in my drawer, but it fell into the hands of my mother while she was cleaning out my desk. She read the story and the annotations of the teacher, saw the big round zero in red ink like a hanging noose, came up to where I sat and said: 'The story is beautiful, Nawal. That teacher is an idiot.'

Her words pulled me out of the chasm of self-doubt into which I had fallen, for a teacher in school to us was like a god.

We could never have doubts about him. It was much easier to
doubt ourselves.

Then my father read the story. I sat next to him as he read,
my eyes fixed on the movements of his face, trying to catch the
feelings that might appear on it before he became aware of them
himself, watching the gleam in his eyes grow stronger or fade
away, the frown on his forehead coming and going every now
and then, the smile hovering around his lips, or turning into a
tightening of the muscles of his mouth.

My father, unlike my mother, did not express what he thought
immediately. He was slower by nature, or perhaps his slowness
was intended. Maybe he could read in my face that burning
desire to know which I felt, and decided to continue sitting on
the sofa as silent as the Sphinx. Maybe he enjoyed torturing me
for a while, for now I remembered what he used to do when I
was still a child and the circus came to Menouf, as though he
took pleasure in wasting time at crucial moments of my life, in
waiting, and waiting, and waiting until I had lost all patience
and was ready to explode.

He sat there for what seemed to me an eternity. Then the
Sphinx came out of his silence and I heard him say: 'Bravo,
Nawal, you really have talent!' At these words I could have leapt
in the air, jumped on him and wrapped my arms around him. Yet
despite the wild emotions that took hold of me, I kept my calm,
unable to overcome the norms of behaviour rooted in me. The
words of my father have always lived with me. 'Nawal, you really
have talent!' They swept away the comments of the teacher, his
crossings out, his zero circled in red ink. I was in love with the
letters of the language, with its words. What I could not stand
was the teacher, the rules of grammar and religion. These three
things were capable of killing any budding talent.

No-one ever made me hate religion more than those who
taught it to us. They seemed to take pleasure in picking out
the most difficult verses in Allah's book, the words that curled
up in one's throat like a knot and stopped there, in choosing

meanings that one's reason refused, explanations that made things more confused, in proffering threats of hell-fire, or hopes of a paradise where there was nothing to do except loll on sofas, or sleep, or eat.

On one occasion I asked the teacher if in paradise there would be pens and notebooks for those who might want to write. The girls burst out laughing and the teacher sent me out of the class. But despite everything, I loved school. What I loved most was to be away from everything, to escape to the library where I could read and write. I also adored running and playing with the girls in the courtyard. We skipped and played basketball and volleyball, but my favourite game was tennis. A school-mate of mine called Safeya played with me. She was fair, with a round face and green eyes, and was the only one among the girls who played tennis. I adored moving my body in the open air under the sunshine, sang with happiness, moved my legs as though ready to fly at any moment.

In the music room I sang and danced with the girls to the tunes which Fatma played on the piano. She was one of the girls who slept in my dormitory and she loved music and songs. She often sang some of Um Koulsoum's songs, like 'Is it true that love is irresistible?' or 'Be happy, O heart of mine.' She had a beautiful, husky voice which made our hearts flutter with joy.

Before the bell rang for bedtime we went into the showers. Under the water I would sing, 'When the night falls and the stars are scattered over the sky, ask the night when will my star come out.' From behind the partition which separated us I would hear Fatma singing the same song. Tears would flow from my eyes with the water drops on my face.

In our life there was no-one capable of making us more miserable than the superintendent. Her name was Abla Aziza. She resembled a jailer holding a big bunch of keys for the punishment cells. She wore heavy black shoes with thick crêpe or rubber soles which stifled the sound of her footsteps as she walked around like Miss Hamer used to do in my school in Menouf.

Thursday nights in boarding school were the most wonderful of all. School would be without a superintendent, for she would have picked up her yellow bag and left for the weekend. We watched her until she disappeared through the door, and then let out shrieks and whistles of joy, and a few seconds later were busy putting everything in the dormitory upside down, so that it could be changed into a ballroom for dancing and singing, or into a theatre auditorium.

A new world was opening up for me, a world where I lived in common with other girls of my age. I had not known this kind of a happiness before, for in the other schools there was no opportunity to live in a group like that. Class followed class, one after the other, and then we raced for home, afraid to be late. But in boarding school we had time, were not afraid to be late in getting home. I adored this life with other girls where there were no parents I had to return to. My school-mates had become my family, and school for me was better than any home. The courtyard had space in which I could run at will. Sun came in through the large windows of the dormitory, and at night moonlight crept over my bed, and I could see a gleam in the eyes of the girls as they looked out from the row of beds.

In the morning we jumped out of bed, ran up and down the corridors, skated on the tiled floor with our slippers and clogs into the open bathrooms provided with only half a wall as partition, splashed one another with water like children on the beach in Alexandria, and once again I had memories of my childhood before the age of seven, images of a child lifted up by the waves to the blue sky, of my mother beside me, swimming in the water like a fish, her eyes shining with the light of golden honey, her arms ready to reach out to me at any moment if I sank.

At night, I stood at the window and looked out at the moon, gazed at the stars all alone while the girls slept quietly in their beds, searched the sky for my star, full of a great longing, of the memory of that first love that had never left me. Sometimes Safeya opened her eyes, got out of bed and walked to the window to stand by my side and look out at the moon with me. Around her neck hung a golden chain with a casket containing a tiny Qur'an, and something else also made of gold but heart-shaped, which she opened with her fingers, and from which she extracted a strand of jet black hair, lifted it to her face, touched it with her lips, and then slipped it back to the heart-shaped casket which closed with a small click of its lock. Her first and her last love, she said to me. This strand of hair was a memory of him, and in exchange she had given a small lock of her hair. She would never forget him, never marry anyone else. His name was Morcos.[*] She made me swear on the Qur'an never to mention his name to anyone. Her father was a Muslim whose name was Muhammad, and when she said that the tears rolled down her face, shimmering in the moonlight.

'He is the only one I love in this whole world, Nawal. I love him more than my father and mother. He is going to become a doctor, as beautiful as the moon,[†] more beautiful than anything else in the world. I will never marry anyone else. What does it matter if he's a Copt?[‡] My maternal uncle Mahmoud is married to Evelyn, the cousin of Morcos. Why should he be allowed to marry a Copt?'

On Thursdays Safeya took her bag, and went off to spend the weekend in her maternal uncle's house in Abbasseya. Morcos was accustomed to visit his cousin Evelyn on Fridays. Safeya would come back on Saturdays, her face radiant with joy, and start counting the days on her fingers until the coming Thursday.

I spent the weekend in school with the girls who had no parents or relatives in Cairo. I never went out of the school door except to take the train to Menouf on the eve of the Eid, or at the end of the year when the summer holidays began.

---

[*] Marcus or Mark, a Coptic Christian name.
[†] In Egyptian and Arabic folklore, the moon has a special place, and so beautiful people, whether young adults or children, male or female, are described as being like the moon (*zay al-amar*).
[‡] From Gypt (Egypt).

On Thursday nights the bedtime bell did not ring, and the lights did not go out. This was the only night of the week when we could stay up until morning, the only night we could sing and dance without the superintendent pouncing on us, the only night we could spend acting one of the stories I had written. Then the beds were all pushed up to one side and the dormitory transformed into a theatre. A space at one end was left to become the stage of the theatre, and the audience composed of the girls from the other dormitories whom we had invited squatted in rows on the ground in front of it.

At the beginning, I took all the roles. I was the playwright, the director of the theatre, the actress, and the one who distributed the tickets. Tickets were free, and were made of small rectangles of paper torn out of one of my notebooks. On each rectangle was written the name of the play and the address of the theatre, that is, Dormitory 3. But later on, the girls in the other dormitories started to call it Freedom Theatre.

One of the teachers in the school, named Miss Saneya, taught us English. She was tall and slender, and was the only one among the teachers who played tennis, and also the only one who talked to us after class, or sat with us in the school-yard and discussed the English novels included in our syllabus.

Amongst them was a novel called *Adam Bede*. In this novel the heroine becomes pregnant with an illegitimate baby. It reminded me of the servant-girl Shalabeya, who had worked in my late grandfather's house, and this suggested itself to me as a play which I then wrote under the title *A Scream in the Night*. After it was finished we put it on for one Friday night in Freedom Theatre.

Plays used to begin after we had supper and had gone upstairs to our dormitory from the dining-room which looked out onto the courtyard. The day before we distributed the tickets, which were no longer free scraps of paper. The price of each ticket was now one millime. When we went round the dormitories selling them the girls yoo-yood with delight.

After that, we laid blankets on the floor for the audience to squat on. Whatever accessories were necessary we bought with the piastres we had collected selling tickets: things such as masks made out of cardboard, powders with which to colour the faces of the different characters, melon seeds and peanuts to eat during the show.

In this play, Safeya acted the role of the heroine who has an illegitimate pregnancy. She flees in the night wearing a wide, loose garment to conceal her swollen belly (which we made by stuffing old clothes under her long dress), sits on the bank of the Nile full of a deep sadness, contemplating suicide.

That night the theatre was completely dark since we had put out all the lights, and hung blankets on the windows to keep out any light filtering in from the moon, or the outer corridors. The audience squatted on the floor holding its breath in expectation of what might happen, since the child had matured in its mother's belly, and was ready to come out into the world.

Suddenly there was a scream from the mother, just one choking scream, followed by the cries of the new-born baby, whose part was being played by Fikreya concealed behind the curtains, letting out sharp screaming cries which cut through the silence of the night like an air-raid siren.

At that very moment the door of the dormitory opened and Abla Aziza burst in holding the pocket searchlight in her hand. To our misfortune she had spent her weekend in the school, and had not gone out as usual. Walking down the corridor outside her room, she had heard the screams of a child and to her it seemed as though one of the girls was having a baby.

The world was suddenly turned upside down in the Helwan Secondary School for Girls. We were supposed to be virgins who knew nothing about sex or illegitimate pregnancies. Such words were not even supposed to be pronounced by us in the Arabic language, either secretly or in public. If they were part of our English language classes, we could pronounce them in English, in English only, and in class but certainly not in the dormitory.

We had no way of knowing how normal pregnancies took place, let alone illegitimate pregnancies. Lessons were given to us on what was called child-care, as a part of the syllabus in girls' schools only. In these classes we used to go down to the underground cellar in the school buildings where there was a big room with something like a bath tub filled with water. There was also a baby made of some yellow plastic material, which Abla Hikmat slung under her arm as she explained to us the way to give it a bath without drowning it in the water, or letting the soap get into its eyes. She did not explain to us how this baby had come into the world.

Abla Hikmat also gave us another class called health and biology, in which she explained to us how fertilization occurred in flowers, bees and worms. But as regards fertilization in human beings, this was a dangerous area, a thing about which we were not supposed to know anything.

Next morning I stood in the headmistress's office, trembling. In her hand she held tickets which said: 'Freedom Theatre presents *A Scream in the Night*, written by Nawal El Saadawi.' Here was material proof of my crime being waved in my face. Her eyes bulged behind her glass spectacles, like those of Tante Fahima, drops of her saliva scattered over my face as she screamed in fury:

'A girl like you, tall [mature] as a door, how could you do such a horrible thing?'

'Abla Headmistress, it's only a story. It's imaginary, something...'

'Imaginary? You want it to be a true story? You really are a girl who lacks proper manners.'

After calling me to her office she took the decision to expel me from boarding school but to allow me into classes. In addition she downgraded my rating for 'behaviour and good manners' by three points.

Miss Saneya intervened in an attempt to lighten the punishment I had been given. She told the headmistress that I was gifted and that I was the best girl in her class. But the headmistress was not to be convinced. 'What do you mean by gifted, Sitti Saneya? Good behaviour is more important for a girl than anything else. She's brazen and can sow bad behaviour amongst the girls in the boarding house.'

The headmistress refused to change her decision until my father came to see her; then I was allowed to remain as a boarder. But that was the end of Freedom Theatre. We had to do with singing only on Friday nights, or standing at the windows like prisoners, or lying awake in the moonlight and recalling memories, or hovering way up in dreams about the future, or gathering around Fatma as she sang, 'Is it true that love is irresistible?', and answering in chorus with the refrain 'I do not know.' Sometimes we went down to the music room where Fatma would play the piano and Safeya would tie a belt around her buttocks and start dancing, with us joining in until we poured with sweat.

26

Wasted Lives

Samia did not join in with us when we were having fun. She would pout her lips in disdain and say: 'The country is in a crisis and here you are playing away!'

She always made me feel guilty, as though we were responsible for the British occupation of Egypt, or the corruption of the king, or for the widespread poverty, ignorance and disease known at that time by the term 'triple scourge'. So all the girls in the dormitory insisted on calling her Bo'o Bo'o Effendi.

My friendship with Fikreya grew. Drawing and painting were, for her, like writing for me. I read her the things I wrote, and she showed me the pictures she painted. At night when the lights went off she pushed her bed up against mine and we started whispering. She said to me: 'I will go to the School of Fine Arts and become a famous painter.'

Later on, Fikreya managed to fulfil the first part of her dream. After obtaining her secondary-school certificate, she was admitted to the School of Fine Arts. Then fifteen years went by without any news of her. I looked for her name among the painters in vain. In the summer of 1961, I was at the beach in Alexandria playing with my small daughter Mona, swimming in the blue waters, lifting her up over the waves and paddling with her like my mother used to do with me. I spotted Fikreya walking barefoot on the sand, holding her shoes in her hands. Her eyes were gazing at something far away, and her lips were, as usual, pouted disdainfully at everything in the world around her. She smiled when she saw me in the water, her white teeth shining in the sunlight. We ran towards each other with the warmth of friends who had not met for fifteen years. I asked her about her painting. The smile on her face vanished and her eyes avoided me, and she said: 'You see, I married.' She let go a small, dry, sarcastic laugh and added, 'My husband is a well-known artist and he paints for both of us.' I laughed in turn and said: 'Like the story of Gandhi with King George, you mean.' She asked me what Gandhi had to do with painting, so I told her that when Gandhi travelled to London to negotiate with the British he went to Buckingham Palace. The king was surprised to see him half-naked, dressed only in his loincloth, and asked him why he was not wearing clothes. Gandhi answered: 'Your Majesty is dressed for both of us.'

Fatma, the girl with the beautiful voice that could fill us with joy, or bring tears to our eyes, had only one dream: to become the star of the east like Um Koulsoum. After she finished her secondary schooling she went to the School of Fine Arts. There she married a professor twenty years older than her, went to Kuwait or maybe Saudi Arabia and I lost all trace of her for more than a quarter of a century. Then suddenly in the autumn of 1975 her voice came to me over the telephone. She had read something about me in the newspapers and after some searching was able to discover my telephone number. Her voice sounded sad, and weak, and she told me that she was sick in bed.

I went to her house in the University City, Dokki, built specially for university professors. It was a beautiful house surrounded by a big garden, and guarded by a wolf-dog, like the one in the house of my late grandfather. The manservant, who wore a kaftan and a red waist-band, led me into a spacious drawing-room full of rare pieces and beautiful ornaments with indoor plants all over the place. Then he took me up marble stairs and along a long corridor to her room.

There I found her lying in a huge bed that reminded me of a picture I had seen of Queen Nazli's bed. Her face was as white as the sheet, her honey-coloured eyes were covered by a grey mist like those of my grandmother Amna. Her husband was away in some Gulf oil country making money. He had married another woman from Kuwait or maybe Saudi Arabia. Sadness had accumulated in a cyst embedded in her left breast right over her heart. She pointed with her thin white finger to where she felt the pain. 'The doctor told me it's a benign fibroid swelling but I feel he is not telling me the truth.' She said: 'Give me your hand Nawal, yes here, and please don't hide anything from me.'

It was a malignant cancer of the third degree. I lied to her as I had lied to my mother and Tante Ni'mat, and all the other patients with the same disease. I cursed the day I had entered the school of medicine and been led to see people only when they were sick or dying, to see eyes that had lost their shine and were full of sorrow. Her eyes had been pure honey, her voice soared when she sang 'Be happy, O heart of mine.' She had dreamt of becoming the star of the east but she had married and her husband had built her a marble tomb on which he had inscribed not her name, but his: 'Mrs X, the wife of Mr X.'

Fatma died at the age of forty-five, the same age at which my mother died, and her name sank into oblivion. She had done nothing with her life, just hours of waiting in her luxurious house remembering her old dreams.

Samia, my third school-friend, was always silent, her lips tightly closed, unsmiling. If we sat under the moonlight talking about dreams, or about memories of first love, she would give us a jaundiced look from her staring eyes. She did not believe in dreams, or in love, or in the fantasies of our imagination. 'The country is going through a serious crisis', she would say, 'and you continue to live in a world of imagination. This is nothing but childish romanticism.'

In response Fikreya would stick out her lower lip or put out her tongue at her. Samia's defence was to cover herself up completely under the blankets until nothing of her was showing. This made Fikreya laugh so much that tears showed in her eyes. 'That's right, Bo'o Bo'o Effendi, go to sleep and make sure that no whiff of air gets into you', she taunted. At that, Samia would uncover her head, stick out her tongue at Fikreya, and quickly slip under the covers again, not leaving a single loophole through which air could reach her.

We did not understand how she could breathe all covered up like that. She slept deeply, right through the night, curled up around herself like an embryo. In the morning she woke up, crept out of bed without a sound and walked with cautious steps towards the bathroom muttering to herself in low tones.

But one morning her voice rang out loudly in the dormitory, and we heard her saying: 'Tomorrow there will be a very big demonstration in which all schools will be participating. Our school must join in because it's a patriotic demonstration, a national demonstration.'

'A patriotic demonstration.' The words rang in my ears, echoed in my father's voice. Once more I was the little girl sitting on the northern balcony of our house in Alexandria listening in wonderment. The tall giant who is my father strikes at the enemy fearlessly. A bullet flies through the air, hits him in the chest, and his red blood spills on the black tarmac of the road. I wake up from my sleep full of fear, tiptoe out of my bed to the door of the room in which my father and mother are asleep. The door is slightly ajar and I can hear my father's snores. I realize he is asleep and that what I saw was only a dream. I go back to bed, fall asleep and start dreaming again, but this time it's to avenge my father's death, put on a bullet-proof jacket, hold up my sword, and smite the enemy like Joan of Arc, but the sword in my hand resembles a fly spray, and the enemies drop in front of it like flies. My body becomes lighter and lighter and I rise in the air like a butterfly moving my arms like wings. The air changes into blue water and I swim in the sea like a fish. The waves mount up to the sky then fall down with me right to the bottom, but my mother's arm reaches out and carries me to the surface.

'The national demonstration is for tomorrow.' Now it's my voice vibrating with enthusiasm as I make the rounds of the dormitories. The blood kept rushing up to my head then down to my feet. My body seemed on fire. I was a flaming torch walking on bare feet as I opened the doors of the dormitories, one after the other, and called out: 'Tomorrow it's the demonstration, girls.' It was the same voice with which I called out, 'Tomorrow it's the play, girls', the same enthusiasm. The world stretched out in front of my eyes like a huge stage. Tickets had become leaflets, elongated pieces of paper torn out of our notebooks on which we had written: 'Evacuation by Blood'.*

In our dormitory there were ten big windows in two rows of five. The inner row looked out over the inner courtyard. The outer row looked out at the desert and the sky. The night before the demonstration we stood at the windows making badges, square pieces of material on which we embroidered in red silk thread: 'Evacuation by Blood'. We worked on the badges throughout the night; all of us, except Samia.

Standing with me at the window were Fikreya, Fatma and Safeya engrossed in embroidering. The night breeze in Helwan is gentle and warm like a mother's caress. A longing for our parents seized hold of us. We could see the street lamps leading far away to the railway station, the high stone wall surrounding the big playground, the desert stretched out to an invisible horizon. The smell of sulphur coming from the natural wells floated towards us on the air. Behind the sand dunes crouched the barracks housing the British soldiers, like wild animals waiting to be let out.

---

* 'We will shed our blood to force the British to evacuate.' Later the slogan changed to 'Armed struggle'.

The night in Helwan was silent except for the sound, rarely repeated, of a cannon, or an occasional burst of gunfire followed by the barking of dogs, or the heavy tread of British soldiers wearing iron-heeled boots. In their hands they used to carry searchlights, directed them to our windows and called out to the girls with their ugly voices. The girls shouted back in chorus :'Evacuation by Blood'.

During the day as far as our eyes could see were scattered masses of towering trees, and behind them stretched the Japanese gardens. The air in Helwan was gentle and dry, and filled our hearts with a deep yearning. Our eyes lost themselves in the infinite space of the universe stretched before us, giving us a feeling of exile, of loneliness. We stood resting our chins on the window-sills holding hands, dissipating the loneliness with this feeling of being together, with the warmth of our bodies touching, with our mutual support in the face of an unknown world. In our imagination, intermingled the face of a mother, of a father, of a first love, flowing into this love of country. We sang together: 'My land, my land, to you I give my love, my heart.'

Nights in Helwan were usually different from that night in the year 1946. On that night the hands of the clock seemed to have jumped from two to four, for the light of dawn started to break through, as we stood at the windows embroidering the badges to be pinned on the left side of our breasts, over our hearts.

Samia was the only one in the dormitory who slept through the night. She did not believe in staying awake in the moonlight, and to her mind embroidery was too slow a process. She wrote 'Evacuation by Blood' with red ink on her badge in half a minute and pinned it on her chest. She believed in practical things, in quick results. Whenever she said anything it started with 'The fact is' or 'I'm sure'. 'The fact is, girls, sleep is much more important than what you are doing now.' 'I'm sure girls that Abla Aziza is going to pounce on us at any moment and she'll give us hell.'

Apart from me, Samia had no friend in the dormitory. Her tight lips and silent character surrounded her with an aura of mystery which attracted me, and because her bed was next to mine we started to talk: 'What use is imagination, Nawal?' she said to me, 'what's the use of all these stories you read? The country is going though a crisis and all you do is read novels.'

The way she spoke was always critical, always blaming. It made me feel guilty, feel as though I was letting down my country, was a traitor because I loved literature and art. I said to her that imagination for me was like air. I had to breathe it, so all she did was pout her lips disdainfully. There was no way I would convince her with my words. Language was like a barrier standing between us. She was fond of saying complicated things I found difficult to understand: 'It looks as though I will have to explain to you what dialectics means, Nawal.' The word dialectics made me feel depressed, because Samia was never able to explain to me what it meant. Every time she heard Samia pronounce this word, Fikreya would burst out laughing, and each night before we went to sleep Safeya would call out to her from her bed: 'May you wake up to a good day of dialectics.'* We hid under the covers suffocating with laughter. Samia pouted in disgust and before she curled up under the covers declared in a ringing voice: 'The fact is, girls, you are ignorant, and will never do anything with your lives.'

That night before the demonstration we did not sleep a wink. The wake-up bell rang followed by the breakfast bell, and we leapt down the stairs, racing one another to the dining-room, and sat on our benches, breathing in the smell of baked bread and fresh milk, once more children screaming with delight.

After breakfast we gathered in the courtyard, wearing grey uniforms, with the badges pinned to our breast and with the slogan embroidered in red letters standing out: 'Evacuation by Blood'. The girls who were not boarders thronged in to the courtyard and took their places in the lines. We could hear the sound of slogans being shouted at a distance. The Helwan School

---

* The usual goodnight in Egypt is 'May you wake to a day of bounty.'

for Boys had gone down into the streets, and the primary schools
had followed. The girls began to shout: 'We want to join the
demonstration. Primary-school boys are not better than us.' A
girl climbed to the shoulders of her school-mates and started to
call out 'Evacuation by Blood', repeating the slogan at the top
of her voice, and the girls gathered in the courtyard repeated
in a chorus made by hundreds of voices: 'Evacuation by Blood'.
A moment later another girl climbed on the shoulder of her
colleagues and began to shout: 'Down with the English. Down
with the government.'

The headmistress reacted by issuing an order that the outer
gate be closed with a heavy lock and chain, and the superintend-
ents spread out in the courtyard, holding sticks, like shepherds
herding their sheep as they beat them from behind to drive them
inside the animal pen.

But the slogans had had their effect on the girls. They were no
longer docile, no longer sheep. They had become human beings
who showed anger, began to sing: 'Our beloved Misr, you are
unique, a land of wonderful things.' It was the song I had heard
for the first time in primary school and which has continued to
resonate with memories throughout my life.

Suddenly the girls launched themselves in a headlong rush
against the gates. Hundreds of young strong bodies became a
single powerful body beating, pushing, straining against the
huge door. The iron chain and the hinges started to give away
under the pressure with a screeching noise. The hundreds of
arms became a single powerful arm that twisted the metal,
snapped it with the strength of an anger building up since the
day they were born, with the force of a dream suppressed since
childhood, with the power of a great love imprisoned in the
chest, with all the pent-up hatred against doors, and chains,
and locks, with all the hope of a coming freedom, and all the
despair.

I was one of those girls and my body had become a part of
them. Nothing, not even death could now separate us. For at

moments like this the subconscious, the giant dormant under the conscious mind, bursts out. Maybe it is closer to the genius of spontaneous nature, more conscious than the conscious mind. If this were not so, from where would it derive its extraordinary power? For at that moment I realized how powerful I had become. My fingers twisted the rusty chain until it snapped, the iron lock rolled to the ground, and hundreds of feet trod over it. The huge gates opened wide, reeled back with a noise like an explosion and the girls swept through like a torrent, shouting: 'Evacuation by Blood'.

In the street we were joined by school-boys, by shopkeepers, and passers-by. At the railway station the engine driver and the ticket collectors mingled with us and we took over the train. We did not need tickets. The ruling system was being overthrown.

When I was a child I used to dream of another world in which there were no tickets for riding trains or entering the circus, no need for money to buy roasted melon seeds and peanuts.

I sat near the window as the train raced through the stations without stopping. Everything looked different, even the blue of the sky, even the sand dunes in the desert. The blue of the sky was bluer than the sea, and the sand dunes had a golden colour under the sun. My heart was big with the freedom I was living as though I now possessed it, held it firmly in my two hands, like the window-sill onto which I was holding. I flew along breathing in the fresh air, my hair blowing in the wind, the voices of the girls resounding in my ears as they chanted in unison, 'Long live Egypt in Freedom', then sang, 'My country, my country I give you my heart and my love', with the sound of the wheels racing over the rails to the rhythm of the song, and the train letting out sharp whistles like a trumpet or a flute.

We got down from the train at Bab Al-Louk station and plunged into rivers of people. Egypt, government and people, rulers and ruled, seemed to be on the streets that day. There were government employees dressed in suits and fezzes, men wearing *gallabeyas* and kaftans, university students with long trousers and fezzes, school-boys in short trousers above the knees, school-girls in uniforms made of linen or calico from Mahalla,* women dressed in long black robes, and *milayas*,† factory workers in blue dungarees, male and female nurses in white coats, peasant women carrying their children close to their breasts, invalids walking on crutches with a foot wrapped in gauze or in a plaster cast.

Flows of people poured out of the lanes and side-streets into the squares. Other people crowded on balconies and roofs, or climbed up trees. Forty-eight years have passed since that day, but every detail remains vivid in my mind. The first national demonstration in my life, the first time I understood the meaning of the word homeland, the first time I felt love for my country sweep me along, break down the barriers between dream and reality, between body and mind, uniting the parts with the whole, the earth with heaven. Life was no longer separated from death, pleasure from pain. The human being was now capable of flying in the air, of swimming to the depths of the sea, of doing anything.

I had never before experienced this feeling of a happiness without limit, like a flood, uncontrollable. I experienced the same feeling later in other demonstrations and during the short moment when I looked into the eyes of my newly born daughter and, years after, of my son for the first time.

This was the mighty torrent suppressed since the age of slavery, since the time when a woman giving birth to a child was a punishment and a desecration requiring that the child be baptized, since the time when the masters were given land and the slaves deprived of it.

I kept looking around me in amazement. The huge square was like an ocean of people. I do not remember now whether it was Ismaileya Square or Abdine Square. The voices which chanted

---

* A small city in the Delta renowned for the size and quality of its spinning and weaving industry.

† A long wide sheet of black material, sometimes silk, wound around the head and the body and worn by women in popular urban districts.

in unison: 'Evacuation by Blood', sounded in my ears like the beating of a drum, echoed by the beat of my heart under my ribs. They resounded like thunder again and again: 'Evacuation by Blood', 'Down with Sidky',* 'Down with Bevin.'

I did not know who Sidky was and I had never heard of Bevin, but there I was in the middle of this human ocean, with row upon row of people in the huge square. Beside me in the row were Fikreya, Safeya, Fatma and Samia and at one moment I looked around and noticed three men heading towards us. They were wearing black uniforms, their faces looked grim, and they advanced with a gait that resembled that of soldiers. When they came up to us one of them said: 'We want a delegate from your school.'

The word delegate was another word I had never heard before. I turned towards Samia since she could have been the one who understood what it meant, but there was no Samia anymore. She had disappeared like that, in the wink of an eye, 'dissolved like a grain of salt in water'.† We looked around but she was nowhere to be seen. And yet just a moment ago she had been right here. We heard one of the men repeating: 'We want a delegate. Come on, choose somebody quickly.' We looked at one another silently, nonplussed. Someone said, I don't know who, perhaps Fikreya or Safeya or one of the girls standing there. 'Nawal is our delegate.' 'Please oblige us by coming with us Miss Nawal', said the same man.

Miss? That was the first time the word miss had ever preceded my name. I had been transformed from a school-girl in the third year of secondary school to a miss. I straightened my back and, as I walked away with them, I discovered that I was almost the same height as they were. As they walked they hit their heels on the tarmac of the square, so I did the same, lifting my head

---

* Prime minister in 1946. He was notorious for having abolished the constitution in 1930, and for firing on the railway workers later; for his attempts to maintain the British occupation of Egypt in 1946 by a new treaty, closing down fifteen newspapers, seven associations and arresting hundreds of people who opposed his policies.

† A popular saying used to describe people who disappear in a crisis.

up proudly in the air, as though I had now reached the age of maturity, had become a miss delegate. But the beating of my heart told me how scared I was. Where were these men taking me? On my chest shone the bright red letters spelling out 'Evacuation by Blood'. My voice had become hoarse with the chanting of slogans. I parted my lips to ask where they were taking me but my voice refused to emerge, just as it used to do in some of my dreams.

We climbed up steps to a magnificent building. Was this the king's palace? Reality and imagination seemed to be mixed together, so that I could no longer distinguish between them. The moments floated by as though removed from time and place, as though I had lived all this when I was only six years old.

I found myself in a huge hall covered with red carpets. Crystal chandeliers hung from the ceiling, gilt-framed paintings looked down from sculptured walls, and the faces of kings and sultans frowned on me as I walked up to a large table with gold carvings and inscriptions. On it was a big open book with a cover on which were written words in letters of gold. I thought it was the book of Allah but they called it a ceremonial register. They asked me to write down my triple name* in it. My hand trembled as I wrote my father's name. I felt the government might arrest him, or even shoot him. As for me, I would certainly be expelled from school, and sent back home to Menouf. When I thought of that I felt that prison, or a bullet, was a better fate, and wondered whether that was what had made Samia run away.

On the way back I sat among the girls with bent head. We kept exchanging glances in silence, unable to understand what had happened. It was as though the mountain had given birth to a mouse. Was it possible that the huge demonstration had ended like this, in nothing? With just a name written down in a ceremonial register?

I saw tears in Safeya's eyes and realized that she had been weeping silently. 'What's the matter, Safeya?' I asked. 'Has

* Full name, composed of surname, first name and name of the father.

something happened?' 'Nothing, Nawal, it's nothing', she answered. 'It's just that I remembered my brother. Where did Samia go, Nawal? You have no idea? Frankly the mouse is playing in my bosom.'*

'What's that you are saying, Safeya? A mouse is playing in your bosom?' I almost screamed, but Safeya started laughing. At first I had thought that a mouse had crept from under the seat of the train, up her clothes. I had never heard the expression before, but Safeya allayed my fears, then the tears started to flow from her eyes again: 'You're really so innocent Nawal, so naïve. But Samia is water under dry fodder.'†

After it was all over, I was the only girl in school who was taken to task. I was accused of causing a riot, for in the language of the headmistress a patriotic demonstration was nothing but a riot. Samia kept away from school for seven days. She had been careful to avoid drawing attention to herself, and neither her name, nor her father's or grandfather's name had been noted down in the archives of the police. She had even avoided distributing leaflets to the girls in the dormitories with me.

I stood in the headmistress's office. She was shaking with fury and I was shaking with fear. 'I interrogated the girls and all of them said that you were the one who incited them to riot.' I tried to open my mouth and say something, say that it was a patriotic demonstration and not a riot, but my voice failed me. Perhaps I had an inflammation of the throat and vocal cords from all that shouting 'Down with the government', and now it was I who was really in trouble and not the government, or Samia who had been the first to incite us to join the demonstration. She was the one who had started by coming to us and saying: 'Tomorrow is the big demonstration.' She had pushed me into the trap, into doing what I did, and then abandoned me. And those girls, how could they point an accusing finger at me when they were

---

* A popular expression which a person uses when he or she is becoming suspicious of something, having doubts.
† Meaning she is unfathomable, cunning, scheming, another popular expression.

asked by the headmistress! Had they not all participated in the demonstration?

The voice of the headmistress resonated in the room: 'Do you dare to say it's not you who incited the girls to riot? Is there any other girl apart from you who did the same thing? Give me her name immediately and I will punish her.' I pressed my lips together tightly, bent my head, and was silent. I did not pronounce the name Samia. I gave the headmistress a quick look out of the corner of my eye. The whites of her eyes were red like the faces of the British soldiers, her voice coarse like theirs when they shouted ugly words from their barracks in the night. At that moment I hated Samia but I hated the headmistress even more, and maybe that was why I did not say anything.

The headmistress reached out with her long arm and ripped off the badge from my breast, threw it on the floor and stamped on it. I watched as the words embroidered in the colour of blood under the light of the moon were crushed beneath her feet. She reached out again and pulled off my jacket. The cold air went through my shirt. I shivered with cold and fear as she picked up the ruler in her right hand and lifted it high up in the air. I covered my right hand with my left hand to hide the scratches made by the iron chain on my fingers as she landed the edge of the ruler on their tips like a knife.

She went on lifting the ruler as high as she could, as though hitting at the sky, then bringing it down on my fingers with all her force. Her jaws were clenched with fury, and I could hear her teeth grind against each other with a sound like that of the ruler landing on my knuckles. Her panting breath wheezed like the whistle of a train, or steam passing though a narrow hole.

She was short and fat like a well-fed duck, her eyes bulging behind thick glass spectacles. On the heels of her shoes she had nailed iron crescents, the shape of horseshoes, and when she walked she struck the floor with them, making a metallic sound. She did not wear black like Nabaweya Moussa but her clothes were drab and colourless like those of all headmistresses. I had never seen a smile on the face of any of these women. Instead hanging over it there was always a high forehead with a frown furrowed deeply, as though it would be there for ever.

Was there a law that obliged headmistresses to look like that? Something that changed their faces into a rigid square box closed on itself? Despite the powder and the make-up, the lipstick and the expensive spectacles, there was something that could not be concealed, something that escaped from the hole in the middle or from the two holes in the head, something under pressure, a violent emotion stored up, held in, like dynamite capable of destroying them from within, a desire to destroy others showing in the bloodshot eyes, in a suppressed fury looking out from behind the black pupils lodged in the greying whites of the eyes.

The voice of the headmistress continued to echo in both my sleeping and my waking hours: 'Consider yourself no longer a pupil at this school.'

School, despite the headmistress, was the only road to freedom, and to me freedom was more important than the liberation of my country. Nation was a word we chanted with our slogans, but I was not a word. I was my body, the living flesh that was being beaten with the edge of the ruler, the blood dripping from my swollen fingers, the joints between my bones that were wincing with pain.

The headmistress had concentrated her blows on my right hand, on the hand with which I used to write. Perhaps she wanted to prevent me from writing. Maybe the teacher had told her that I had once written a story in which I said that the heavens were unjust.

To expel me from school the headmistress had to speak to the person in whose charge I was, and that was my father. So my father came to school. I saw him coming in tall, his head held up as always, the tread of his feet on the ground powerful, steady. He had a characteristic way of walking, moving one foot forwards slowly, deciding exactly where to put it down before he lifted the other foot and trod with all the weight of his body on the ground as though he feared no-one, neither king, nor government nor even the headmistress, as though God was the only one he feared.

I ran towards him like an orphan seeking protection. He caressed my shoulder with his big gentle hand: 'Don't be afraid. Come with me, Nawal', he said. I walked behind him, almost holding on to the tail of his jacket, like I used to hold on to my mother's dress when I was a child, hid behind his big body as we entered the office of the headmistress.

She stood up when he came in and received him with a show of respect: 'Welcome, Al-Saadawi Bey. Please sit down.' He sat down, his body filling the chair. He lit a cigarette, began to talk to her about the political situation.

'The Sidky–Bevin Treaty does not benefit Egypt in any way', he said. 'It gives us neither independence, nor leads to the evacuation of British troops. It maintains the occupation of Egypt, Oustaza Aziza.'

'Yes Al-Saadawi Bey, but you are in the Ministry of Education and you know that the Ministry has forbidden all demonstrations.'

'The government is about to fall', he said, 'and after the huge demonstration which took place recently it's only a matter of days. The whole country took part in it, even school-children and housewives.'

'But there must be respect for law and order. Can you imagine that your daughter, who pretends to be as innocent as a kitten incited the girls to break down the door of the school, and take to the streets. Adolescent girls in school breaking down the door and going out into the streets. What have they left for others to do?'

'It was a political demonstration', he said. 'Nawal is my daughter and I know her. She would never incite the girls to do anything bad. Besides she's among the top girls in the school.'

'But being the top girl in the school and instigating riots are two different things, and I have orders from the Ministry which I must execute or else I am liable to questioning.'

'I am in the Ministry and know the situation perfectly', he said. 'Oustaza Aziza, all the high officials in the Ministry gave their support to the demonstration, and I have just come from the office of the undersecretary, Fahmy Bey.'

There must have been something like magic in the name of Fahmy Bey. Her face changed, and the tone of her voice became almost gentle. 'O, so your excellency is acquainted with Fahmi Bey?' 'Yes, he was my colleague in the college of Dar Al-Oloum. He's a relative of Sanhoury; that's why he was promoted before his time.'

She rang the bell, ordered a cup of coffee for my father, asked me in the same gentle tone: 'What would you like to drink my child?' My throat was parched and sore. I wanted to ask for a glass of tea with milk, but once more my voice refused to come to my rescue.

27

Cholera, Ageing
and Death

In 1947 I was in my fifth year in secondary school. It was the year in which the epidemic of cholera broke out. Our house in Menouf became like a fortress guarding itself against the disease. The windows were covered with fine wire netting, which prevented flies and mosquitoes from getting in. Empty tins of spray, Tox, Flit and DDT were piled up with empty bottles of Lysol, potassium permanganate, and ethyl alcohol in the corner of the kitchen.

My mother travelled to the village and came back accompanied by Sittil Hajja. Cholera was killing men and women in the village like an epidemic of diarrhoea among chickens. My father wanted to save at least his mother from the disease.

Sittil Hajja could not even pronounce the word. She called it 'chorera', which made us laugh. She would join in our laughter until tears came to her eyes, picked up the edge of her *tarha* and wiped them off. But a moment later she would begin to sob in a shaking voice: 'I want to go back to the *kafr* (village). I'm afraid my daughter Zaynab will catch the *shota*.* Mother asked her, using her first name: 'But why Zaynab in particular, Hajja

---

* Diarrhoea in epidemic form, used also for chickens and children.

Mabrouka?' 'Because she's better than all the others and has the kindest heart in the world. And chorera takes only the most kind-hearted', she answered before beginning to sob quietly again, as though her daughter had already died of cholera.

One morning before the sun had risen we found Sittil Hajja standing upright in her long black robe, as though ready to leave. As soon as my father woke up she said to him 'Take me back to the *kafr*, son. My heart has been eating itself away, all night, over Zaynab. I'm afraid something may have happened to her.'

My father put on his suit and went off with her to the village. He returned two days later, his face pale and his eyes red. His sister Zaynab had died of cholera. With every gasp of breath, she kept repeating deliriously: 'Bring me my mother, I want to see her.' Sittil Hajja arrived just in time. Zaynab opened her eyes, her lips parted in a smile, and suddenly her eyes were full of light before she closed them and died.

The cholera-stricken village wept for her. The disease swept away a number of women and men in our family, but the sadness of people over her was greater than it was over anyone else. She was the closest of her sisters to my father, the most loved by Sittil Hajja of her daughters. She was tall like her mother, with a beautiful bronzed complexion, and with eyes green as clover. She had a son called Nagah (Success) and a baby daughter who died in the arms of her dying mother.

Sittil Hajja changed overnight into an old woman. She no longer laughed as she used to do, and her face became covered in wrinkles. She sat on the threshold of her house cuddling Nagah, looking into his eyes, as green as the eyes of his mother. Now he was the orphan, apple of his grandmother's eye. 'May Allah take the chorera and those who brought it to us', she would say.

In Menouf, the epidemic brought many deaths. My mother became like an army officer on guard. She kept picking up the fly spray as though it were a machine gun and bringing down the flies. The moment the illness broke out she declared war on it and fought it with vigour. She boiled the water before we drank it, washed the vegetables thoroughly, and soaked them in a solution of potassium permanganate, heated the bread on the burner before we ate it, to kill any germs. She sterilized everything my father bought. As soon as he entered the house she made him take off his clothes so that she could soak them in a sterilizing solution. If any one of us entered the toilet more than once in the same day she was seized with panic. The radio broadcast instructions telling people what to do. She listened to these broadcasts attentively or wrote them down in her notebook: 'The signs of cholera are diarrhoea and vomiting, with rice-water stools. All the body secretions are highly infectious, and the authorities must be notified immediately if anyone shows signs such as these so that the ill person maybe isolated in the hospital.'

We lived for months hearing nothing except news about death. When the epidemic was over my mother continued to take certain precautions and sterilize things. To this day I still heat my bread on the burner as my mother used to do forty-seven years ago in Menouf.

I remember my father's pale face and his red eyes the day he came back from the village, still hear the voice of Sittil Hajja as she stood at the door wearing her black *gallabeya*: 'My heart keeps eating me all night over Zaynab.' How had she felt that her daughter was dying despite the distance that separated them? Why among all her five daughters had Zaynab been the only one she mentioned, and why had Zaynab been the only one who was afflicted with cholera? Had she heard her voice calling out to her in the night? Had it reached her across space and made her decide to leave at once, so that she would be at her side when she took her last breaths and died? Father called this telepathy, which is the ability to sense others who are far away. His grandmother, the woman from Gaza, was said to have had this unusual ability, and perhaps Sittil Hajja had inherited it from her mother.

Sittil Hajja's grandson Nagah became the heart of her life. Her eyes might have lost their glow, but they followed him wherever he went. She would sit there on the threshold of her house watching him playing. She deprived herself of food to be able to pay his school fees, repeating what she used to do for my father and his step-brother, Sheikh Muhammad, when she sent them to study in Cairo many years before.

When Nagah was admitted to secondary school, he was living with relatives in Matareya or Ain Shams. He took the train every day from Zeitoun station. It was the same train I used to take from Zeitoun station every morning when I was living in my grandfather's house, the same train that ran over a number of poor school-boys and killed or maimed them under its wheels.

Nagah fell under the train as he was racing to catch it one morning, the same way as I used to race for it when I was a school-girl his age. He was wearing a pair of brand new leather shoes which Sittil Hajja had bought for him, and his foot slipped. He fell under the train and it cut off both his legs. I visited him in Demerdash hospital, saw him lying under the covers without legs, a look of surprise in his large green eyes as he looked around and asked: 'Where have my new shoes gone?'

Sittil Hajja's heart broke and she died a short while after. Before she died she said to my paternal aunt: 'Fatna,˙ send to your brother Al-Sayed and tell him to come.' 'Why, mother?' Fatima asked. 'I'm going to die, Fatna, and I want to see him.' 'What do you mean die, mother, and God's will being great you're as strong as a horse.' 'Girl send for your brother, I want to see him before I die', Sittil Hajja said.

Sittil Hajja died in her house in her village, Kafr Tahla. After she died people went on talking about her death, just as years ago they had talked about her mother's death.

I was not there when she died, but I visited the village two years later. My paternal aunt Fatima was still telling the story, and as soon as I arrived she sat me down next to her, brought her mouth up to my ear, and told it to me from beginning to end. She

---

* The name Fatima is often pronounced this way by illiterate village and town people.

continued to tell it over and over again, day after day, without ever wearying until the day she also died, and I can still hear her voice floating through the night as it did over forty years ago:

Your Sittil Hajja died a death that everyone would wish for themselves. That day she woke up at dawn as usual, did her ablutions, prayed, and then called out to me. I woke up to her voice repeating, 'Fatna, Fatna.' I said, 'What do you want mother?' She said, 'Daughter, it looks as though life is over for me. Go call your brothers and sisters all of them and find someone who can travel to Misr, and tell your brother to come immediately, tell him your mother wants to see you before she dies.' I said. 'Mother, evil be far from you, you're as fine as ever.'

She got up as usual, God's will is great, swept the house, sprayed water on the floor of the Ka'a,* put on the black silk *gallabeya* which your father bought her for the big Eid, saying, 'So that I meet God with my new *gallabeya*', frankincensed the earthenware water jug, and put drops of rosewater in it, so that my brother Al-Sayed could drink from it when he came, since, as she said, her beloved son never drank water unless there were drops of rosewater in it. Then she lay down on the straw mat with her head pointing towards Al-Kibla,† saying: 'So that when I die my head will be pointing to the holy city of Mecca, and the tomb of the Prophet, the Prophets prayers, a thousand prayers be on it, and so that, my beloved son, when you come to see your mother die, you'll find her lying like this, but this time you must harden you heart, and not worry, apple of my eye, because I'm going straight to Paradise. I've visited the Prophet's tomb,‡ and have done good all my life, and brought up five orphan girls, and their brother, and his half brother born of your father.§ Fatna, go now and slaughter a chicken and cook some *mulukheya* for your brother Al-Sayed when he comes, and call Nefissa to light the oven and make a couple of pastry loaves, and let Zaynab, the daughter of Baheya, go to the fields and gather some figs.'

---

* A central room in a peasant's house where during the day most things are done, like preparing dough, washing clothes, preparing meals, chatting, etc. Since it usually has a dust floor, water is sprayed on it.
 † The direction in which Moslems face when they pray and which points to the city of Mecca.
 ‡ That is, done the pilgrimage to Mecca, one of the five main tenets of Islam.
 § Since her husband Habash died.

And Sittil Hajja went on like that from the moment she woke up at dawn until the sun set. She would fall silent for a little while, and we would say, it's over, she's dead, but a moment later she'd come back and recite the verse of Yasseen and talk to Azraeen* as though he were standing in front of her: 'Keep away, Azraeen, until my son gets here, I want to see him before I die, and you'll never take me away, Azraeen, until I've seen my son Al-Sayed. Get up, Fatna, and go see why your brother hasn't got here yet and you, lad, yes you, Hosni, take this *bariza* (ten piastres) and go buy a packet of tea and some sugar from your uncle Al-Hajj Afifi's store, for your uncle Al-Sayed Bey and the men when they fill up the house, and you child, yes you, Na'eema, chase the flies away from your face so that your uncle will say that you are a pretty girl, and a clean one too. And you, Nageya, take the water jar and go fill it from the river because the water in the *za'laa*† is almost finished.'

And Sittil Hajja kept on like that the whole day long. For long moments she would be silent as though she had died, and we'd recite Al-Fatiha over her, but she'd suddenly come to again and say 'Shoo away from me, Azraeen, may God take you.' Hasn't my son Al-Sayed come yet? I can see him there at the railway crossing. Get up, Fatna, and go meet your brother at the crossing.' And I got up and did as my mother told me, and found my brother coming towards the crossing on foot. Poor apple of his mother's eye, his face was as pale as a lemon. He had taken the first train to Benha, then got into a taxi. The taxi had broken down a little distance after Tahla and so he had to walk all the way to the crossing, but Sittil Hajja had made up her mind that one way or another she would not let Azraeen come anywhere near her until she had seen her son. So I quickly embraced him at the crossing and said to him your mother's waiting for you, brother, and by the time we entered the house they had recited Al-Fatiha over the body of Sittil Hajja and pulled the covers over her, but as soon as she heard your father's voice she pushed the cover aside, opened her eyes and took him into her arms, the same way as she had always done, all the while repeating, 'Why were you late, my son?' He said, 'the taxi broke down on the way, mother', and she said 'It's a blessing that you've come son', and those were the last words she ever pronounced

---

* The angel of death. The way illiterate village or town people pronounce 'Israel'.

† A big earthenware pot kept in the house for storing water.

before dying, her head pointing towards Al-Kibla and the light of the Prophet shining all around her, and there's nothing better than the blessings of the Prophet.

As I listened to the voice of my aunt Fatima, my eyes kept glancing around the house as though the spirit of Sittil Hajja was still alive in it, for I could see her standing at the door, or hovering near the oven, or sitting straight-backed on the threshold of the house, or on the straw mat, chasing Azraeen away, and covering her mouth with the edge of her *tarha* as she laughed until the tears came to her eyes from so much laughter, then whispering, 'God will that it be good.'

Sittil Hajja's spirit did not disappear until my father died. Perhaps she was waiting for him until he went with her to the other world. By that time I had grown older, and knew that the spirit is not separated from the body, and does not come back after death. I had by then studied medicine, but I also read a lot in other areas. My mind was rid of superstitions, but nevertheless Sittil Hajja's spirit seemed different from other spirits, seemed to have a will of its own which made it capable of appearing whenever it wanted, as though it were made of a special spiritual substance, out of which only gods are made. Perhaps her grandmother, the woman from Gaza, had bequeathed to her the spirit she had inherited from Ashtar,* her nature, her fertility, or from Noon,† the goddess of the universe, born before all masculine gods.

In 1947, I obtained my fifth-year secondary-school certificate, known at that time as the 'cultural certificate', and was moved up to the sixth and final year of secondary schooling called *al-tawgeheya*.‡ I opted for the sciences, having decided not to go in for mathematics or the humanities. I preferred studying chemistry and physics to geometry and algebra and the other

---

* A Mesopotanian female goddess akin in folklore to Isis.
† An ancient Egyptian female goddess.
‡ Meaning the year which directs one to sciences or mathematics or the humanities.

subjects taught under mathematics, or to history, geography and the other subjects taught in the humanities.

The stage of secondary schooling lasted five years for boys but for girls it was six years. I asked my father why this discrimination between boys and girls. He told me that the Ministry of Education seemed to consider that girls had less brain than boys and their 'faith' was weaker. There were also additional subjects that were not taught to boys, subjects like child-care, sewing and embroidery, cooking and making cakes or pastries, as well as cleaning windows and toilets, and scrubbing floors!

I usually pretended sickness in order to absent myself from these additional classes, tied a black band around my head, like women mourning a recent death, stayed in bed so that the school nurse would come to see me. She was a short fat woman who walked slowly over the ground like a duck, sat on the edge of my bed, and did no more than rest her plump hand on my forehead. I closed my eyelids so that she would not notice the black eyes I was hiding behind them, eyes sparkling with life and health, with the burning desire to continue the novel hidden under my pillow. 'My child, you have a slight temperature and all you need is some rest, and an aspirin and tomorrow if God wills, you'll be fine.' She gave me three small white tablets in the palm of my hand which I threw in the toilet bowl before returning to continue my reading.

The story I was reading was written in English and was called *Jane Eyre*. Miss Saneya had given it to us as a text. She was the only teacher who smiled at me when we met; the only teacher I heard say 'Nawal is gifted'; the only teacher who, when she came, brought the sunshine with her and, when she left, took it away.

My heart beat more strongly during English classes. I was not sure whether it was my love for literature or for Miss Saneya. She resembled Miss Yvonne, my school-teacher in Menouf, the same slender body, the same light step, but she was taller, her complexion was not so dark, and for her my heart beat even stronger. She reminded me of the letter *F*, of my first love. To me she was like a spirit that floated through the air without a body, only the eyes, and of the eyes only the quick shine, the colour of pure honey like the eyes of my mother.

She used to walk up and down in the class as she read from a novel by Charlotte Brontë or Jane Austen, or Emily Brontë, three women writers whom we studied in the English class. In the Arabic class, we did not study a single woman writer, and in the library of the school I did not come across a single book by an Arab woman.

I loved the Arabic language and was in the habit of writing in Arabic. I dreamt of becoming like Taha Hussayn. I searched through history in vain for the woman of my dreams, so I was left only with Taha Hussayn.

But Miss Saneya started to have a place in my imagination. My heart beat every time I saw her. Her honey-coloured eyes reminded me of my mother. Was I looking for the mother left behind in Menouf, or for my first love suppressed but still alive in me? I did not perceive her as someone with a body, she was neither a man, nor a woman for me. My love had nothing to do with sex. It was a different kind of need, need for the type of human being, for the kind of God I had looked for in vain when I was a child. It was the need for a just God who did not give my brother twice my share just because he was a male.

Miss Saneya did not pronounce the words of the English language in the same way as English people did. She seemed to be always doing things in her own special way, creating her own special voice, her own special way of walking, and the special shine that showed in her eyes when she saw me, a shine that swept me out of my feeling of alienation with the world. The loneliness I lived, the profound undefined sadness within me disappeared. I was transformed suddenly into a happy human being who laughed, sang, and danced, whose voice rang through the universe. Now I could almost embrace the sun, as I ran and ran and ran in the big courtyard of the school as though nothing except the high stone wall could stop me.

And because I have never known how to conceal things, how to be secretive, the whole school got to know about my love story. No sooner did Miss Saneya open the door of her room in the boarding school, than the girls started a race with one another to find me, to make me dump whatever I was doing, and run as fast as I could to see her as she walked down the corridor towards the toilets reserved for the teachers, or as she went down the stairs on her way to one of her classes, or to the courtyard or to any other place in the whole wide world.

Love stories between the school-girls and the teachers occurred quite often. Sometimes three or four girls would be in love with one teacher. Hearts would burn with jealousy, with the heat of competition, and the greater the number of girls in love with her the more the teacher would swell with conceit.

Most of the girls were in love with Abla Nefissa, the teacher who gave classes in drawing. In their opinion she was the most beautiful, the most smartly dressed and the most striking of all the teachers. I did not feel attracted to her. She looked to me more like a doll, or a picture drawn on canvas. Her features were so perfect, so carefully cut and exact that they lost that special thing which is attraction. Her personality, like her features, lacked the unusual, the extraordinary. Abla Nefissa was ordinary, submissive, incapable of firing my imagination. She belonged to the type of women who are princesses or wives of kings, or presidents, women who never appear except with complete make-up, and always walk in the shadow of a man, disappearing once he has ceased to be there. They are addressed as madam, or her highness, or the wife of his excellency, or of his highness, or the First Lady.

But Miss Saneya was different in a way I could not exactly define. The main difference was that she did not look like any of the other women, especially the ones we could call shadow women. She always appeared without make-up, or a hair-do, and never walked in the wake of the headmistress, or the minister when he paid a visit to our school.

I learnt to love English literature because she was the one who taught it. I waited for the lesson like someone thirsty in the desert waits for a drop of water. I picked up every word that fell from her lips as though it were a pearl. Whatever she taught us stuck to my memory. I had no need to study her lessons, I knew them all by heart without needing to read. It was enough for me to listen with my eyes fixed on her as though drawn by a magnet, and my ears open so as not to miss a single one of her words. Safeya, who sat next to me, would keep digging me with her elbow but it was as though I were not there. A fire could have broken out in class without my noticing. My senses, my mind, my imagination were gathered together in an undivided concentration, on a single circumscribed spot in the universe where she happened to be.

Then came the shock which dispelled the spell and with it the love. We were at the beginning of the summer of 1948. The final examinations were closing in on us and like the other boarders I was accustomed to walk up and down the long corridors in front of our dormitory holding a book in my hand, going over the lessons in it. There was a corridor that circled round the teachers' rooms, and it was a favourite with the girls for reasons everyone knew, but I never went anywhere near it. I was afraid Miss Saneya might open her door, find me there and imagine that I was hoping for an opportunity to see her. I used to long to see her every single moment of the day and night on condition that it never looked as though I had been seeking this chance. I wanted to appear aloof, indifferent, and not flighty or emotional like the other girls.

It was a Friday and Miss Saneya, like other teachers, did not spend her Fridays in the school. She used to pick up her small bag on Thursdays after classes were over, leave, and not reappear before Saturday morning. So on Fridays I walked up and down that corridor without fear. I used to lift my eyes from the book, stare at her closed door for a moment, and then come back to the book. I knew she was not in her room or in any other part of the school. Her room was empty, and it made me feel that the whole world was empty too, was without meaning.

Suddenly her door opened just I was passing in front of it, and there she was a short distance from where I was standing. I stood stock still, unable to move, so I had time to see her well. She was wearing her nightdress with a towel slung over her shoulder, and a bar of soap in her hand. A very ordinary sight, and yet to me it was as though I had been struck by a thunderbolt, maybe because it was so ordinary. But in addition to that her nightdress was open below the neck, and I glimpsed the thing that stands out on the chest of women and which people commonly call a breast. My conscious mind told me that she was a woman and that she had to have a breast and a womb, and everything else that women have. But all these were only abstract thoughts like the existence of God and the devil and other matters of a similar nature. That these thoughts should be transformed into flesh and blood, that was the real catastrophe.

The ecstasy of love disappeared like a fine summer cloud under the sun. It no longer possessed that wonderful magic of before. So were things at that time, yet years after a special relationship continued to link me to her. The first image of her in my mind remained with me after I left school. I kept a photograph of her in a drawer, tall, slender smiling like radiant sunshine.

Four years went by and I met her by accident as I was walking down Kasr Al-Aini street. For a long moment I did not recognize her. In four years she had been transformed into an ageing, limping woman. Then she lifted her face to me and smiled. I recognized the smile and the shine of her honey-coloured eyes. 'What a wonderful coincidence. It's really you, Miss Saneya', I exclaimed.

At one time the mere idea of pronouncing her name was enough to tie my tongue and bring my heart to a stop. 'Where are you now, Nawal?', she asked. 'I'm in the School of Medicine, here in Kasr Al-Aini Street.' 'So you're going to be a doctor, not a writer, then?' I did not know what to answer, as though by going to the school of Medicine I had betrayed her. 'Nawal, you have a gift, and it's a pity that you've chosen medicine.' 'And where are you now, Miss Saneya?' I asked her in turn. 'I've moved to the Institute of Music. It's also here in Kasr Al-Aini Street.'

She was about two minutes' walk from where I was. I used to visit her in the institute and each time I saw her her condition seemed worse. She had rheumatoid arthritis and no-one knew how to treat it, since the exact cause was unknown.

The last time we met was in 1955. I had become a resident doctor in Kasr Al-Aini hospital. She could hardly move the joints of her hands or feet. Despite everything, her face would light up when she saw me, and her honey-coloured eyes would begin to shine. It hurt my heart to think that she of all persons had this illness which prevented her from moving. She died one year before my mother.

28

The Qur'an Betrayed

In Helwan school I became well-known for my love of prose, poetry and literature. Whenever there was a school celebration I was asked to stand on the platform, and give a speech, or recite a poem. The biggest celebrations were those organized for the king's birthday, or the anniversary of the birth of the Prophet, or on the occasion of the Prophet's migration from Mecca to Madina (the city of light) which was called Eid Al-Hajira (the festival of emigration).

In the year 1948, the school organized the usual celebration of Eid Al-Hajira and I was asked to prepare a speech for the occasion. So I closed the door on myself in the library and started to read everything there was about the life of Muhammad. I found out that his mother was called Amina Bint (daughter of) Wahb. She died when he was still nursing at her breast, and his uncle Abd Al-Mottalib took him in charge. He became a camel driver travelling through the desert, and was known for his honesty, so people called him Al-Amin, the honest one, and his popularity amongst the members of his tribe Koraish (the ruling tribe of Mecca) became great. Al-Sayeda (Lady) Khadija, who came from a noble family in the tribe, married him and after their marriage she entrusted her money to him, and he managed her trade for her so successfully that she became very rich. But after this he started to isolate himself in the mountain caverns of Ghar Hera'a in order to meditate and worship the gods, and the Angel Gabriel descended on him with the Qur'an and said to him, 'Recite in the name of Allah the creator. He created man from a worm. Recite in the name of Allah the most bountiful. He taught us to write with a pen.'

Prophet Muhammad did not understand what Gabriel meant by these words, was seized with a great fear, and went back to his wife, his teeth chattering, his body trembling all over. He said to her, 'Wrap me up, wrap me up.' Al-Sayeda Khadija calmed him down and said to him, 'Allah has sent Gabriel to you with a message that you are the prophet of Islam. Go out to the people and carry his message to them.'

Al-Sayeda Khadija was the first Muslim convert to believe in Muhammad. After that people flocked to Islam, but were it not for her, her husband might not have engaged in his mission and founded Islam. That's what my father explained to me, and it made me feel proud, for she was a woman like me. I often referred to her to challenge my uncle Sheikh Muhammad when he used to say that in the Qur'an Allah did not address himself to women, and had not mentioned a single woman apart from Mary the mother of our Lord Jesus, peace be upon him.

I decided to read the Qur'an right through from beginning to end. Then I realized that what my uncle Sheikh Muhammad had said was true. Allah did not address Eve except through her spouse, Adam, and the name of Khadija was not mentioned once although she had participated in the founding of Islam, and was the one who directed her husband to the path that made him become the prophet of Islam. Why had God ignored Al-Sayeda Khadija and other women who had fought and died, martyrs on the battlefields of Islam? Why did God address himself only to men, and if he did address himself to women, why was it always through men? Why should a man's share be double that of a woman? Why were men made 'responsible for women' and why had God mentioned men who were much less worthy than Al-Sayeda Khadija, men like Lot, Majuj and Yajuj, or Isaac and Jacob? And why was King Solomon's name mentioned in the Qur'an, whereas that of Belkis, Queen of Sheba, was completely neglected although she was known for her greater knowledge, and for her more profound thought and culture.

Lots of questions began to go round in my head, but when I asked my father, he did not have the answer to them. He was satisfied with repeating things like, 'It's God's wisdom', or 'There are things in religion we believe with our hearts because the human mind is incapable of penetrating God's wisdom.'

I had just turned seventeen, but in my mind I was not convinced by what my father was saying. If God's wisdom could not be understood by human beings, how could it be wisdom, and to whom then was it directed? If God was not just in his dealings with people irrespective of race or sex, how could we ask people to be more just than he was? If God had created man and woman from the same living thing, why should he discriminate between them?

I began to suffer from chronic headache and was unable to find out the reason. The nurse told me I was 'overflowing', because I had reached puberty, and she gave me aspirin and different pills. The headache sometimes disappeared but then I would often have pains in different parts of my body, and they increased when I had my periods. The Qur'an said: 'And they ask you about the menses. Say it is an offence, and keep away from the women until they are cleansed.' So I used to stay in bed during my periods, and isolate myself from everybody. I said to myself: 'It shall be by my hand, and not by that of Amr.'* I would rather shun the whole world than let the whole world shun me. My body was rebelling against my body, the muscles of my inner

---

* A well-known saying which means, 'I can do it to myself but let no-one do it to me.' When Amr Ibn Al-Aas ruled in Egypt, an opponent of his said: 'I prefer to kill myself rather than submit', and expressed it in these words.

organs developed spasms, and I suffered with painful colic. The moment I saw blood in my underclothes, I was seized with nausea and could not eat. If I ate something I vomited it immediately. I could not bear either the sight or the odour of the offence inflicted on me by God, spoke to him with anger in my dreams, waved my clenched fist at the heavens. Was there no cleaner way of telling girls that they had reached the age of maturity? Why this offence, O God in Heaven?

To my good luck, my period was over by the time the anniversary of Emigration Day arrived. I was scared lest this sacred occasion would fall on a day when I was still impure. Our teachers kept repeating that when women had their periods they should not stand before God in prayer, should not repeat a single word of the Qur'an, or of the Prophet's sayings in an audible voice, or even under their breath. So when I had my periods, during the class I used to tremble when I was asked to read something from the holy texts. Death seemed easier to me than to admit in class that I had the menses. Ever since I had been assailed by 'this offence', I had concealed it from everybody, including my mother and the other members of our household.

Since the moment I had been asked to make the speech at the celebration I had kept praying to God that he keep the offence away from me on that particular day. How could I stand up on the platform and talk in a loud voice to hundreds of people about the emigration of the holy Prophet, how could I quote verses from the Qur'an, or sayings by the Prophet when I was guilty of having the offence, of being afflicted with what he imposed upon women, that they be isolated until they were cleansed of it? During the long hours spent in the library preparing my speech I had continued in secret to commit the sin by touching the Holy Qur'an and the Prophet's words with fingers which had not yet been cleansed. Ever since I was a child I had been convinced that God saw everything I did, knew when I had my periods, was watching me when I was in the toilets. These were thoughts that had never left my head.

I had learnt the speech I was going to give that day by heart. In it I said that the tribe of Koraish had continued to believe in stone idols which could do neither good nor harm to people, whereas Sayedna (Our Lord) Muhammad asked everyone to believe in God, in the one and only God, and in the Holy Qur'an. Koraish planned to murder the Prophet, so he fled from the city in the dark of night, and his cousin, Ali Ibn Abou Talib, slept in his place to mislead his assailants. On the way to Al-Madina, the Prophet and his followers hid in an abandoned cave, and God sent a spider to spin its web over the opening to the cave. The pagans from Koraish who were pursuing Muhammad saw the spider's web covering the opening, and their thinking led them to imagine that no-one could have gone into the cave, or else the web would have been swept away. God had saved his Prophet by one of his miracles and so Muhammad and his followers arrived safely in Al-Madina where crowds of their partisans flocked to receive them, and celebrate their arrival with joy.

I was alone on the platform in front of the hall crowded with school-girls, the teachers sitting in the front row with the head-mistress and visitors from the Ministry of Education in the middle. I stood there straight as an arrow, my face lifted to the heavens, delivering my speech in a tone that resembled that of my father. My voice trembled with holy fervour when I pronounced the name of Allah the Almighty, and when I said that the arrival of the spider to weave a web over the opening of the cave at that particular time was a miracle of God I lifted both arms to the heavens, pronounced each phrase, each word with a special emphasis, prolonged the word spider so that it became 'spiiiider' to make it stand out as a sign of absolute faith in God's miraculous powers. I felt my heart flutter under my ribs, and the tears gather in my eyes. Applause echoed in the hall, so I repeated the part about the spider imitating Um Koulsoum and Abdel Wahab when they sang *mawals* (wandering minstrels' songs) or Sheikh Muhammad Riffa'at reciting the Qur'an on the radio.

I now had an excellent reputation in school. People pointed to me admiringly: 'She is a model pupil, combines science with religious faith" is outstanding in chemistry, physics and rhetoric. Her eloquence is remarkable, and she writes both poetry and prose, and knows the Qur'an and the Prophet's sayings by heart.'

In my mind Arabic literature became linked to Islam. Religious belief became a part of my deepest feelings together with my love for my father. I forgot my childhood, how I do not know. From a child who had doubts about the justice of God, I was transformed into a reasonable, deeply religious girl. I lost my natural gift for seeing paradoxes. God no longer appeared in my dreams in a human or a semi-human form, and the devil also disappeared from them. The echo of repeated applause crept to my ears from under the pillow. I opened my mouth as wide as possible as though yawning when I repeated the story of the cobweb, and praised God's miraculous powers. But in my sleep my child's mind would emerge to question: Is this what you call a miracle? And if it was a miracle, couldn't the miracle have happened in Mecca, and then there would have been no need for emigration, and for all the troubles our Prophet Muhammad had to go through, no need for him to be chasing around like that?

I would open my eyes in the middle of the night with a feeling of guilt, creep out of bed to the bathroom, do my ablutions, and tiptoe back to the dormitory, lay a piece of clothing on the tiled floor to serve as a prayer carpet, and start praying fervently to God, prostrating myself again and again. Then I would recite verses of the Holy Qur'an, verses which sounded like music, like a poem with rhyme and rhythm.

There was a verse which I was fond of repeating to myself as if it were a refrain: 'And if the female child buried alive is asked for what sin she was killed.'[†] My eyes filled with tears as though

---

[*] Many years later Sadat's slogan after he came to power!
[†] Pre-Islamic Arab tribes often buried a newly born child alive if it turned out to be a female.

I was that child, had been buried alive since I was born, and was being asked the question. At times, while reciting, I used to add words of my own to the words of God to improve the meaning or the rhythm.

In the Arabic language classes the teacher was in the habit of saying that eloquence meant an economy in words, that repetition and stuffing with unnecessary words resulted in bad style. So I started to delete the repetitions and the unnecessary words from the Qur'an. But the teacher strongly forbade me to do that and said to me: 'You stupid ass. The Qur'an is the most miraculous of all God's miracles and no human being can write anything that is anywhere near as splendid, so how do you dare make changes in it?' I reminded him of what he had said about stuffing with words and repetition. He shouted angrily: 'You stupid ass, there's no stuffing with words, or repetition in the Qur'an.'

My childhood was on its way to disappearing completely. The pure, mature, idealistic young girl was taking over my body and mind. The phantom of my first love had become autonomous with the shadow of the devil, with original sin. Religious faith had swept away the last vestiges of doubt. I started my descent to an absolute belief with the steady step of my father, became a model of piety and moral behaviour to the girls, prayed regularly, fasted the month of Ramadan, pronounced my words in an eloquent classical Arabic style, supported what I said with verses from the Holy Qur'an, and the sayings of the Prophet, peace be on him.

29

British English and
Holy Arabic

I passed my secondary-school certificate with distinction. I wanted to go to the School of Literature, to become a writer, but my father told me that graduates from this school became either government civil servants or clerks: 'And besides, Nawal', he said, 'what future have people of letters in this country? They live and die in poverty like the poet Al-Deeb. In one of his poems he has a line which says: I am a wall on which is written, 'O man with a full bladder, piss here.' My mother laughed, was silent for a moment, then said: 'You know, Nawal, who seeks admission to the School of Literature. Those who are no good at school or have low grades. But you got the highest grades. Go to the School of Medicine. You may become a famous doctor like Ali Ibrahim [one of the first and foremost surgeons of Egypt] and you'll be able to look after us free.'

But in my dreams I continued to imagine myself becoming a writer like Taha Hussayn. I loved the Arabic language, its letters, its words, their rhythmic music in my ears. I believed it was God who had created it, given it a higher status than all other languages by sending the Qur'an down to people in Arabic, whereas the English language had been created by human beings, by the British. Arabic was a divine language, it had in it the spirit of Almighty God, since it was a divine creation, and the Arab nation was the greatest of all the nations with which God had peopled the earth. It looked down on other nations from a throne up high. They spoke languages which were ordinary, human, belonged to inferior nations which were not even mentioned in Allah's holy book. But at night the silent child would wake up in my dreams and, no longer dumb, would ask: 'If God loves us more than he loves other nations, why did he let them discover the energy which is in steam and electricity, and invent the radio, the telegraph, the aeroplanes and the submarine?'

I was admitted to medical school in the autumn of 1948. The first year was called preparatory year and we attended our lectures in the School of Sciences, which was located in the main building of the university.

The word university for years had had a magic ring in my ears, and here I was a student in Fouad Al-Awal University in Giza. The main building had a dome which looked down on me as I stood in the grounds, and in the middle of the huge dome was the clock which gave out rich, deep, awe-inspiring chimes that made me start when I heard them.

When it first opened its doors, the university accepted only male students, but after many years had passed, in the second half of the 1930s, it began to accept female students. The mere thought that the girls sat next to the boys in the auditorium made my heart thump. Was it possible for girls and boys, for the two sexes, to mix? There were still many words that made the blood rush to my face, and words like sex and men were among them.

Co-education was only allowed in kindergartens, and at the university, which means that in the primary and secondary schools the sexes were not permitted to mix. I had, therefore, spent a total of ten years, four in primary school and six in secondary school, without mixing with boys. My heart fluttered as I walked down the street to the main gate as though I would fall in love with the first boy I met in the university. I lifted up my shoulders, straightened my back, and gave my face a serious expression by frowning slightly and tightening my lips, so that everybody would think I was a serious girl with model behaviour. Was I not now a mature girl seventeen years old? God! Seventeen years! The number seventeen when I whispered it under my breath made me sound very old, more like seventy, or seven hundred. Since I had reached the age of seventeen people had started to describe me as grown-up, as the eldest of the girls in the family. All the other girls in the Al-Saadawi and the Shoukri Bey families had been married off, and had become mothers by the time they reached the age of seventeen.

My uncle Sheikh Muhammad had a daughter called Fawzeya living in Kafr Tahla. She could have gone to the university, but he married her to a teacher from a nearby village called Biltan. 'Girls rubbing shoulders with boys in the university is dangerous for the girls', he used to whisper to my father, in a voice that hissed like Satan. My mother would protest and say in a loud voice so that everyone could hear: 'You can throw our daughter Nawal in the fire and she will come back safe. Nawal is not like other girls, Sheikh Muhammad.'

My mother's words used to lift me high up above the heads of the girls, in the same way as her arms used to lift me above the waves when I was a child. Since I was admitted to the School of Medicine she had started to address me as Dr Nawal. My father gave me this title only in the presence of guests. My uncle Sheikh Muhammad would pout in disapproval whenever my father did this, as though between him and me there was some old feud, an animosity of unknown origin handed down from past generations. He never called me by name, always used the word 'girl' when he spoke to me, addressing me as 'you girl', and I always refused to answer him. 'I'm speaking to you girl', he would say, 'answer me'. I would turn my back on him, ignoring him completely, as though he were not there, upon which he would say 'Where are you going, girl? Come recite the verse of "The Cow" [a passage in the Qur'an] to me. Have you memorized the Qur'an or not? Allah's book will be more important to you than your books on medicine. The Qur'an has everything in it, includes all knowledge, and all sciences. And you, boy, yes you, Tala'at, come here next to me and recite the verse of "The Cow".'

My brother Tala'at was more cheeky than I was, and would answer back: 'I am Oustaz Tala'at, the great musician, and I prefer the buffalo to the cow, your highness the Sheikh', at which Sheikh Muhammad would almost fall off the sofa on which he was squatting, as though bitten by a snake. His big turban swayed wildly on his head so he would lift up his two hands to steady it, all the time asking God under his breath to protect him from the evil Satan (prevent him from losing his temper) before he walked away hurriedly in his wide, loose kaftan. His walk resembled that of his second wife, was very much like that of a well-fed duck. He was short and fat and had a big high belly like a pregnant woman. His legs were thin and he staggered a little when he walked to the small table on which he had put his cane, picked it up and tried to run after my brother shouting, 'Come here you rascal.'

In these tussles all he ever ended up with was to choke from a loss of breath. When he collapsed back on the sofa we could hear the sound of air blowing in and out of his mouth and nose. Sometimes, it blew out of his backside too, for his second wife never stopped feeding him with lambs' feet, stuffed cabbages, and *fetta* with garlic, and every time he went to the toilet my brother would block his ears with his fingers, and burst out into endless peals of laughter. My brother only got up to these tricks when my mother was not there. She would be away in the kitchen, or somewhere else, but when she heard Sheikh Muhammad scolding us in a loud voice she'd come out to see what was happening. I used to share in these little games with my brother since they were a source of great delight to us.

My uncle Sheikh Muhammad was completely different to my father, perhaps because he was not the son of Sittil Hajja.

Father inherited her tall stature and her natural intelligence. Both he and Sheikh Muhammad studied at Al-Azhar University together and they graduated at the same time. My uncle stayed on to become a teacher at Al-Azhar University and never understood anything in Islam apart from its rituals and its very limiting jurisprudence, but my father broke away from these limitations and went to Dar Al-Oloum and other schools. He even taught himself a little French, perhaps to woo my mother. He could have become Minister of Education if he had agreed to join the game of political parties, but he despised hypocrisy and all attempts to reach power and be in a position of authority at the expense of dignity, self-respect and the right to voice his own opinion freely. In the home of my uncle Sheikh Muhammad there were no books apart from the Qur'an, books on religion, and religious jurisprudence. But my father had a library in which there were novels, poetry, books on literature and literary criticism, philosophy, history and some translated works.

Fawzeya, the daughter of Sheikh Muhammad, like Zaynab the daughter of my paternal aunt Baheya, dreamt of becoming an important Oustaza. Instead she became the wife of a teacher in Biltan, and gave birth to a number of boys and girls. Sometimes I used to drop in to her house on my way to Kafr Tahla. Her sad, pale face reminded me of her mother. She sat in front of the primus stove stirring the big pot from which arose a cloud of steam with a ladle. Her eldest daughter sat beside her. 'Mother, I want to be a doctor like Auntie Nawal', she would say, and I could see her eyes shine. Her mother would stare at me in silence for a long moment, suck her lips, then hide her face in the pot cooking on the fire, and start to stir again, while her daughter took me into a small room, lifted the mattress of her bed, brought out a small notebook which resembled the diary I used to keep when I was her age, and opened it with her long, slender fingers. Between the pages was a dried white butterfly and a small folded piece of paper which she opened to reveal a newspaper clipping with my picture on it. Below was an article, and the title said: 'A woman is a human being and she thinks.' 'I want to write like you, Auntie Nawal', she said.

Years later I was passing through Biltan and remembered the little girl who had shown me the newspaper clipping with my picture on it. After asking several people, I managed to find her house. There were children playing around and one of them took me in through the open door of a small, ugly red brick house. On the floor of the parlour squatted a woman in front of a pot stirring it with a long-handled spoon. By her side stood a little girl with curly hair wearing a yellow dress and sandals. I walked in and it was the living image of Fawzeya that looked up at me.

During the year 1948, the same year in which I was admitted to the university, my father was transferred from Menouf to Giza. He had sent a complaint to the Minister of Education. He said that it had become clear to him that promotions in the ministry did not depend on work, or on performance but on personal relations and recommendations, and that he had the intention of publishing his letter in the newspapers, with examples.

At that time political opposition within the country was growing, and its influence on events increasing. Rumours about the corruption of the king and the political system were rampant. The pressures on people, due to the rise in the cost of living, were becoming difficult to support, and leading to more and more dissatisfaction. The national movement was attracting increasing numbers of people to its ranks, especially students and youth. Strikes and demonstrations kept breaking out in different parts of the country.

After the complaint, my father was promoted and became general inspector of education in the province of Giza. He was able to rent a single-storey house surrounded by a small garden in a new and quiet residential area called Omraneya at the beginning of Shar'i Al-Haram, the main road leading to the Pyramids. The house looked out on a stream called Tir'it Al-Zoumour, which flowed for a long distance with flowering trees on either side, and continued on the other side of Al-Haram Road by passing under a small bridge.

In this area there were no tall buildings or shops, and the roar of traffic in the main road on its way to the Auberge (a well-known nightclub) and the Pyramids, or going in the opposite direction to pass under the railway bridge built for trains travelling to Upper Egypt, and then on to Abbas Bridge or Shar'i Al-Gama'a (University Road) and the zoo, did not reach us.

My mother could not stand living in a high building, or a flat without a garden. She liked to open the windows in the morning to sunshine, to the colour of green, and the rustle of trees. Green was as necessary to her as the air she breathed, as the rays of the sun warming her face. My father, too, had been brought up in the midst of fields with growing crops, had always had a longing for the village, for the house of his mother surrounded by endless expanses of green.

I walked every day from home to the university, and from the university to, a distance which took me one hour in the early morning and another hour at the end of the day. I walked with a long, quick stride wearing strong leather shoes like the shoes men wore, and a grey skirt and jacket made of the same wool out of which my father made his suits. In my hand, I carried a black leather bag like the bags carried by doctors.

This daily walk was a form of exercise in the cold, exhilarating morning air which became indispensable to me. I stepped out of our house into a small street for a short distance, then walked along Tir'it Al-Zoumour up to Al-Haram Road, turned left to pass under the railway bridge on to Giza Square, then turned left again into Shar'i Al-Gama'a. Shar'i Al-Gama'a was a very big road with tall trees on either side, and the first day I experienced a feeling close to awe as I walked down it. The trees in the zoo could be seen from it as they rose high above the iron railings of its fence, and in the early morning the incessant chirping of hundreds of birds filled the air. Sometimes I could hear the lion roaring in his cage.

On the other side of the road, opposite to the zoo was Al-Sa'adeya Secondary School for Boys, to which my brother Tala'at went after the family moved from Menouf. The road was always full of school and university students, a sea of bodies filling the road, and overflowing on to the pavements, so that cars found it difficult, or almost impossible to pass. But all these masses of students were male, and I rarely spotted a girl like myself among them. I felt alienated in the midst of all these boys, walking along with a serious mien on their faces. Sometimes one of them would say in a low voice, 'Good morning, beautiful', especially in front of the entrance to the School of Agriculture, where a group of boys started to wait for me every day. When he saw me approach one of them would say 'Here comes Samia Gamal' (a well-known belly-dancer and actress). Another group of students waited in front of the School of Engineering. They called me Esther Williams. I asked my girl colleagues who Esther Williams was and one of them told me she was the heroine of a film called *The Beautiful Swimmers*, or *Mermaids of the Water*, or something like that. And one day the film was showing so I went to see it. There she was on the screen, tall and slender, swimming like a fish. Samia Gamal, whom I saw in films several times, was tall and slender too, but had black hair and a brown skin more like me. But I was happy to feel that I resembled them both, even a bit proud.

But I also heard sarcastic remarks about the way I walked with a long, rapid stride or about my height. A student who was rather short, once walked up to me and said: 'Say, what's the air like up there?' When I got home I would tell my mother and father about the events of the day. They laughed a lot when I told them about the short student and what he had said. And after that my mother would sometimes look at me and say, 'I wonder what the air is like up there?' For my mother was not tall, and even when she put on high-heeled shoes she still remained shorter than me. She would stand on tiptoe and say, 'I wish I was as tall as you, Nawal.'

At the university I used to catch the students' eyes as they stared at me. Deep down I felt there was something that made people look at me, some kind of unknown attraction, not the usual feminine attraction but something else, different, my instinct said to me. I started to develop friendships with some of my new colleagues. Of my previous school-mates in Helwan only Safeya was admitted to the School of Medicine. Samia went to the School of Pharmacology, Fatma to the School of Literature, but we used to meet in the cafeteria of the School of Literature because it was the only one which girls frequented, probably because there were more of them studying literature.

In those days girls were rarely encouraged to enter the sciences, or attend schools of medicine or engineering, or pure science. The word 'sciences' in Arabic was a masculine noun and had a masculine ring to it but *aadaab* (literature) was feminine, and its letters were similar to those of *adab*, which means good manners, well-behaved, docile. An oft-repeated saying was 'Good manners are preferred to science' (meaning knowledge). Good manners and good behaviour were expected of girls, but not necessarily of boys. For boys the common saying was, 'Nothing shames a man but his pocket' (in other words, not to have money is the only thing which a man need be ashamed about!).

One of my new friends was called Camelia, but the nickname by which she was known was Batta (duck). She lived at the beginning of Shari' Al-Haram, near our house. She was short with a square body, and a broad face with large eyes. She darkened her eyelashes with a pencil, and sometimes with *kohl*, which was jet black. She had a dark complexion which she tried to conceal with a thick layer of white powder, and full lips which she coloured red with lipstick. She wore tight skirts which became even narrower above her full knees, so she had to walk with short, slow steps, often faltering on her thin, high heels.

Batta was considered a model of feminine beauty. Her voice was soft, caressing, and she turned the thick guttural sounds of some of the Arabic letters into finer, more feminine sounds.

So with her the thick *d*s, *t*s and *s*s* became finer, more delicate, 'pansy-like' sounds. She pronounced the Arabic *r* as it is pronounced in Parisian French. Batta had a paternal or perhaps maternal uncle who was a pasha with a post in the king's court. Sometimes his picture appeared in the newspaper and then she would stick up her nose even higher in the air.

In those days the university was the scene of almost continuous demonstrations. The students pulled down pictures of the king, threw them on the ground and stamped on them with their feet. My heart beat with happiness whenever I passed through the entrance of the university to find that the students had gathered together in the grounds, and were chanting slogans: 'Down with the British. Down with the King.' It reminded me of my childhood days when I longed that the world would change, that lots of things would collapse.

The female students, apart from a few in the School of Literature and one or two other schools, did not participate in demonstrations. The girls studying medicine or the sciences kept away from politics and concentrated only on their studies. Very often I heard professors in our school say, 'Politics is nothing but clowning and nonsense, good for students of literature who have nothing to do.' But my father always followed what was happening in the country. He read government and opposition newspapers, always talked about the corruption of the king and the ruling class, about British colonial rule and the military occupation of Egypt. He used to say the riches of our country went to the foreigners and to the handful of dishonest pashas who ruled the country. He called Egypt the country of 2 per cent (meaning that 2 per cent of the population owned almost everything, leaving the rest of the population hungry, sick and ignorant). 'It's a chronic triple misery and there's no solution to it without a change in the regime. People must wake up, must rebel', he would say.

---

* In Arabic there are letters which are like twins, close in the way they are pronounced but one has a thin and the other a thick tone.

A Daughter of Isis

Whenever I recalled what my father used to say my heart ached, and I could feel the blood coursing through my body with anger, an anger that had continued to grow since I was a child. Was I not one of the people about whom my father had spoken? One of the people who had to wake up and rebel? So whenever there was a demonstration I could be found amidst the students chanting with them, 'Down with the King. Down with the British', or stamping the pictures of the king, the pashas and the British under my feet. And in May 1943, I discovered a new enemy, the state of Israel, and a new cause, the liberation of Palestine.

Yet for me politics remained a dark world I knew little about. I participated in demonstrations impelled by the love I had for my country, my voice hoarse, my hair all mussed up. In one of these demonstrations, a stone hit my head, close to the eye and I could easily have lost it. Mother started to caution me: 'Nawal, keep away from demonstrations. It's dangerous for you to be always in them.' My father also started to warn me, and I felt he was retreating from the things he had said to me before: 'Demonstrations and what not, that's all nonsense, Nawal. Concentrate on your studies, you need to give them all your time.'

However he did not stop reading the newspapers. In the morning and in the evening I could see him sitting on the verandah, sipping his coffee and smoking a cigarette as he read the news in *Al-Ahram*.* Near him sat my mother, also sipping coffee and leaning over to try and read some of the headlines: 'Dissolution of the Muslim Brotherhood',† 'Hassan Al-Banna shot dead.' At the top of each page there was a picture of King Farouk inside a big frame with a caption undermeath: 'The picture of our beloved King Farouk is engraved on the hearts of our people. The loyal and faithful people of Egypt today celebrate the an-

---

* Was and still is the most important governmental newspaper in Egypt.
† The major fundamentalist movement in Egypt, founded in 1923 by Hassan Al-Banna, a school-teacher and its 'supreme guide' until he was shot dead in retaliation for the assassination of Nokrashi Pasha.

niversary of the birth of our King with hearts full of joy, loyalty and obedience to him.'

I sit in my room studying. I can hear my father's voice rising in anger: 'These newspapers deserve to be burnt. Loyalty and obedience, my foot! These hypocrites who write stuff like that in *Al-Ahram*! The end of this King is in sight. The purchase of outdated arms to make money, and the defeat of our army in Palestine, should be enough to bring him down.'

On my desk were piled my new books and the notebooks in which I took down the lectures. I picked up my scalpel, cut out the picture of the king and the words loyalty and obedience printed under it, and tore it into small pieces.

I looked up the two words 'loyalty and obedience' in my father's special Arabic dictionary. I discovered that they went back to the beginning of slavery. With slavery, came defence of the land, loyalty and obedience to the landowner, to the master. And at the beginning of the month of March 1890, *Al-Ahram* on the occasion of the anniversary of the birth of the Khedive, had written the following: 'The letters of the words love, loyalty and obedience are engraved on the hearts of all Egyptians. The loyal, faithful people of Egypt are overwhelmed with immense joy on the occasion of the anniversary of the birth of our great Khedive, the words submission and obedience are written by loyal hands on the heart of every patriotic Egyptian.'

The word 'love' was therefore linked to submission and slavery, and slavery was linked to loyalty and obedience. But between the years 1890 and that year of 1948 the word slavery was gradually being deleted from the dictionary used by the Egyptian peoples. The power of the slaves was growing, and the national movement was threatening the ruling regime. But *Al-Ahram* was still upholding the regime in the name of what it called our traditions, even if these traditions had proved themselves to be no more than corrupt values that had to be abolished from our lives. *Al-Ahram* was one of the pillars of the regime, an instrument used to corrupt and mislead. It's emblem was the

Pyramids built of stone carried on the backs of slaves thousands of years ago, in order to house the tomb of the Pharaohs, and today the piles of newspapers coming out of its press were being carried on the backs of young boys who ran around the streets selling them for a wage of hunger, as they called out, '*Al-Ahram, Al-Ahram*, read the president's speech.'

In 1949 I entered the main building of the School of Medicine in Kasr Al-Aini Street for the first time, after completing the preparatory pre-medical year in the School of Sciences in Giza. I was now in the first year of Al-Mashraha,* and now it was the word Al-Mashraha that carried a magical ring with it, perhaps even more magical than the first chimes of the university clock that had floated to my ears in Giza. My imagination wandered wildly as I approached the entrance to the building. How could I cut up a human body? How could I cut through the muscle called my heart that never stopped beating under the ribs throughout life? How could I cut through the cells in that brain that never ceased asking questions, and bringing back memories of childhood?

In the preparatory pre-medical year I had dissected only frogs, or cockroaches, or beetles. Since the day I was born my eyes had never fallen on a dead body. A shudder went through my body at the mere mention of the word 'corpse'. I glimpsed the door of the dissecting hall at a distance. My heart beat quickly and for a moment my breathing stopped. Would I meet with spirits and devils in that hall? A penetrating smell was carried up my nose as I drew near. Was that the smell of death?

But my curiosity overcame my fear. I walked in, followed behind by Batta and Safeya. In the hall, marble-topped tables were arranged in long rows. On each table was a body surrounded by a group of students. After a short while we realized that they were groups of eight and then somebody told us that there were seniors who were second-year students, and juniors

---

* The dissecting hall, meaning the year in which students study anatomy and physiology of the normal human body in addition to pharmacology and parasitology.

Nawal (*centre*) in the dissecting room at the Faculty
of Medicine, Cairo University, in 1951.

who were first-year students like us. And so we became a group
of eight students sitting around a table with a dead body, or part
of one, lying on it. Then one of the senior students came up to
explain things to us. That was the tradition in the dissecting
hall, the older students giving a hand to the freshers and vying
with one another over who would explain to the girl students the
mysteries of dissection.

When we were in the dissecting hall we sat on stools. Four
of us sat around the upper part of the body, that is the head
and neck, and four around the lower part, what we called the
lower limbs. In one of the corners of the dissecting hall, near
the door were two huge wooden chests filled with formalin to
prevent the bodies in them from rotting. They were like wooden
tombs crouching in the corner, with the dead floating in that
fluid with a penetrating smell. They were closely guarded by an
orderly called Am Osman, in charge of the dissecting hall. He
had narrow eyes that glinted like those of a hawk. The skin on

his hands was cracked by the formalin in which he kept immersing them, to throw bodies in, or take them out, or push them around. His features were burnt by the sun to a dark pallor, like the faces of the peasants in my village.

Am Osman used to lock the huge chests with keys, as though they contained the riches of the earth, then he would stand in front of them haughtily as though he was Lord Radwan, the guardian angel of Paradise. He smiled only when a rich student went up to him to buy a corpse from him. The price of these corpses was three pounds apiece. He used to steal them in connivance with the undertaker and usually paid him fifty piastres for three dead bodies. During the night he crept into cemeteries and collected the bones of the dead which he sold to the students by the piece.

In the morning I used to see him standing in the courtyard wearing his white coat covered with formalin stains, straining his ears to catch the shrieks of the women as they followed behind the coffin of some relative. The body of the deceased was still warm but he would walk in the funeral procession, as far as the cemetery, to clinch a deal. The students said he had more money and owned more buildings than Mooro, the Dean of Medical School.

When I returned home at the end of the first day, my mother almost shrieked with fear as I came in through the door, as though I had brought back the spirits of the dead in my bag. She made me put the bag with the clothes I was wearing outside the door, then she put my white coat and my dissecting instruments, together with my clothes, in a tin full of water to boil.

In the first few days, I used to shudder whenever I cut into the body with my scalpel for I could not forget that this was human flesh I was dissecting. I stopped eating any kind of meat, and when I saw any floating in the soup tureen I had nausea. It reminded me of a dead limb floating in the formalin. Mother used to prepare a small meal for me and put it in a box, so that I could take it with me in my bag. Sandwiches of egg or meat for protein, green vegetables and fresh fruit rich in vitamins, and bread. I used to throw the box with its contents into a refuse bin, and spend the whole day without eating, except for a glass of tea with mint or lemon which Am Muhammad, the orderly, prepared for me in the female students' room.

I was seized with wonder at the sight of seniors holding a scalpel in one hand, and a sandwich into which they munched in the other, while they stood at our table explaining certain things to us. But soon the wonder evaporated and we juniors started to imitate the seniors. My female colleagues began to eat as they sat around the dissecting table with the body on it. And I started to devour the meat sandwiches that mother prepared for me. My appetite for food returned stronger than before, perhaps because the lust for life becomes greater in the proximity of death, just as light shines more brilliant in the midst of darkness.

One of the professors in the school was a relative of my colleague Batta, whether on her mother's or her father's side, I was not sure. Consequently, Am Osman never refused her any of the treasures stored in his chests, and he once gave her a complete human skeleton for half the usual price. She lived in a two-storied house on Al-Haram Road. Her mother put the skeleton together on the lower floor using wooden supports to hold it up, and Batta used to invite me to her house so that we could go over what we had to study together. This helped me because she could afford to buy whatever corpses or books were required. I, on the other hand, could not purchase from Am Osman anything more than a few pieces of bone belonging to the hand or the foot.

My father's government salary was not small but he had to pay for the education of nine boys and girls in school. He had a small piece of land in Kaft Tahla which he sold little by little to pay off money he owed. The expenses for the School of Medicine were higher than for other schools and books cost a lot. In addition, the cost of living was rising rapidly. As a result I was late paying for the fees of the pre-medical year, and again when I moved to the first year in medical school, and my father received a letter warning him that if he did not pay the fees that were long due his 'honourable daughter' would be expelled.

The day came when my father gave me the envelope containing the first instalment of my fees. I noticed the slight tremor in his fingers as he handed it to me. He was saving on the food of my brothers and sisters to keep me in medical school. Every day he went out early in the morning, worked hard all day and came home in the evening exhausted. At the beginning of each month he handed over his salary to my mother. With it she paid what was owed to the grocer, the butcher, the fruiterer, the vegetable shop, the bakery and the drug store. After that, little was left. We lived for almost half the month on what mother called *shoukouk.** She had a small notebook in which she wrote down everything we owed, day by day.

Before I went out in the morning she used to give me the money to ride the bus or the tramcar. Often I would walk, and give it back to her at the end of the day, or save up to buy a book, or some bones, or a joint from Am Osman. I was sorry for my mother and my father, for the load they both were bearing, and did my best to make it lighter for them.

Mother worked hard all day in the house, helped by a small servant-girl like Sa'adeya. I used to stand at the sink and help her with the plates and sometimes on Fridays when I was home, I cleaned the whole house, or cooked instead of her, or prepared the table, or performed other domestic tasks.

How much I hated the repeated horrid chores I did in those days! No sooner had I finished preparing breakfast, than it was time for lunch, and no sooner had we finished lunch than it was time to prepare for supper. No sooner had I finished cleaning the floor than it was covered with dust again. The sink emptied of plates was soon full of them again. It seemed like a never-ending struggle to prevent the earth from revolving around itself, or against the movement of dust particles through the universe,

---

* What is bought but not paid for until later, usually the beginning of the month.

or against the contraction of the muscles of the stomach and the intestines inside our bellies.

On the day when my father gave me the envelope with the first instalment of my fees, and I saw his hand tremble, saw the print of his fingers on the banknote smelling of sweat, my heart was heavy with sadness as I walked down the street, carrying it in my bag, as though it was my father with his huge body that I carried in my bag, or as though I was carrying the whole world on my shoulders as I walked. Maybe it was the feeling of guilt, an uneasy conscience, for how could my small brothers and sisters go hungry, grow weak and anaemic, so that I could graduate as a doctor?

I had never carried such a big sum of money in my bag. I pushed the envelope between the pages of a notebook to hide it and put it in my bag, locked the bag and walked along holding it tightly under my arm. People seemed to be staring at me in a strange way as though they had the eyes of thieves which could penetrate through leather, and as though they had noses that could smell the odour of money at a distance.

I did not ride in a bus or a tramcar that day, for riding in them there were always pickpockets with nimble fingers capable of stealing the envelope in the wink of an eye like jinnis or hidden spirits. I walked all the way from Giza to Kasr Al-Aini Street, slipped into the building which housed the administration and stood in front of the official responsible for student affairs.

There was a long line of students waiting. The official kept leaving his desk and disappearing for a long time in some other office. In addition, he was not respecting the line. Every time one of the students gave him a card, probably with a recommendation on it from someone whom the official considered important, he would deal with him before his turn, or if one of the professors or a high official came in he would jump to his feet to finish his business for him. But none of the students protested. They just stood there looking frustrated or commenting in a low voice. I heard one of the students standing behind me saying:

'It's chaos here in this school as it is everywhere else in the country. The money we pay is all wasted because of corruption. If I had an important relative or a recommendation to the dean I could be exempted from paying fees.'

Exempted from paying fees! The phrase struck a bell in my mind. I had passed my secondary-school examinations with distinction so why was I not exempt from paying fees? Chaos or no chaos, this was not going to stop me. Suddenly I felt furious and my body seemed to propel itself out of the line. I asked someone standing there where the dean's office was located. It was somewhere along the corridor or further inside. But when I got to the door of his room, it was closed and there was a red lamp burning above it. I went back to the director of his office. Sitting behind his desk with his fez tilted on one side and a cigarette in his mouth he told me that the dean was having an important meeting, then hesitating for a moment he asked me if I had a recommendation which he could take to the dean, for then he might be able to meet me after a while. I asked whether a student in the school had to have a recommendation to meet the dean. He stared at me as though I had insulted him, or broken the law. Then a bell rang above his head and he leapt to his feet, buttoned his jacket quickly and adjusted his fez on his head before hurrying to the door of the dean's room.

The door closed behind him as I stood there with my bag tight under my arm, my eyes fixed on the red lamp burning above the door. I could see my father's fingers tremble as he handed me the envelope that I was still carrying in my bag. A voice seemed to whisper inside me, 'I have no recommendation with me, nor have I a relative who is a pasha, but I'm going in.'

This time my body propelled itself with all the force of my anger, my fear, my hope and my despair in the direction of the closed door. Behind this door was my fate and I could face it, face anything, even death. I no longer cared what might happen, exemption from my fees, or expulsion from the school. What did it matter? What mattered now was to open the door which remained closed in my face no matter what could happen. The anger, the fear, the hope and despair, all the turbulent feelings inside me had disappeared, leaving a calm, a loss of feeling, a paralysis of the senses, a state which I realized later precedes every courageous act, even if that act were to throw oneself under the wheels of a train.

I found myself inside a huge room that reminded me of the day when I walked in to Abdine Palace. The enormous chandelier hanging from the ceiling, the thick red carpet, the gold-framed pictures looking down on me from the walls. At the far end of the room was a big black desk made of ebony with carved edges and legs and behind the desk the bright red colour of a fez, a white collar with a neck-tie, the upper part of a black suit, and large black eyes that opened wide as they stared at my face. Above the desk on the wall was a picture of King Farouk, dressed in an army suit with medals on his chest.

The man I saw was alone; there was no important meeting or anything of the sort. The director of the office stood to one side of him, trembling. I blurted out, 'He stopped me from coming to you although I've come here for something very important, Doctor.' Doctor seemed an appropriate title for the dean of a school of medicine, but the director corrected me quickly, muttering in a low voice, 'He's called his excellency the pasha dean.' But it was as though I hadn't heard what he said. I was too preoccupied wondering what to do, now that I was in the dean's room. I stood staring at him not knowing what to say, but his voice came to me across the desk as though from a distance. I heard him asking, 'What's the problem, my child,' in a low hoarse voice. The word child combined with the quiet tone of his voice gave his question a fatherly quality. The words came out of me in a rush. 'I deserve to be exempted from paying fees because of my high grades in school. There are students who have not done half as well as I have done, who have been exempted because they have a recommendation from someone.' The word recommendation rang out in the room and the director gave a start and intervened again quickly 'His excellency the dean does not accept recommendations. Please, you entered here without permission and his excellency the dean is busy.'

I did not move. I had got in and that was it. No one was going to make me leave. I would fight to the last breath. 'What's your name, child', asked the dean. His voice was kind, yet had he not installed this hyena of a man in front of his door? I felt encouraged, told him my name was Nawal El Saadawi, that my father was called Al-Sayed Al-Saadawi, and added with a note of pride that he had participated in the 1919 revolution, was in the Ministry of Education and had nine sons and daughters all of whom were in school because he did not discriminate between girls and boys. I spoke as though I were up on a platform making a speech. I saw him smiling. 'Where do you come among the nine, my child?' he asked. 'I'm number two', I answered. 'I have one brother who is older than me, but I've always been first in class.'

My meeting with the dean lasted not more than five minutes. He made me write an application for exemption from the payment of fees, then wrote in red ink on it at the bottom: 'The student is to be awarded an exemption from the payment of fees throughout her period of study in the School of Medicine', then he signed, The Dean, Mostapha Omar.

I do not remember how I walked out of his office or how I got home. I felt that I was just flying through the air, that I had become so light that my feet hardly touched the ground, but one thing I remember. I still held my bag tight under my arm, and moved fast eager for the moment I would stretch out my hand and give back the envelope to my father. I kept imagining the moment when I would reach home, imagining my father's face, and his eyes opening wide filling with a light that shone over the whole world like the light of the sun.

When I got home, my father was sitting on the verandah dressed in his pyjamas. Mother was in the kitchen preparing a glass of tea and a cake freshly baked in the oven for him. I can still remember the aroma of the cake in my nostrils as I came in.

My father's face is still engraved in my memory: the muscles of his face drooping a little with exhaustion, a slight pallor in his features, as though something were troubling him, a slight bending of the shoulders where he sat as though he were carrying a weight, his pyjamas white in colour with a bluish tint from the bleach my mother used in the washing, its buttons made of a kind of yellow onyx, the size of a piastre, with one button missing over his chest, and the trousers sagging. For this was a moment I could not forget and its details would remain forever living.

I told my father what had happened, and my story, as I told it, sounded to me unreal, as though I had imagined it, made it up. And my father, too, looked at me as though he did not believe what I was telling him, as though I were inventing it, until I brought out the envelope and gave it to him, until he opened it with trembling fingers as though afraid he would find it empty. When he brought out the banknotes, looked at them, touched them with his fingers, he stood up, held out his hands to me, took mine and said, 'Bravo Nawal. By God, you're really great, really to be depended on. Come, Zaynab', he called out, 'come see what your daughter has been able to do.'

It was a day of great rejoicing in our home. I had risen in my father's eyes, to another level. He began to call me doctor, and when my mother was tired he would wake up in the morning to prepare tea and breakfast for me, or a lunch box to take with me.

I could now obtain books and a skull from Am Osman. I put it inside my leather bag together with my books and the day's lectures and brought it home. When my mother saw it she gave a scream: 'You have brought home a dead man. My God, this is a black day', and she closed the door of my room on me, on the bag, and on the dead man. Every time I opened my door she hid her eyes with her hands lest she see it, as though the spirit of the dead man was just waiting to spring on her at any moment.

My younger sister Leila shared my room with me. No sooner had I brought my skull in than she went out with her bed, small

desk and everything. Nobody in the house came into my room
any more. So there I was sleeping the whole night through with a
dead stranger: his head looking down on me from the desk, close
to my bed; his eyes, two big gaps in the bones of his skull.

Before going to sleep, my mother now recited the verse of
Yasseen to chase evil spirits away from the house. But soon the
ordinary course of life resumed its ascendancy, and the unusual became habitual. My mother once more entered my room,
removed the dust from my books and papers, wiped the head of
the skull with a yellow cloth, and pushed its edge into the gaps
of the eyes, the ears, the nose and the mouth, to remove any dust
that might be there. She looked into the two empty holes where
the eyes used to be and sighed, 'The world is ephemeral and in
the end the human being is turned into dust.' Sadness would
cover her eyes like a cloud, but the moment she looked at me it
disappeared, swept away by something like golden sunlight. Her
laughter rang out before she said, 'The world doesn't deserve our
being sad over things or taking them too seriously.'

Her laughter continued to ring out, the childish laugh of old
that we had not heard for some time, like the ring of pure water
in a silver vessel. She took off her house dress and slippers, put
on the yellow silk dress with the thin straps that showed off the
white marble of her shoulders, sat down in front of her dressing
table, put black mascara on her lashes, moved the small brush
over her prominent cheeks until they were coloured like petals
of roses, pressed lipstick over her lips so that they looked like
cherries in her face as fair and round as a full moon. After that,
she hooked her diamond earrings in the lobes of her ears, and
they hung down on each side, long and slender, their stones
flashing with every movement of her head; freed the long tresses
of her chestnut hair and left them to fall over her naked shoulders; encircled her neck with the diamond necklace she called a
pendantif; closed her golden bracelets called *al-shabka*˙ around

---

˙ The present bought by the husband. Literally means the thing that hooks
together.

her forearms; slipped her small diamond watch on her wrist, the ring with a single stone called solitaire on one finger, and the wedding-ring on another. She put on her shoes with the thin, high heels which made her feet arch with a beautiful curve, and stood up, looked in the mirror one last time and started to move restlessly from one room to the other until she finally settled on the verandah. There she sat for a while looking over the tops of the distant trees at the sky, then went inside to make herself a glass of orange or lemon juice and returned to her seat, sipping slowly from her drink, her eyes glistening as though she were drinking wine. Her ears strained to hear the ring of the front-door bell, for she knew my father's ring, knew to the minute what time he would be home, knew that he was as accurate as a clock always on time, that he had nothing but his government job, nine children and one wife.

I used to see them sitting on the verandah, sipping orange or lemon juice as though getting drunk on it, laughing with a laughter that filled every corner of the house. Sometimes they would play cards or backgammon, or chess. My mother always lost and my father would then swell up like a peacock, stretch out his long legs, and begin to remember his heroic moments. The revolution of 1919 always came first, then when he had graduated with honours from Dar Al-Ouloum, and finally how he had succeeded in marrying my mother despite the obstacles put in his way by her father, Shoukry Bey.

My mother would laugh, toss her golden chestnut hair behind her neck and say: 'Do you remember, Sayed, when my late father told you to marry Fahima instead of Zaynab, and you said either Zaynab or nothing?' Then she would laugh softly again and again with that sound like water flowing interruptedly from a delicate porcelain jug. Then she'd ask, 'But why Zaynab, Sayed. Had you ever seen what I looked like?' My father's eyes shone as he followed the contours of her feminine body sitting beside him. 'Where was I going to see you, Zaynab? But my mother Hajja Mabrouka described you to me in detail and sometimes the ear loves before the eye.' At this stage love would have reached a peak, so father and mother would get up and disappear into their room. From behind the closed door would come whispers, then a crackling sound from the bed mingled with sounds of laughter, gasps and long sighs, like sobs and laughter chasing one another.

30

The Name of Marx

In front of the female students' room was a small garden completely dry and bare except for a eucalyptus tree under which I
used to sit sipping my tea with mint. The buildings of the School
of Pharmacology were nearby. Samia and Safeya would join me
and we would sit recalling old memories. Sometimes Batta also
came along, or it could be other colleagues of ours from one or
both of the two schools. We sat drinking tea with mint, or coffee
and milk, and telling stories.

Love stories in Al-Mashraha were more frequent than in the
School of Pharmacology. Senior students fell in love with junior
girls easily. Over the dead bodies eyes would meet, and hearts
would leap or beat faster under the ribs. Love and death would
join at one table like twins, as though they were the children
of one mother, but of different fathers, at opposite poles, like
rivals, yet unaware that they were rivals, unaware of the existence of one another yet competing, antagonistic with nothing
in common, with nothing to bring them together except that
common mother.

Over the dissecting bodies the heads of the girl students
would draw close, and then the whispering and the hidden talk

never ceased, interspersed with suppressed, interrupted gasps of laughter over the jokes. Batta would tell us the latest one and we would die of laughter, and the male students would die of jealousy, or perhaps envy. Letters would come and go between the folds of a notebook, or between the pages of Cunningham, the dissection manual, carrying the scent of love and formalin. A male student often borrowed the lecture notes of a girl student. He would walk up to her hesitant, shy, the blood rushing to his face like a young virgin, and ask, 'May I borrow your notebook? I missed Professor Batrawi's last lecture.' 'Yes, you may.' 'Thank you very much.' Then up would come another student whose eyes had fallen on another girl, 'I forgot my Cunningham at home. I wonder if I can borrow yours, doctor?' 'Yes doctor, of course.' 'Thank you very much doctor.'

Ever since we had come to Al-Mashraha we had never stopped exchanging books, lecture notes and the title of doctor with one another. As soon as one of us girls had received her lecture notes or her book back it would disappear somewhere behind the cadaver, on her knees below the dissecting table. She would open it secretively, hide the letter in her pocket or her bag, bring it out every now and then, to breathe in its odour. 'My God, what a beautiful smell of formalin, girls', one of us would say and there would be a burst of choking laughter, jokes, and gasps and glances from eyes gleaming with curiosity.

One of the senior students kept coming to our table. He would hold the scalpel between the tips of his fingers, imitating the professor. 'No, you're not holding the scalpel in the right way. That's not how you should dissect. Give me, I will show you', or 'No doctor, not like that, that's not the way to hold the tweezers. Pardon me, these are for dissecting not for plucking the eyebrows.'

The girls held their laughter while the student threw glances at the girl for whom he had come, avoiding looking at her directly as though he had not noticed that she was there. But we knew, love could not conceal itself no matter how much it tried.

He would stick to our table, reluctant to leave, go on explaining what he'd already explained. 'Yes, yes, we've understood, doctor.' Then he'd take his scalpel and go back to his dissecting table, but his eyes would continue to hover around us from a distance, go round and round the hall looking at different faces, but end by settling on the girl at our table.

Batta would give me a nudge with her elbow and ask, 'Can you see that senior boy over there?' 'Yes, what about him?' 'He's got his eyes on Safeya.' 'Shame on you, Batta he's a good boy.' 'You mean he's stupid?' 'No, I don't mean that.' 'It's stupid people who fall in love. The clever ones are as clever as monkeys. They've got their eyes fixed on five things.' 'What five things, Batta?' 'To own a clinic, a car, a farm, a building and a bride.' Batta would gurgle with laughter before adding 'Of course, the bride comes last. After he's saved up money from the building and the clinic, he goes off to ask for her hand from the pasha without bothering about love, or other trifles of that sort.'

In the year 1951, we moved up to the second year of Al-Mashraha without needing to go through any examinations. Examinations were held at the end of the two years and were rather difficult because they covered all the subjects we had studied during that period, including anatomy.

The biggest auditorium in the School was called Ali Pasha Ibrahim's auditorium and accommodated hundreds of students. We attended lectures in it, but often seminars, meetings, or celebrations were organized there. I participated with the students in these extra-curricular activities, as well as in the increasing number of demonstrations against King Farouk and the British.

For the festival of the Hegira, the leader of the Muslim Brothers asked me to make a speech. When we celebrated the abrogation of the treaty of 1936, the leader of the Wafdist students invited me to speak, and when it was Workers' Day the representative of the communist students suggested that I write an article in their magazine *Al-Gami'i* (All of Us Together). If there was a seminar dealing with culture or art I would be asked to write a short story or a piece of prose.

I was the only girl student in the school who made speeches on different occasions, or wrote stories and articles. The medical students, like their colleagues in other schools of the university, published magazines, and I preferred literature and art to medicine. Since I was in secondary school, I had continued to write short stories, and keep a diary. In my dreams I saw myself as a writer rather than as a medical doctor. When I said that, my colleagues smiled sarcastically. 'What nonsense are you talking about? Writing won't feed you, Nawal.'

Most of the student leaders were in the fifth or final year of medicine. We, who were still in the second year, looked up to them as though they were giants compared to us. The final year of medicine seemed so far away, further away from us than the stars. Among them were two students who published a magazine called *Students of Kasr Al-Aini*. One of them was tall with a lean body, and his name was Kamal Al-Kashmiri. The second was short and squat and was called Ahmed Younes. They never separated, were always together, like twins, and would walk into the dissecting hall together, come up to our table and say 'We want you to write an article, or a short story for the next issue of our magazine'.

The first time I ever saw my name in print was in this magazine. I gazed at the black letters printed on the white paper as though my name had been written on the moon, as though cast in lead on an everlasting sky to become one of the planets or the stars. Every time I saw a student holding the magazine, I imagined he was reading my article, 'The students in Medical School as I see them.' My father kept bursting into peals of laughter as he read it. I do not remember how I described the students but my father said I had an acute sense of observation.

The general atmosphere in medical school was not to my liking. Most of the students were book-worms, learnt everything by heart, fought to get into the auditorium before the others and sit in the front row, stepped on the feet of the girl students to reserve the best benches for themselves, wrote down every word that dropped from the mouth of the professor, their faces almost glued to their notebooks. At the end of the year, their eyes were red, their lids swollen, their faces pale, as they rushed panting from auditorium to auditorium. Nothing seemed to occupy their minds other than the phantom of the coming examinations.

I also described some of the student leaders. The leader of the Muslim Brothers was short and fat. He had a fair complexion and a big square head like that of the sphinx, and when he made a speech it was always in a very loud voice, and the speech went on for a very long time. On the anniversary of the Hegira he used to tell the story of the spider. Every now and then he brought his fist down with a bang on the table, or waved his arms in the air. Throughout the speech he kept his eyelids lowered in piety, wetted his lips with his tongue. Sometimes he raised his eyes to the ceiling, as though addressing the heavens upon which the students would seize the opportunity and start leaving, but he would go on speaking to the empty auditorium.

The leader of the Wafdist students was tall and lean with drooping shoulders and a dark complexion. He would jump up on the platform suddenly, pull the microphone out of the hands of whoever was speaking and shout into it as loud as he could: 'Long live Nahas Pasha', but nobody ever paid any attention to him. Sometimes one of the students would say, 'We don't want slogans. We want to listen to something of interest to us.' So the leader of the National Party, feeling that this was a good opportunity would climb up on the platform. He had already graduated, and was a junior resident in the University Hospital. He was tall and slender, walked upright, strutting like a cock, and always wore a smart suit. On the platform he stood silent for a moment holding the microphone in his hand, then suddenly his voice would resonate in the auditorium. Many years later, in the late 1970s he became prime minister under Sadat, and died in his office one day suddenly, with his face flat on the desk. He was usually

followed by a colleague of ours called Ibrahim Al-Sherbini, who
was not so tall, nor so smart, yet his voice was no lower. The
years passed and the day came in the early 1960s when we found
ourselves sharing the same office in the Ministry of Health.

The magazine *Al-Gami'i* was edited by a final-year student
who was known to be a communist. He used to cross the big
courtyard with long, rapid strides, his arms moving freely, his
head bent as though he was going to butt into someone with it.
When he came into the dissecting hall he strode immediately
to our table which was reserved for the female students. He
spoke in a classical Arabic and tended to emphasize the ends of
his words, 'Nawal', he would say, 'I am enlisting all those who
have talent to write in our magazine. I want you to write a short
story or an article about the recent demonstration. My name is
Youssef.' His name had sounded to us as though it was Yousri.
Part of it, probably the *f*, was lost in the din coming from the
courtyard and outside the dissecting hall. That day there were
students gathering for a demonstration. Demonstrations had not
ceased since the abrogation of the Anglo-Egyptian Treaty by the
Wafdist government in October 1951.

My female colleagues refused adamantly to participate in
any demonstration. They refused anything related to politics
and political parties. But what provoked and scared them most
was when 'the communist' used to enter the dissecting hall,
and come to our table. As soon as they spotted him they would
exclaim, almost in one breath, 'Here comes Yusri the communist, Nawal. It's going to be our ruin.' Safeya shot up and down
on her stool, assailed by memories of what had happened to her
brother: 'Listen Nawal, we don't want to raise the suspicions of
people here. I have had enough trouble already.' 'He has a stare
in his eyes like someone who's just committed a murder', added
Batta. We all burst out laughing. 'It's true by God. He's got a look
on him that's really scary, like a killer.'

One day Batta asked him in her simpering tones, 'Are you
really a communist, Yusri?' His gleaming eyes stared straight

at her before he replied 'If you want to know really, my name is Youssef and not Yusri.' Everybody laughed and that was how we discovered that his name was Youssef Idris, and that he was the editor responsible for the magazine *Al-Gami'i*. Later he became a famous literary writer in Egypt.

Even at that time I did not know what the word communism meant. My female colleagues believed that it was a combination of atheism, heresy, corruption and immorality. Samia was the first communist I had befriended. She used to sit with us in the women's room absolutely silent, her lips shut tight, never parting them in a smile. The girls would be bursting out in fits of laughter all the time but she would remain serious. They told one another stories about love, about the love-letters hidden between the pages of their notebooks, but she would pout her lips scornfully just as she used to do when we were in Helwan school, and say, 'The fact is, girls, that the country is in a crisis and you are busy with all that nonsense. Love is a kid's game, Nawal', she kept repeating, 'romantic nonsense. Childish stuff for adolescents, bourgeois sentments. Listen, Nawal, it's time you began to know something about Marx.'

It was the first time I had heard the name Marx. It sounded to my ears like Marcus, or Morcos, especially when Batta pronounced it. Morcos was the first love of Safeya, when she was in Helwan school. For days I thought Samia, like Safeya, had fallen in love with a Copt, and for the first time since I had known her, Samia burst out laughing, and it was real laughter. 'He's the founder of Communism, not a Copt, Nawal.' 'My God, Samia, that's terrible. A Copt is much better, at least he believes in God's book, but a communist is an atheist, a heretic.'

There was another magazine in the School of Medicine called *Sho'lat Al-Tahreer* (Flame of Liberation). The student who edited it was in his fourth or fifth year in the school, and his name was Ahmed Helmi. He never came to the dissecting hall or spoke to the girl students. He was one of the student leaders and used to speak on national occasions, but there was a difference. He always spoke in a quiet voice, never shouted, and the students listened to him with attention. His eyes were hidden behind sunglasses, and later we heard he became one of the guerrilla fighters in the Suez Canal Zone. We rarely saw him in school, and he was surrounded by a kind of halo.

Some of the professors had interests outside the field of medicine. Amongst them was Dr Said Abdou, the professor of public health. He used to write a column in an important weekly magazine. The column was entitled, 'They mislead you and say.' He was fond of literature and poetry. The professor of biochemistry was called Dr Shafeek Al-Ridi, and sometimes he used to attend cultural meetings, or celebrations, and concerts where there was music and singing. One of the students used to play the lute and sing. He was short and fat with a squarish body, and his name was Hassouna. He composed a song which went as follows: 'Ridi, Ridi, put on your sunglasses to hide your captivating eyes. Ridi, Ridi, Oh my Ridi.'

Dr Ridi was famed for the beauty of his eyes. They were a blue green with something like sunshine looking out of them. All the students, male and female, were attracted by his eyes, his hair shot with strands of grey, and his haughty features when he strutted across the courtyard to get into his car. The girls followed him from the windows of the dissecting hall and Batta would say with a gasp, 'Look at him, sisters, isn't he cute and really handsome', and the other girls would chorus in a single breath, 'By Allah, he's a moon.'

I was not attracted by Al-Ridi, or by the type of handsomeness the girls saw in him, so I would go on dissecting while they looked out of the window. Batta would snatch the scalpel from my hand and say, 'Look at him and let your eyes enjoy the pleasure of seeing him, before we all die and become like this corpse.' 'Give me the scalpel, Batta, and stop your clowning. The exams are getting nearer.' 'Exams my foot, all this rubbish. What I want is a bridegroom like Al-Ridi, or no bridegroom at all. Look at his car! It drives me crazy. Is it a Cadillac or what,

Nawal?' 'I don't know anything about cars. Give me the scalpel.' 'What d'you know about then, wizard? Demonstrations and liberating the country. Country my foot. It's all shit. I want to get married, Ridi, Ridi, Oh my Ridi', followed by a deep sigh and the laughter of the girls.

Her real name was Camelia. I don't know who nicknamed her Batta, but she really was like a duck, short, fat and squat, swaying over thin high heels as she walked, clucking like a hen, her voice rising to a high pitch when she tried to speak loudly, her full fleshy lips painted red, her hands small, smooth and plump, her nails covered with a coating of red lacquer and pointed like claws. Batta never picked up a scalpel during the two years we spent in Al-Mashraha. She was afraid the formalin might spoil the skin of her delicate fingers. Caustic fluids made the skin rough and cracked, and dulled the lustre of the nails. As a matter of fact not one of the girls ever took hold of a scalpel. They were satisfied to sit and watch the cadaver being dissected, or to read in Cunningham and look at the illustrations.

Dr Batrawi used to make a round of the tables in the dissecting hall. He had a tall upright stature like my father, his hair was greying, his forehead high and he had a slightly husky voice which for me added to his attraction. He used to see me standing over the cadaver with the scalpel in my hand while the other girls sat around the table. He would say to them: 'Isn't there a single one of you who is prepared to hold a scalpel in her hand? Of course not, you're all worried about your delicate fingers. But how are you going to practise as doctors, ladies?'

His laughter rolled out in the dissecting hall filling the air with a boisterous gaiety. He would look at me the way my father used to do and say: 'Bravo. You're the only serious one amongst them, Show me what you have done. That's fine. But one of these flower pots here should give you a hand.' The girls would shrink together on their stools like frightened hens, hide their mouths behind their hands and chortle with laughter. He would join in their laughter, lift his foot up and rest it on an empty stool and say: 'Or what do you think, Ya Sit Batta?' 'Don't be too harsh on us', was her usual answer, the words pronounced in a mincing way so that they sounded as though spoken by someone from a high-class family. 'My God, what kind of doctor are you going to be if you speak to patients that way? How are you going to speak to villagers, or people in Upper Egypt. They won't understand a word,* or what do you think Dr Amr?'

Next to him would be standing the tutor, Dr Amr, at attention like a soldier in the presence of his officer, his arms folded over his chest, his head nodding in agreement to every word that came out of Dr Batrawi's mouth. As soon as Dr Batrawi went off, he unfolded his arms, lifted his head, and began to strut up and down imitating Dr Batrawi in the way he walked and talked, laughing out loudly and calling the girls flower pots. He owned a long car, like Dr Ridi, but there were no grey hairs in his head, and no engagement or wedding ring around his finger. Batta followed him with her black, mascaraed, eyes, commenting 'There, that's a suitable bridegroom for you, not these students. They are just a bunch of kids. The only one that's worth anything is Hisham Mooro.'

Hisham Mooro was our colleague in Al-Mashraha and was assigned to the adjoining dissection table. His father was Mooro Pasha, who later became Dean of the School of Medicine. He was tall and slender with fair hair and a rosy face, always dressed smartly. He never put on a white coat, was rarely to be seen, and did not attend lectures, hold a pen or a scalpel, or join in demonstrations.

As soon as Batta caught sight of him she would pull the scalpel out of my hand. 'Enough dissecting. wizard. I suppose you think, you're going to be top over us. No my dear, nothing doing. Here we are in medical school, and in medical school if your father is the dean, or one of these big professors, you can come out top straight away without straining your eyes reading through

---

* People speak with a thick guttural and sometimes clipped pronunciation in Southern Egypt.

Cunningham, or dirtying your hand in this formalin shit.' Batta knew things we had never thought of. A relative of her mother or father was a professor in the school. She called him Uncle Mahmoud. He might have been only a distant cousin to her mother, but she used to speak about him almost as though he were her father.

The girls often talked about their families as we sat around the dissecting table, went in detail through the various branches, especially if some of the members were in different departments of the school. Then the conversation shifted to engagement and marriage. One of them had become engaged to a lecturer in the school, so she brought us her *shabka* and showed it around. Batta pinched her in the arm and leg for luck, and said: 'So that it will be my turn next', then added 'and all my furniture will come from Pontremoli.' So the conversation would shift from the *shabka*, to furniture bought for the bride, to clothes and fashion, to different cars and their makes, to different kinds of footwear, ranging from clogs to stiletto-heeled shoes for nights out, to leather, silver and even aluminium, before ending in the different shades of lipstick, the light 'natural', the dark carmine and the purple.

Safeya was the closest of my colleagues to me. She did not put on lipstick or wear high-heeled shoes, and she played tennis or ping-pong with me every Thursday. To get to the tennis courts, we crossed a small bridge over a subsidiary branch of the Nile which flowed between the old and the new Kasr Al-Aini hospitals (the new one was later called Al-Manial University Hospital), then crossed through gardens with rows of trees and flower beds. A clock-tower rose high up in front of us, overlooking a flight of wide arching marble steps. The sports grounds of the school were to the left, a large expanse of green, surrounded by a high stone wall. We changed our clothes and put on our rubber shoes in a small dressing room. Custom did not allow us to wear shorts and

---

* A very expensive furniture store in the centre of Cairo, originally owned by an Italian.

show our thighs. We wore pleated skirts, or long shorts which reached below the knees.

Some of the male students used to join us, including a colleague of ours named Hussein Kamel Baha' Al-Dine. He had smooth black hair which he parted on one side, walked with bent head, his eyes on the ground. Safeya called him the domesticated student. He was silent by nature, spoke little and did not participate in political meetings or demonstrations but later he became a professional politician and worked with Ali Sabri* at the time of Gamal Abdel Nasser's presidency and then, after many years, became Minister of Education under Mobarak.

Another colleague of mine was called Ahmed Al-Menissi. He shared my table in the biochemistry laboratory, so we kept exchanging bottles of chemicals and test-tubes and I remember that his fingers trembled a little when he held them. He never lifted his eyes to my face, and he would blush furiously if we exchanged a few words. One day without turning his face towards me, he asked 'May I borrow your biochemistry notes? I want to copy the lecture which I missed yesterday.' I gave him my notebook and next day he returned it. Between the pages I found a small, folded letter, and I opened it to read the only sentence written on it: 'Your face will be before my eyes as I fight for my country and Islam.' At night I thought about that word 'fight'. Was he going to join the guerrillas who were fighting the British forces in the Canal Zone? Would he hold a gun in his hand and kill, the hand that trembled when he held a test-tube? When I looked at his nose from the side it looked sharply arched, held up in the air. Was that the nose of the *feda'iyin* (resistance fighters).

The word *feda'iyin* had a magic ring, and my heart beat fast when I heard it. In my dreams I saw him standing upright, his sword in his hand, smiting the enemies, one after the other. He was tall, like my father, and people carried him up on their

---

* Director of Gamal Abdel Nasser's office and later prime minister. Air-force pilot and one of the Free Officers in the revolution of July 1952.

shoulders but suddenly a bullet flew through the air towards him, he was hit in the chest, and toppled to the ground, bleeding. People lifted him from the ground and laid him on a horse-cart. And as he lay there he put his hand under his ribs, on his heart, and held something out to me with trembling fingers. When he opened his fingers I saw it was my photograph.

I had very few pictures of myself. This was one of them. It was taken by a photographer in Menouf when I was awarded my secondary-school certificate. He was a man with a huge body who limped on two swollen legs that bent backwards when he walked. Perhaps he had been afflicted with some disease like elephantiasis when he was young, and I shook with fear whenever I met him on the street on my way to school. He came to our home carrying his box on his back, like someone carrying his cross. He made me stand in a field with the sun in my eyes, put his head inside the box, and the upper half of his body disappeared under a black tent, then he lifted his right arm in the air and shrieked in a voice like an air-raid siren: 'Attention. One, two, three.' At that precise moment, according to his instructions, I was supposed to close my mouth, open my eyes and not make any movement, not even breathe. But what happened was just the opposite, because, I do not know why, the ground seemed to shake under my feet, and the strong burning sun looked out at me from the bulging magic eye of the black box.

I used to give this picture to my friends whenever we exchanged photographs, writing on the back in memory of something or other. Friendships were created only between people of the same sex, and there was nothing called friendship between the sexes. A girl would never give her photograph to a man who was not her husband, or at least engaged to her, but in love sometimes things did happen that overstepped the bounds of custom and tradition. So a girl might give her picture to a boy but without ever writing a single word on it, for if the picture fell into the hands of someone else, this was sufficient for the girl to lose her reputation.

After he wrote his small letter and put it in my notebook, I saw Al-Menissi only once. One day in the biochemistry lab something very unexpected happened. He turned his face towards me and smiled, and when he smiled his eyes lit up, his thick black lashes trembled but his hand was steady around the test-tube. He opened his lips and said something which I barely heard, his voice was so low: 'I want to take your picture with me.'

I was a model of a young girl, who never gave her picture to anyone even if she was in love, and in any case my heart was not beating at that moment the way it had done with my first love. Despite the gleam in his eyes, there was something humble, something submissive in the way he looked at me, like the look I saw in the eyes of girls. I disliked that look in the eyes of the girls, let alone in the eyes of boys.

The laboratory was on the third floor and there were no stools for us to sit on. We stood hour after hour on our feet in front of the long wooden counter mixing the chemicals in the test-tubes, then heating them over a flame to speed up whatever process it was. Gases would rise up in the air, most of them harmless, but some toxic.

Suddenly, as we stood working, we heard an explosion. A test-tube had burst in the hands of one of our colleagues, and the laboratory was filled with smoke. We rushed out coughing and sneezing, and ran down the stairs to the courtyard. 'My God, I've forgotten my bag in the lab, and I can't get home without it', I exclaimed. 'I'll go upstairs and get it', said Al-Menissi, handing me his bag to hold until he got back. He leapt up the stairs through fire and flame, not fearing death, and came back with my bag. We exchanged bags without a word, but in the quick exchange his finger tips brushed against my hand, and he said: 'Sorry.'

There he stood in front of me pronouncing that word 'sorry' and I was not able to say a word. I should have put my arms around him, or if I could not do that, I should at least have shaken hands with him, and thanked him. But I stood there like a statue unable to do anything. I was being held back by something I did not know, by chains that tied me down, by obstacles that separated me from him. He was still panting a little after leaping up, then down three flights of stairs almost in the wink of an eye. His face was red, his teeth bit into his lower lips, and he said nothing but that one word, 'sorry'. Was he apologizing for the letter he had slipped into my notebook, or because his fingers had accidentally brushed against my hand? Then I heard his voice again, heard him saying something, caught the words with difficulty amidst the deafening noise in the courtyard, the roar of traffic, the loud voices, the wind laden with dust and sand sounding like a prolonged sharp whistle in my ears, as he put out his hand with its fingers cold around mine. Then he said: 'I leave you in Allah's care', and he was gone.

On the way home his voice kept coming back to me. I leave you in Allah's care. What did he mean? Something weighed heavily on my heart. Perhaps it was my conscience. Had I unknowingly hurt his feelings? Why hadn't I opened my mouth at least to thank him? Why?

31

The Brush of History

When fresh demonstrations broke out, Menissi was no longer among the students. Had he left with the *feda'iyin* groups for the Canal Zone, I wondered? Since the treaty of 1936 had been abrogated, the British occupation of Egypt had lost any lawful standing. Students and youth were now engaged in armed resistance, and the Wafdist government secretly encouraged the resistance fighters.

When I joined the demonstrations I was sometimes the only girl amidst thousands of male students. In my imagination I still carried a childhood dream of myself bearing a sword and smiting the enemy, and of people hoisting me up on their shoulders as I shouted, 'Long live Free Egypt'. As I sat at the dissecting table or in the auditorium, or in the laboratory, something like electricity went through my body, made me start as though I had received a shock. My body would be propelled by some hidden force to rush out and join them, and as I advanced with the crowds my heart would beat strongly, rhythmically, as though once again I was living my first love.

My voice would choke as I shouted, 'Long live Free Egypt' and tears flowed from my eyes, sweeping away the sadness that had lived in me since the day I was born. My body grew lighter as though it had thrown off a weight, as though it were shedding itself as I advanced in the crowd without a body, or a name, or a father, or a mother, or a family. These people were my family, my parents, my home.

Were these feelings what people call love of one's country? Was it a longing for love, for my first and only love? I could not tell. They seemed to be mingled together in a single torrent of feeling, like a flood breaking through all obstacles, and overflowing its banks. I forgot that the people around me were men, of a different sex. We became one sex. We fused to become one body, or one spirit with no body.

The biggest demonstration was the one that took place on 14 November 1951. It was called the silent demonstration, and sometimes silence can be much more eloquent than slogans shouted out loudly. Hundreds of students gathered in the big courtyard of the School of Medicine. They brought big banners made of calico on which they proceeded to write in big black *naskh*⃰ letters, 'Long live the struggle of the *feda'iyin*', 'No to negotiations with the British', 'The medical students are one with the people', 'Long live the People's Armed Struggle', 'Long live Free Egypt.' A group of students was wearing the army fatigues of the *feda'iyin*. Another group with badges pinned to their chests was organizing the students in rows.

Student leaders walked up and down calling out every now and then: 'We need order, comrades, and chanting slogans is not allowed. This demonstration is to celebrate the anniversary of the first People's Delegation that went to meet the British administration and demand the evacuation of British troops from Egypt. It will be the most important demonstration in the history of Egypt, and the first time that the people and the government are united because it is a Wafdist government.'

⃰ In Arabic there are different calligraphies: *naskh* is the simplest and the most common.

Here voices were raised shouting, 'Long live Nahas Pasha', but the harangue went on: 'Please no shouting of slogans. The country is passing through a very critical phase and if this demonstration fails there will be dangerous complications. The British are preparing to strike a powerful blow in the Canal Zone, and we must show them today that the people are firmly united. We are to march in single step and no-one should break the line. Perhaps agents of the British or the king will try to infiltrate our ranks and cause trouble, so we must be vigilant, and maintain silence and order throughout the demonstration.'

The demonstrators moved out through the door into the street without a sound like a huge crocodile moving over the ground. Rivers of people flowed out from the side-streets to join in one mighty river that poured into Ismailia Square, for there were demonstrations coming from everywhere forming a huge mass of people, one huge body advancing on innumerable feet and carrying innumerable heads. Waves of people rising and falling in an endless sea. Millions of breaths mingling to create the single breath of the crowd. An immense silence that echoed in the ears more powerful than the sound of thunder.

Two female students from Al-Mashraha had joined me. One of the organizers came up to us and said, 'We want you girls to walk in the first row and carry this banner. Can you do that?' It was a long piece of calico on which had been written a sentence in black ink which said, 'The girl students of the School of Medicine support armed resistance to liberate our country', and fixed to the banner were two long wooden poles. I held up one pole while another girl held up the other with the help of her brother, who was also in the medical school. We lifted the banner high and advanced with it to the front of the demonstration.

The whole of Egypt was in the streets that day, and every inch of ground was covered with people. People climbed the trees when there was no room on the ground. The roofs and windows of houses were filled with people, their eyes watching what looked like the day of reckoning, when it is said that people will be resurrected by millions and walk on their legs.

Nobody held back from the demonstration, not even small pupils and children. There were housewives in their *milayat* holding children to their breasts, villagers wearing *gallabeyas*, and skull caps on their heads, factory workers wearing blue dungarees stained with oil and dark grease, old people moving on crutches, beggars wearing torn *gallabeyas*, street hawkers carrying baskets on their heads, carts drawn by donkeys, patients who had walked out of the hospitals wearing their white gowns, male and female nurses and doctors with white coats, most of them with stethoscopes dangling from their necks, religious shiekhs wearing kaftans and white turbans, priests in black robes and black cassocks, lawyers, also in black robes, judges wearing their sashes, hawkers selling combs, street boys with an arm or leg missing, and on one side a boy with amputated legs rolling along on a wooden board with small wheels, propelling himself with a push of both palms along the tarmac road. All the shops on either side were closed and locked, their owners in the demonstration or up on a roof, or a balcony, looking down on it.

I advanced, holding the pole of the banner up in my right hand, hour after hour without tiring, as though in a dream, holding up the torch of liberation above our heads, as though I were Joan of Arc, or Zarq'a Al-Yamama leading her country to freedom. A caressing voice seemed to reach my ears, floating in the air, like a song being sung to the rhythm of the *ood* in the midst of the warm blue sea, its waves rocking me gently up and down, like the arms of my mother when she held me on her knees and sang 'Sleep, sleep, sweet child.'

I closed my eyes as though walking in my sleep. Suddenly I heard a noise, opened my eyes as though I had awakened from my sleep. What was that? Could it be a bullet? The sun in my eyes seemed to be tinted red. I ran to hide behind a wall and then a voice called out, 'Nawal'. Reality and dream seemed to mingle in my mind, for the red sunlight had changed to a red liquid flowing under my feet, like a red ribbon laid out on the black tarmac. I felt my arms and my legs. Everything seemed intact, in its place. I could still walk, still lift one foot after the other and place it on the ground. The sun was now hidden behind a cloud of dust, then the cloud disappeared revealing a face I had seen before. He walked towards me with a quiet, confident step. He wore sunglasses on his eyes but a light seemed to radiate from them. 'Nawal?' Was that my name I heard being called? How had he been able to pick it out, to chose it from the millions of names in the universe?

I did not know where the gun had been fired. I was in a big street, a street the name of which I did not know. I knew very few streets in the city of Cairo. Transportation was at a standstill. No buses, no tramcars, no taxis, no donkey-carts. Nothing with wheels that could roll over the ground, nothing but human feet that had started to scatter, without a sound, without the chanting of a single slogan. And once the masses of people had scattered, the streets and the lanes had swallowed them up.

'Nawal, there's no way you can get home, except walking', he said. He pronounced my name with an ease that sounded strange to me, as though he knew me, had called out to me many times before. I walked beside him silent, hearing nothing but the tread of our feet on the tarmac road. My shoes were solid black leather like his. His foot was big like mine, his height tall like mine. He wore an open shirt with no tie, no jacket, no pullover. His tread on the ground was strong, challenging. Could he be one of the *feda'iyin*?

Our walk home was like a journey through a dream. I came to only when I found myself in Kasr Al-Aini Street. I stopped and said, 'I know the way back to the school from here', as though I realized suddenly that I had been walking with him. He stretched out his hand and shook mine. His hand was a big, strong, self-confident hand. 'Alright, Nawal, peace be with you', he said.

Once more he had pronounced the name Nawal, but now in my ears it had a different ring to it as though there was no other name that was anything like it, as though there was nothing anywhere near it in this world of people. Was it really my name? And why did it echo like this in the universe, why did it have this new ring?

Living in Resistance

I finished this autobiography in the winter of 1995. I was still in exile far away from my country and my people. But why did I stop at this relatively early period of my life? When I thought it over, I realized that the years I had written about had been very important in the direction that my life later took. I had met and married my second love. He became a victim of the guerrilla struggle against the British and the king, of political machinations he knew nothing about. Later on he was able to settle down and resume his life. I bore my first child, a girl we named Mona, from him. When Mona was four months old, on 23 July 1956, a voice on the radio announced in ringing tones that the Suez Canal Company had been nationalized and happiness seemed to radiate out from our little home to the whole of the country of which we were a part. The ship *Ivan Gibb* steamed out of Port Said carrying the last British soldiers away from our shores, ending the occupation of Egypt which had lasted seventy-two years.

After four months the soldiers came back, parachuted from the air, or travelling over land from Israel. I was a village doctor. I took off my white coat and put on army fatigues ready to go

My son Atef, a cinema director, with my daughter
Mona, 1988. His father is Sherif Hetata.

off and fight. I wanted to join the ranks of the resistance in Port
Said but the war ended before I was able to get there. The United
Nations issued a resolution which enforced a ceasefire, and on
23 December 1956 the British, French and Israeli troops were
obliged to evacuate.

As a rural doctor I lived close to village people, shared their
experiences, learnt about their lives, witnessed what the triple
scourge of poverty, ignorance and sickness did to them. Women
bore a double burden since they also suffered from the oppression exercised on them by fathers and husbands, brothers and
uncles and other men. I saw young girls burn themselves alive,
or throw themselves into the waters of the Nile and drown, in
order to escape a father's, or a husband's tyranny. I tried to
help them but the men with power in the village in agreement
with the state authorities had me transferred somewhere else,
accusing me of not respecting the traditional values of their
community, of inciting women to rebel against religion and
its laws.

Nawal as a village doctor, Tahla, 1957.

This accusation now followed me wherever I went, in whatever I wrote as I moved through the dark corridors of the government bureaucracy under Abd Al-Nasser, then under Al-Sadat, and now under Mubarak. Under Al-Sadat, I was put in prison, but he was assassinated one month later. When I was released, my name was shifted from a black list to a grey list which is more ambiguous and gives the authorities more latitude.

I was not attracted by the medical profession. It seemed unable to do much in face of the sufferings imposed on people. I realized how sickness and poverty are linked to politics, to money and power, that medical practice was removed from our everyday life. Writing became a weapon with which to fight the system, which draws its authority from the autocratic power exercised by the ruler of the state, and that of the father or the husband in the family. The written word for me became an act of rebellion against injustice exercised in the name of religion, or morals, or love.

Dr Nawal El Saadawi among male doctors,
Ministry of Health, Cairo 1963.

Words should not seek to please, should not hide the wounds
in our bodies, the shameful moments in our lives. Sometimes
words shock us, give us pain, but they can provoke us to face
ourselves, to question what we have accepted for thousands of
years. There still remains a lot to say about my life. I have not
sat down to write it yet.

Creativity is linked to memory. Through it I discover the
shining moments in my life. They started to scintillate when I
found myself in exile far away from home, like stars that died
out many years ago, but their light still reaches us.

My husband, Sherif Hetata, has shared my exile. He is a
writer, is creative in what he does, whether medical writing
or politics. That is why he spent fifteen years in jail and a few
years in exile on his own. We have been together for a long
time, walked side by side for many miles, over the green grass
of beautiful lands washed by the Atlantic Ocean, beneath the

Nawal inaugurating the Egyptian Women Writers' Association
in Cairo, 1970.

Carolina blue skies, surrounded by friends who made our exile
seem sometimes like a second home.

Perhaps in some ways autobiography is more real, more true
than fiction, more creative, and more steeped in art. Autobiography seeks to reveal the self, what is hidden inside, just as it tries
to see the other. My pen has been a scalpel which cuts though
the outer skin, pushes the muscles aside, probes for the roots
of things. Autobiography has lifted me above the daily grind to
see my life emerge under a different light in which the riches of
the earth, the promises of heaven have shrunk compared with
these sheets of paper covered with my handwriting. As I write,
I experience moments of thrill, of deep pleasure never experienced since I was a child. I lean back, stretch my body, open my
arms to the whole world, walk through the trees in Duke Forest,
and the sunlight touches my face, like the gentle fingers of my
mother when I was a child of five.